Improving Student Achievement

Reforms that Work

a volume in
The Milken Family Foundation Series on Education Policy

The Milken Family Foundation Series on Education Policy

Talented Teachers: The Essential Force for Improving
Student Achievement (2004)
  Lewis C. Solmon and Tamara W. Schiff, editors

Improving Student Achievement

Reforms that Work

Edited by

Lewis C. Solmon
Kimberly Firetag Agam
Tamara W. Schiff
The Milken Family Foundation

MILKEN
FAMILY
FOUNDATION

INFORMATION AGE
PUBLISHING

Greenwich, Connecticut • www.infoagepub.com

Library of Congress Cataloging-in-Publication Data

Milken National Education Conference (2004 : Washington, D.C.)
  Improving student achievement : reforms that work / edited by Lewis C.
Solmon, Kimberly Firetag Agam, Tamara W. Schiff.
      p. cm. -- (Milken Family Foundation series on education policy)
  The major portion of the book is from the proceedings of the 2004 Milken
National Education Conference which was held in Washington, D.C. in May 2004.
  Includes bibliographical references.
  ISBN 1-59311-352-8 (pbk.) -- ISBN 1-59311-353-6 (hardcover)
  1. Academic achievement--United States--Congresses. 2. Teacher
effectiveness--United States--Congresses. 3. Educational change--United
States--Congresses. I. Solmon, Lewis C. II. Agam, Kimberly Firetag. III.
Schiff, Tamara Wingard, 1963- IV. Title. V. Series.
  LB1062.6.M54 2005
  379.73--dc22
                                                        2005006480

Cover Photo:

2004 Milken Educator Michael Aw starts off the day with his sixth graders at Hopedale Memorial Elementary School in Hopedale, Massachusetts.

Printed in the United States of America

MILKEN FAMILY FOUNDATION

Two Decades of Advances in Education and Medical Research

The Milken Family Foundation (MFF) was established by brothers Lowell and Michael Milken in 1982 with the mission to discover and advance inventive and effective ways of helping people help themselves and those around them lead productive and satisfying lives. MFF advances this mission principally through the various programs it initiates and carries out in the areas of education and medical research.

Guided by a belief that "the future belongs to the educated," Lowell Milken created one of MFF's signature initiatives—the Milken National Educator Awards—in 1985 as a means to attract, retain, develop, and motivate high caliber individuals to teaching. The program has evolved from spotlighting a dozen California educators into the nation's largest and most visible teacher recognition program now in 47 states and the District of Columbia, annually honoring outstanding teachers, principals, and specialists with individual, unrestricted $25,000 prizes. They join a national network of over 2,000 Milken Educators committed to excellence in the teaching profession, and in demand as an expert resource base for local, state, and national education policymakers.

The nation's students benefit from the commitment of many capable teachers. Yet experiences with Milken Educators and thousands more teachers in classrooms across America made it increasingly apparent that if every child is to have access to quality teachers K-12, far greater numbers of talented people are needed to teach. Thus in 1999, Lowell Milken introduced the Teacher Advancement Program (TAP) as a complementary initiative to the Milken Educator Awards. TAP is a research-based comprehensive school improvement model to attract, develop, motivate, and retain the best talent for the teaching profession. The program is built on four interrelated elements: *multiple career paths, ongoing applied professional growth, instructionally focused accountability,* and *performance-based compensation.* In just a few short years, the Teacher Advancement Program has been implemented in over 75 TAP schools across the nation with more in the planning stages, and preliminary research findings confirm the value to students and teachers alike of this comprehensive education reform strategy.

The Milken Educator Awards and Teacher Advancement Program are but two of the Milken Family Foundation's education-driven initiatives. Others include the Milken Scholars Program, the Milken Archive of American Jewish Music, and the Milken Festival for Youth. In the realm of medical research, Foundation efforts include the American Epilepsy Society/Milken Family Foundation Epilepsy Research Award, Grant & Fellowship Program, as well as the Prostate Cancer Foundation, created by Michael Milken in 1993 and today the world's largest philanthropic organization dedicated to better treatments and a cure for prostate cancer.

For additional information concerning Milken Family Foundation initiatives in education and medical research, visit *www.mff.org*.

CONTENTS

PART III
TEACHER QUALITY

PART IV
WHAT IT TAKES TO MAKE A PERFORMANCE PAY PLAN WORK

PART V
NO CHILD LEFT BEHIND

PART VI
WHAT WILL MY UNION SAY

PART VII
EVALUATING REFORM

ACKNOWLEDGMENTS

We had the pleasure of working with many talented people in preparing this book. Their hard work and dedication made the project significantly easier and of high quality. First and foremost we appreciate the efforts of Citadelle Priagula who aided us in editing and assembling this publication. Our appreciation goes out to Maggie Bava, Daren Reifsneider, Félice Myers, Jennie Weiner, Debbie White, and Judy Wiederhorn who helped with the editing process. Thank you to Zephran Hamlin who edited the initial conference transcripts to turn the document into a readable form. Much appreciation to Larry Lesser and the Milken Family Foundation Creative Services Department for their technical talents in video taping the conference sessions and then providing us with transcripts of each session. Thank you also to the Milken Family Foundation Communications Department under the leadership of Bonnie Somers for providing input and editorial guidance.

Thank you to all of the contributors to this publication who participated in the Milken Family Foundation's 2004 National Education Conference and helped to bring to fruition the important ideas laid out in this volume. We would also like to thank Information Age Publishing, Inc. for their continued involvement with this project and for investing time, energy, and support for such a worthy cause. Finally, special gratitude goes to Lowell Milken, chairman and co-founder of the Milken Family Foundation for his continued support and contributions to the goal of improving the educational experience for all children.

INTRODUCTION

Lewis C. Solmon, Kimberly Firetag Agam, and Tamara W. Schiff

Education in America has undergone a multitude of reforms over the last 4 decades. Despite countless efforts and billions of dollars spent, student achievement has remained essentially stagnant. In a knowledge-based society such as ours, a quality education is the key to a promising future; thus this trend of mediocrity in our public schools must be eliminated. Past reform efforts appear to have been ineffective; however, some current reforms are promising.

No longer will we accept the fact that student achievement is not increasing; as a result, we are seeing a large push to increase the quality of teachers in our schools. In studying hundreds of such reforms over the past 2 decades, the Milken Family Foundation has learned a great deal about why even the most promising reforms have not succeeded. Most have been isolated efforts, not school-centered; they have been poorly designed and/or poorly implemented; and they have not been comprehensive in nature, often solving one problem only to create another. Too often these reforms have been imposed on teachers without explaining the merits to them or getting their input and buy-in. Furthermore, these reforms have not taken account of the political realities of the education system, including the goals of special interest groups or the priorities of changing leadership; and they lack a scientific research base. Frequently, these reforms have been implemented without an obvious source of ongoing funding, and so are not sustainable in the long run.

In addition to these observations, our extensive research and analysis of school reform has led us to a clear conclusion: no reform will result in sustained student achievement gains without a high-quality teacher in the classroom.

We thought it appropriate, given that this book focuses on Reforms that Work, to begin in the introduction by reviewing a reform that is working: our own Teacher Advancement Program (TAP). Research confirms that the quality of the teacher is the single most important school-related factor driving student performance. So in 1998-1999, as an outgrowth of our studies of other reform efforts and research on teacher quality, we developed the Teacher Advancement Program (TAP), a scientifically based, comprehensive school reform strategy to attract, develop, motivate and retain the best talent to the American teaching profession.

We realized that in order for the teaching profession to attract and retain high-quality human capital in competition with other professions, certain structural changes need to be made. Teachers must be offered powerful opportunities for career advancement, professional growth, and increased compensation, and until the teaching profession offers these prospects, it will continue to find itself hard pressed to attract top talent, let alone retain the talented teachers that are already in the profession and motivate them to excel.

TAP provides these opportunities through its four essential elements: multiple career paths, ongoing applied professional growth, instructionally focused accountability, and performance-based compensation. These elements provide teachers with the ability to move along a career path and, when qualified, take on more responsibilities for increased compensation without leaving the classroom where they are needed most. Under TAP, teachers no longer work in isolation, but collaborate on a regular, weekly basis using student data and classroom evaluations to help guide their professional development. This enables teachers to improve skills, behaviors, and knowledge that specifically impact their students' learning. In addition, TAP teachers are evaluated within a fair, transparent system focused on clearly defined instructional standards. Finally, a portion of the compensation of TAP teachers is based upon the skills, behaviors, and knowledge of the teachers as exhibited through their classroom evaluations, upon their responsibilities, and upon the achievement growth of their students. This is a system that ensures greater teacher accountability and a focus on student achievement.

TAP honors the essence of our public education system while changing its structure to appeal to a broader group of high-quality professionals. It is not a program that has "compromised" reform due to teacher demands, but rather one that has sensibly adapted to their needs, positively impacting teachers and students in over dozens of schools in nine states in just 4 years. And though we continue to make refinements in the program as it expands, we have steadfastly maintained the core principles of TAP, which we have found to be essential to effective school reform.

TAP is gaining momentum, national visibility, and wide support from many different constituencies. Our early results have been very encouraging. In particular, we have found that resistance to change—a major obstacle in any reform effort—has been lower than anticipated. Part of this is due to the fact that we are implementing TAP in a climate in which government officials, parents, and students are demanding higher levels of performance from our schools, making them more open to change. This shifting paradigm provides fertile ground within forward-thinking schools and districts to adopt and implement TAP.

Improving Student Achievement: Reforms that Work expands on the first volume in the Milken Family Foundation series on education policy, *Talented Teachers: The Essential Force for Improving Student Achievement.* The series explains to policymakers, parents, business leaders, and teachers the importance of teacher quality in increasing student achievement. This volume is based primarily on the proceedings from the 2004 Milken National Education Conference (NEC), which was held in Washington, D.C., in May 2004.

In the early 1980s, the Milken families created an awards program to acknowledge educators' crucial contributions to our national well-being. Their main belief was—and is—that an effective way to advance the teaching profession is to reward educators' achievements, enhance their resources and expand their professional interests. The program has grown to national stature with 47 participating states and the District of Columbia and now gives the unrestricted Milken Educator Award of $25,000 to outstanding kindergarten through 12th-grade teachers, principals, counselors, librarians, and other specialists each year, having reached a total of 2,000 in the fall of 2004.

Award recipients are also invited to attend the Milken Family Foundation's annual National Education Conference where they have the opportunity to learn about critical educational issues, policies, and programs. In 2004, for the first time in the program's more than 20-year history, the NEC took place in our nation's capital.

The 2004 NEC, "Improving Student Achievement: Reforms that Work," generated discussions on many of the critical issues relating to teacher quality and improving student achievement. The resulting proceedings comprise a major portion of this book. In addition to the proceedings from the conference, we invited panelists to submit supplemental articles, reflecting in greater depth their examination of these issues. Each chapter begins with the discussions from the conference and concludes with the companion articles. Several of the conference participants have changed employment positions since the completion of this publication; however, given that the narrative is proceedings from a conference, provided titles reflect the position those individuals held at the time of the NEC.

PART I

This book opens with a discussion of the fact that, despite a myriad of reform efforts, schools in the United States have actually undergone little change over the last 3 to 4 decades. The proceedings provide supporting data and reasons explaining a lack of transformation, as well as offer optimism for current reform. The seven panelists and moderator represent a wide variety of political and educational perspectives, and so provide a diversity of views: Lowell Milken, the chair of this session, brings both a business perspective and 2 decades of work in K-12 education; John Boehner, U.S. House of Representatives (R-8th, OH) and chair of the House Education and Workforce Committee, provides a congressional perspective on school reform; Frank T. Brogan is president of Florida Atlantic University and former Florida state education commissioner; Kevin P. Chavous, former District of Columbia City councilmember, provides insight gained through his three terms of promoting education change on the District of Columbia City Council; Dr. Eugene Hickock, former under secretary for the U.S. Department of Education, provides a discussion from the federal government's perspective; Mary Landrieu is a U.S. senator from Louisiana and one of the Senate's foremost leaders on education; and Ted Sanders, a former education chief in three states, is the president of the Education Commission of the States, a nonprofit, nonpartisan organization that provides leaders from all levels of education a forum to exchange information, ideas, and experiences.

Education is often called "the great equalizer." It has the power—if provided and received as part of a rigorous experience—to enable a secure future for every child. Unfortunately, as a nation, we have not achieved this goal despite countless reforms tried over the past 40 years. This panel discusses the various reasons for why these reforms have not worked from resistance to change, the structure of the current system, a lack of vision, teacher quality concerns, and funding issues. Presenters also highlight current efforts they see as steps in the right direction for improving student achievement including No Child Left Behind and, in particular, the accountability measures the law requires from states, districts, schools, teachers, and students. The panel ends with a message of hope that the future will bring positive change in education, rather than the stagnancy in education reform that has played out over the past 40 years.

PART II

The promising outlook for transforming the current education system continues in the presentations from Virginia Governor Mark Warner and Minnesota Governor Tim Pawlenty. The future appears bright, but that does not mean that obstacles do not exist. The governors discuss some of the critical challenges facing public education in America, and specifically in their respective states. They share the actions they are taking in addressing those issues.

One challenge that states are facing is filling positions in hard-to-staff schools with high-quality teachers; Governor Warner informs us on what Virginia is doing to deal with this issue. Governor Pawlenty shares his views on the responsibility of parents in their child's education and continues the discussion of the importance of high-quality teachers in the classroom. He describes the current status in Minnesota and talks about what they are doing to motivate, retain, and recruit teachers. Both governors urge that high-quality teachers are crucial in improving student achievement.

PART III

Part III highlights how teacher quality (TQ) is being addressed in a variety of ways across the nation. At the federal level, No Child Left Behind (NCLB) has led the way, while state initiatives and local efforts including numerous pay-for-performance plans, alternative certification programs like *Teach for America*, district hiring incentive programs such as signing bonuses and mortgage assistance, and programs such as the Teacher Advancement Program (TAP) have all influenced the TQ landscape.

Cheryl Fagnano begins the discussion by reviewing both the No Child Left Behind requirement for all states to develop a plan to ensure that all teachers are highly qualified by 2005-2006 and the specific guidelines the law lays out for determining whether or not a teacher is highly qualified. The panelists address the challenges and promising outcomes of the various TQ efforts in response to NCLB that are underway both nationally and at the state level. Jim Horne, then Florida commissioner of education, argues for the need to make fundamental changes to the teaching profession in order to address the quality issue. Lisa Graham Keegan, then CEO of the Education Leaders Council, shares her ideas about how removing barriers to entry into teaching can help to improve quality. Ray Simon, assistant secretary at the U.S. Department of Education (U.S. ED), reminds the audience that the U.S. ED is a resource to assist states as they embark on teacher quality reform, and Janice Poda, senior director of the South Carolina Department of Education's Division of Teacher Quality, tells us about some of the teacher quality programs and policies that South Carolina had in place before NCLB, such as requiring content area exams for teachers. She then discusses how NCLB has helped the state reexamine what they are doing in terms of teacher quality and concludes with her concerns about the law.

PART IV

One reason often cited for low teacher quality is money. Low salaries often contribute to the limited number of talented teachers entering the profession, as well as to the difficulty of retaining and motivating high-quality teachers once they are there. One idea to address this problem is performance pay. Over the last decade, many plans that link pay to teacher performance have been attempted in school districts across the country. However, most of these programs have been terminated or suspended.

Lewis Solmon begins the discussion by sharing with us why he favors performance pay along with his observations about why performance pay plans have not worked in education, including budgetary constraints and a lack of teacher understanding and support. Solmon argues that all of the problems that arise can be dealt with and performance pay can be successful. He calls on the panelists who have studied, designed, and implemented performance pay plans to offer their perspective on whether such plans are viable and, if so, how they can be successfully implemented in the future to support higher quality teachers and increased student achievement. The group of experts on the subject includes: Frederick Hess, director of Education Policy Studies at the American Enterprise Institute; Alan Krueger; Bendheim Professor of Economics and Public Affairs at Princeton University; Brad Jupp, a teacher in Denver Public Schools who has helped to develop and implement the Denver Classroom Teachers Associate pay-for-performance plan; and John Schacter, president of the Teacher Doctors who formerly worked at the Milken Family Foundation and helped design the details of the TAP performance pay plan.

PART V

No Child Left Behind has been in place for over 2 years, and as schools, districts and states wrestle with implementation, there are both supporters and detractors. Those who support the law cite that this is the first time achievement has been looked at by the subgroups of race, language, socioeconomic status (SES), and special education. They contend that without looking at these important differences, we will not be able to close the achievement gap. The detractors recognize the importance of closing the achievement gap, but feel that too much testing, too little funding and the inflexibility of NCLB outweigh the benefits.

In tackling the pros and cons of NCLB, we hear the perspectives of those trying to implement NCLB at the state and federal level, as well as observations from the media and research. Lewis Solmon opens with a review of the achievement gaps that NCLB seeks to close. Susan Zelman, superintendent of Public Instruction at the Ohio Department of Education, conveys how NCLB has helped her state with its educational agenda. Kenneth James, director of Education in Arkansas, asserts his support for the high standards and accountability that the law calls for, while sharing his concerns such as the breadth of the law coupled with short turnaround times. He also discusses what he feels are key components to successfully meeting the law's requirements. Jay Mathews, education reporter for the *Washington Post*, brings a different outlook to the table and shares his observations gained while traveling around the country, visiting schools and talking with teachers about NCLB. Richard Ingersoll, an associate professor at the University of Pennsylvania, provides a researcher's angle and tells us what data on teacher supply and demand indicates about the prospects of meeting the teacher quality requirements in NCLB. Finally, a panel discussing federal law would be incomplete without representation from the office that administers the law. Nina Rees, deputy under secretary for Innovation and Improvement in the U.S. Department of Education, talks about the progress of NCLB and answers some of the questions raised by those in the field.

PART VI

As a new twist to this proceedings volume, we have included a discussion from a different Milken Family Foundation conference, the Teacher Advancement Program Conference held in Vail, Colorado, November 12-14, 2004. The reason for inclusion is that in talking about education reform and improving student achievement, we would be remiss if we did not include the perspectives of the teachers' union. Joan Baratz-Snowden, director in the Educational Issues Department of the American Federation of Teachers (AFT), reminds us of this point and stresses how the teachers' union can and should be a collaborating force in education reform. She dispels the rumor that unions are "little more than roadblocks" to reform and urges us to call upon them in any reform endeavor. Ms. Baratz-Snowden describes the role that the AFT has taken in efforts to improve schooling and particularly to improve teacher quality; she discusses the union's view on pay-for-performance and finally evaluates TAP against AFT criteria.

PART VII

Evaluation is an integral component of reform. Not only does it tell us of a program's challenges, evaluation also alerts us to policies and programs that are making a positive difference, serving as a very powerful tool when used effectively. In this last chapter, we have included a paper by Dr. Herbert J. Walberg, a professor emeritus of education and psychology at the University of Illinois at Chicago and distinguished visiting fellow of Stanford University's Hoover Institution. Dr. Walberg's studies include the topic of educational effectiveness. His chapter examines the necessary components for a good evaluation. He concludes by evaluating several evaluations of whole school reforms including the Teacher Advancement Program.

IN SUM

Reform of any kind is an arduous process. It requires forward thinking, hard work, collaboration, and commitment on the part of teachers, administrators, policy leaders, and other supporters of the endeavor. Education reform in particular can be especially difficult due to the many ingrained features of our current K-12 system; however, it is vital to learn from our past mistakes and break the cycle of failed efforts in order to fix the system that is the lifeblood of our country's future success. These proceedings provide insights into some of those past efforts as well as some of the current initiatives that provide optimism and hope in schools across the country. From these examples, we recognize that it is imperative that we improve student achievement by embracing reforms that work.

PART I

IMPROVING STUDENT ACHIEVEMENT

CHAPTER 1

IMPROVING STUDENT ACHIEVEMENT

Reforms that Work

Lowell Milken, Congressman John A. Boehner, Frank T. Brogan, Councilmember Kevin P. Chavous, Eugene W. Hickok, Senator Mary L. Landrieu, and Ted Sanders

Introduction by Tom Boysen

The hardest job I ever had was that first year of teaching when I was scrambling just one lesson ahead of my science and geography students, anxious about the parent conference with the owners of the dog that ate Harriet's homework and excited about my team's basketball game that night. Teachers and principals, we celebrate your excellence and your contribution and welcome you to the session.

In our audience today, we have most of the 50 chief state school officers, those state superintendents, commissioners, and directors who carry the torch for education excellence working with legislators, governors, and the professional community to advance educational excellence and opportunity. We say a warm welcome and thank you for your courageous leadership. I had the pleasure of serving as Kentucky commissioner of

Improving Student Achievement: Reforms that Work, 3–42

education in the 1990s and many of you are longtime friends. Indeed, I am proud to consider myself a "recovering chief state school officer."

The goals of the Milken National Educator Awards program are to celebrate, elevate, and activate great educators. *Activate* means to deepen your understanding of policy issues and strengthen your voices in deciding them. Today's panel on education reform is a step in that direction, and it is my pleasure to welcome this very distinguished panel and introduce them to you.

I have a dilemma: "So Much Fame, So Little Time." Our panelists have accomplished so much that I could use most of the hour introducing them. They want to talk about the future, not hear about the past. Therefore, I will give each of them an extremely short introduction while you hold your applause, and then we will give them one extremely loud, uproarious greeting.

In his seventh term as representative of Ohio's Eighth Congressional District, John Boehner has continued to fight for a smaller, more accountable federal government. A leader in education reform issues, he helped pass legislation in 1994 allowing school districts to use Title I funds for public school choice programs. Since January 2001, Congressman Boehner has chaired the House Committee on Education and the Workforce, through which he helped shape and then pass the No Child Left Behind Act with overwhelming bipartisan support. Congressman Boehner now leads his committee on a wide variety of issues including retirement security, special education reform, and expanded school choice.

A lifelong champion of public education, Frank T. Brogan is president of Florida Atlantic University. Over the course of his education career, he has been a fifth-grade teacher, dean of students, assistant principal, principal, and superintendent of schools for Martin County in Florida. In 1994, Mr. Brogan became Florida's youngest-ever commissioner of education, building greater accountability into the state's public school system. He also served as Florida's lieutenant governor under Jeb Bush. A leader in the fight against cancer, Mr. Brogan currently serves as statewide chairman of Florida's Dialogue on Cancer.

Kevin P. Chavous is currently in his third term as a member of the District of Columbia City Council, representing Ward Seven. As chair of the city council's committee on education, libraries, and recreation, he has been at the forefront of promoting change within the D.C. public school system. His efforts have led to nearly 400 million new dollars for public education. An advocate for school choice, Councilmember Chavous has helped guide the charter school movement in the nation's capital. His book, *Serving Our Children: Charter Schools and the Reform of American Public Education*, was just published. In addition to his work on the city council, he is a practicing attorney and teaches education law at American University's Washington College of Law.

Dr. Eugene Hickok is the U.S. undersecretary of education and principal adviser to Secretary of Education Rod Paige. Prior to his appointment, Dr. Hickok spent 6 years as Pennsylvania's secretary of education, during which time he oversaw the state's education system and helped implement a sweeping education reform agenda. An expert on public policy, the U.S. Constitution and Federalism, Dr. Hickok has served as a consultant to the governments of Lithuania, Latvia, and Estonia regarding constitutional, political, and economic reform. He has been on the board of trustees at four universities in Pennsylvania. Dr. Hickok helped conceive the No Child Left Behind Act and is a leader in shaping its success in schools and states.

One of the Senate's foremost leaders in education, Louisiana Senator Mary Landrieu was the first woman from Louisiana elected to a full term in the U.S. Senate. In 2001, she worked across party lines to help craft the No Child Left Behind Act. She also led a successful effort to ensure that federal Title I dollars go to schools with the highest concentration of poor children. As a co-sponsor of the Safe and Stable Families Act, Senator Landrieu helped remove barriers that children face in seeking permanent homes, and established systems that connect children with loving families in a timely manner.

Dr. Ted Sanders is president of the Education Commission of the States (ECS), an interstate compact created in 1965 to improve public education by facilitating the exchange of information, ideas, and experiences among state policymakers and education leaders. A former classroom teacher, Dr. Sanders was state superintendent of education in three states: Illinois, Nevada, and Ohio. In 1989, he became deputy U.S. secretary of education, and then served as acting U.S. secretary of education until March 1991. Dr. Sanders also presided for 5 years as president of Southern Illinois University.

Introducing Lowell Milken is a great pleasure for me. I met him over 10 years ago when I led the Kentucky delegation to a conference like this in Los Angeles. Lowell's vision for American education is the same start in life that he had ... for all students. That start was a first-class public education, which extended from kindergarten through law school attaining the highest honors at every level. Lowell was and is that student that we, as teachers, want sitting in the front row: curious, compassionate, energetic, good-humored, collaborative, and prepared. *No dog* ever ate Lowell's homework.

So after incredible academic and business success, at the age of 33, Lowell co-founded the Milken Family Foundation, and for over 20 years, the Foundation has been advancing its mission by implementing national

programs in education and medical research that identify talented people, provide them with resources and connect them within powerful networks, all to enable individuals to achieve even higher levels of success
and performance.

As a businessman and a keen student of economics, Lowell knows the
importance of human capital and sees schools as the wellspring of talent
and teachers as the currents that lift talent to the top of each student.
Lowell says that in every endeavor, people make the difference.

Lowell is not just a student; he is a visionary and a doer. In the late
1980s, before the World Wide Web was of any consequence, Lowell saw
the potential of technology to support learners and teachers. That insight
led to the Milken Exchange on Education Technology, which initiated
programs and encouraged policies, such as the federal e-rate, that have
led to so much progress in bringing computers and connectivity to American classrooms. In the mid-1990s, Lowell saw ahead to the teacher shortage and the teacher quality crisis. He decided that the next big push of
the Foundation would be to change the structure of the American teaching profession. That dream became the Teacher Advancement Program
(TAP).

When Lowell Milken talks about the future of American education, it is
a good idea to listen.

Lowell Milken

I want to extend a warm welcome to the members of the panel. Your participation makes a powerful statement of your commitment and your dedication to improving K-12 education. The topic of the panel is
"Improving Student Achievement: Reforms that Work."

The panel topic is one of great interest to me and it has been for over 2
decades. Believing as I do, that education is a means most conducive to
building human resources, it is essential that we do everything within our
power to assure that every child in America is afforded a high quality educational experience.

The stakes are extraordinarily high. I say that because millions of
young people, the majority from disadvantaged circumstances, have a
window of opportunity, while they are in school, to develop and nurture
their moral and intellectual character. These goals, if achieved, will yield a
secure future. The means to do this is education, for education has the
power to:

1. Equip every young person with knowledge and the skills of civiliza-
    tion: most notably, literacy and mathematics, but also a broad
    understanding of history and the sciences.

2. Provide young people with the breadth of awareness and confidence to make sound and independent judgments, and to proceed to the next step in learning and life.

3. Prepare young people to be good citizens, to participate in, to defend, to question, and to understand our democratic government, making young people part of our great national narrative. This is crucial in a nation whose bloodlines, languages, religions, and myths have so many sources.

4. Enable every young person to become a productive member of our society, for it provides the knowledge and skills that are key to the knowledge worker.

Yes, the benefits of education are great, but only if they are provided and received as part of a rigorous experience. Tragically, this is not the state of American education today.

Over the past 35 years, the world has undergone significant change. We see it in the workplace and in virtually every major sector of the economy. However, our schools have undergone little change. The result, for the most part, is that U.S. education outcomes show little improvement over this period.

Now, there have been positive developments over these years. For example, as a nation, we have focused efforts through federal legislation to address racial segregation, to meet the needs of special education students, to support disadvantaged youngsters and to provide bilingual schooling for immigrants. We have also seen a marked increase in the number of academic courses taken by high school students (Chart 1.1).

Over the past 2 decades, we have seen an increase in the percentage of students taking higher-level math and higher-level science (Charts 1.2 and 1.3). Progress has also been made in the areas of standards and assessment. Today, more than 80% of states are using criterion-reference assessments, and we estimate that there are at least 15 states now using the same standards-based tests in grades three through eight for both language arts and math.

Yet, when we look at the outcome measures—what the system is producing—the growth is not there. We have not made progress on increasing graduation rates, especially the percentage of students who enter high school in ninth grade and graduate on time (Chart 1.4). In terms of college readiness, studies show that the percentage of high school graduates that possess the basic skills to attend a 4-year college totaled just 32% of all 18-year-olds. For African American students, that percentage is 20%, and for Latino students, 16%.

Employers' and professors' views of academic performance of U.S. high school graduates confirm these findings. A recent public agenda poll

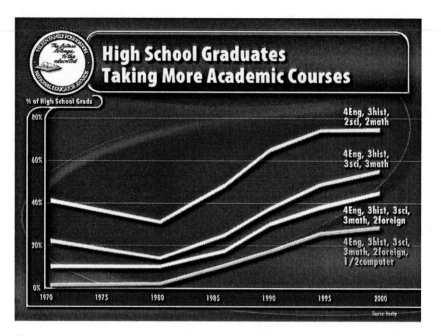

Chart 1.1

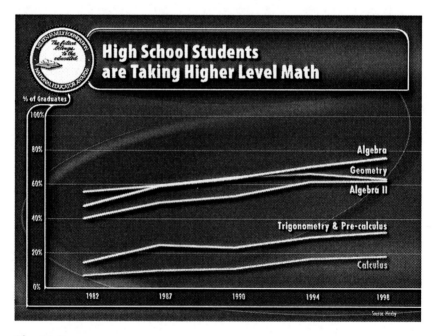

Chart 1.2

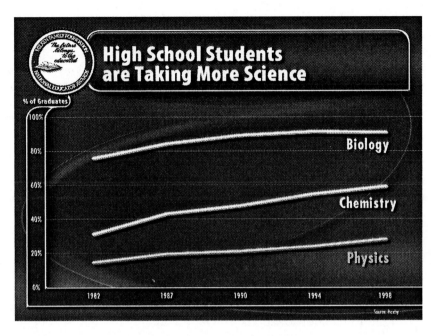

Chart 1.3

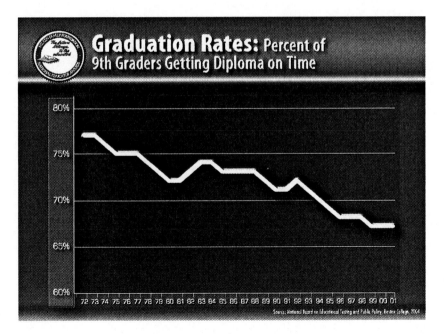

Chart 1.4

shows that a high percentage of employers and professors believe that public school graduates have fair or poor skills when it comes to writing clearly, doing basic math, and grammar, and spelling (Chart 1.5). These results are not surprising when you consider that remediation in English and math remains the fastest growing activity on many college campuses. For example, California State University, with its 23 campuses and more than 400,000 students, threw out 11% of its freshman class in 2003 for failing to master basic English and math skills.

This state of affairs is indeed troubling; after all, the knowledge economy has less and less need for unskilled workers. From 1991 to 2000 alone, the demand for skilled workers increased from 45% to 65% of all jobs in our country. We also see the education and wage disparity in life-time earnings continue to widen (Chart 1.6). Unless U.S. graduates obtain a rigorous education, they are going to be hard-pressed over the coming years to compete for professional and skilled jobs with the ever-increasing number of college graduates from around the world. These graduates will provide very stiff competition for the most talented U.S. graduates, much less those with weaker skills.

In light of the poor to fair skills of all too many U.S. high school graduates, it is not surprising that academic achievement levels in K-12 are

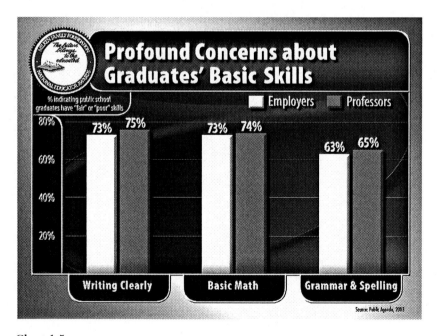

Chart 1.5

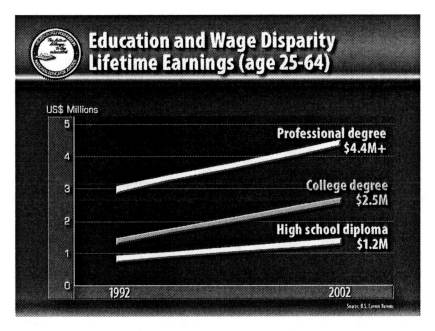

Chart 1.6

lacking. A recent UNICEF report provides an analysis of the gap between low achievers and average students by using test results in reading, math, and science (Chart 1.7). The United States ranked 18 out of 24 countries in terms of having a low percentage of 14- and 15-year-olds below minimum competency in literacy, math, and science. Even more disturbing is the fact that international comparisons show that the longer U.S. students spend in school, the poorer their comparative performance (Chart 1.8). The number of nations scoring higher than the United States on the Third International Math and Science Study (TIMSS) increases as students' progress from Grade 4 to Grade 12.

Why is this so? Some argue that the results are not truly comparable country by country because student populations differ. Others say American students fare poorly because curriculum in American secondary schools is "a mile long and an inch deep." While others argue that because of the high rate of out-of-field teaching in secondary schools, particularly in math and science, the United States simply does not have enough teachers with strong knowledge of the subject matter they are teaching.

Whatever one's views are of the international comparisons, when we look at student achievement growth in K-12 nationally, little progress has

Chart 1.7

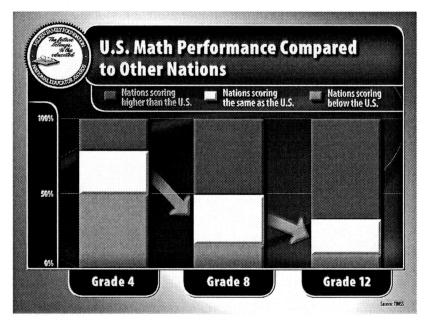

Chart 1.8

been made over the past 35 years. The National Assessment of Educational Progress (NAEP) 2003 reading results show that just 32% of fourth graders and 31% of eighth graders were proficient or better in reading. Over the past few years, with virtually no improvement in moving students to a proficient level in reading, we can better understand the enormity of the task before us if our nation is to reach the goal of moving every young person to a level of proficiency.

Why it is so critical for young people to reach a proficient level in reading. A child in the fourth grade reading at the basic level has the ability to comprehend the overall meaning of what they read. However, this fourth grader does not possess the skills that proficient readers do: to draw conclusions; recognize cause-effect; identify a writer's intent and purpose; analyze similarities and differences; and read actively by summarizing, predicting and clarifying their thinking. A proficient level of achievement is the target achievement level set by No Child Left Behind. It is the level that young people must attain if they are going to be prepared for gainful employment in the twenty-first century.

As I mentioned earlier, only one third of fourth-grade students nationwide can read at a proficient level. This is certainly disappointing. But what is *tragic* are the numbers of children in America that score at an achievement level below basic, which means they cannot read at all. Sixty percent of African American fourth graders who took the NAEP reading assessment scored "below basic," while 56% of Hispanic fourth graders could not read. Although the numbers are better for Asian and Caucasian children, respectively, the number of students who cannot read is clearly a national travesty (Chart 1.9).

In math, results are also disturbing. On the 2003 NAEP mathematics exam, just 33% of fourth graders were "proficient" or better in math. Similarly, only 28% of eighth graders were at or above "proficient." There has been some growth over the past 3 years in students reaching math proficiency (Chart 1.10) in fourth grade. However, even at the current level of progress, it will be still be generations before all students are at proficient levels. There are still extraordinary numbers of students who are at the below-basic-achievement level. Fourth graders who perform below basic levels in math are unable to estimate or use basic facts to perform simple computations with whole numbers, do not show understanding of fractions and decimals, cannot solve real-world problems, nor can they use calculators, rules, and geometric shapes. In the eighth grade, the percentage of students "below basic" is slightly less than that of fourth grade, but only because many of the kids scoring below basic in fourth grade have dropped out of the system by eighth grade.

We know that these low achievement levels are highly correlated with being poor; and because African American and Hispanic children consti-

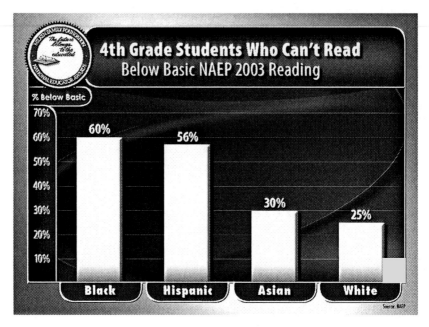

Chart 1.9

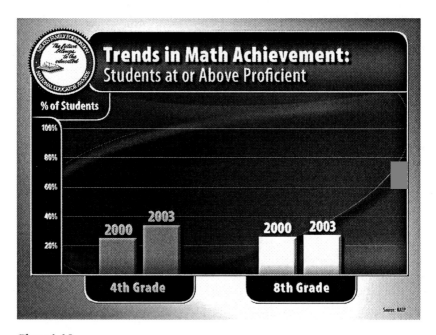

Chart 1.10

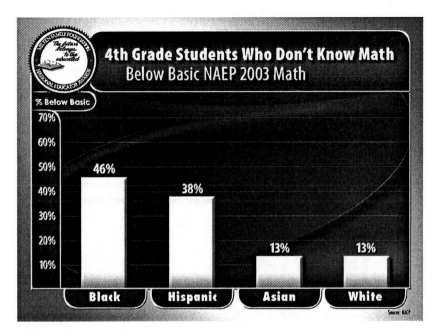

4th Grade Students Who Don't Know Math
Below Basic NAEP 2003 Math

Chart 1.11

tute the majority of those living in poverty, their achievement results are correspondingly low (Chart 1.11). All of this adds up to the fact that as a nation, we have made little progress in closing the achievement gap in the past 2 decades (Chart 1.12).

With respect to educational spending, on a per-pupil basis, the United States outspends most other major industrial countries in both primary and secondary education. Nationally, after inflation, K-12 spending more than tripled between 1960 and 2002 (Chart 1.13). The federal government, as most of us know, only constitutes approximately 8% of total K-12 funding. However, federal education spending itself has increased from $6.5 billion in 1983 to $35.8 billion in 2003, reflecting an annual compounded rate of 8.9%.

In the past 37 years, the federal government has spent more than $180 billion on Title I programs to help disadvantaged children. Yet the K-12 system continues to allocate only minimal funds to research and development and to data collection and management. Of the total funds spent on K-12 education in all forms, less than two tenths of 1% is spent on research and development and on collecting data and then analyzing the data to make informed management decisions, respectively. These allocations do not adequately provide funding for the research that is needed to

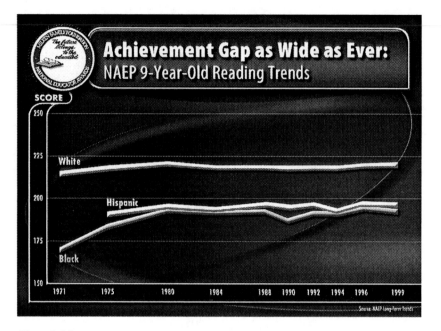

Chart 1.12

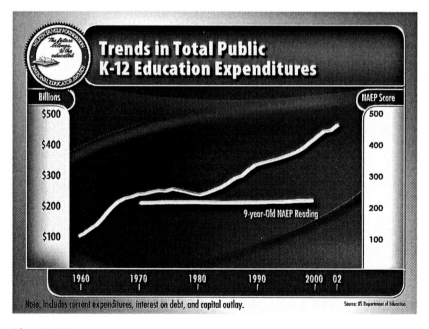

Chart 1.13

develop educational strategies, tools and programs to help students achieve.

Let's turn to the issue of teacher quality. Although research shows that the single most important school-related factor in driving student performance is teacher effectiveness, the profession still has not made the structural changes required to be able to attract large numbers of talented people to the profession and then develop, motivate, and retain them. With so many opportunities and rewards in other professions in the form of career advancement, higher pay and sustained professional growth, it is little wonder that poll after poll and focus group after focus group show that the most talented college graduates have little interest in teaching. Similarly, key concerns of talented teachers have simply not been addressed in the schools, and therefore, attrition rates remain high. Unfortunately, those who do leave the profession generally score highest on subject matter knowledge and pedagogy.

Out-of-field teaching persists, especially in high poverty schools. For example, 64% of physical science teachers in high poverty schools had neither a major nor a minor in the subject matter being taught. From 1982 to 2000, the number of teachers with bachelor's degrees in subject areas declined, and the percentage of teachers who had earned master's degrees in their subject area fell even more, from 17% to 5% (Chart 1.14).

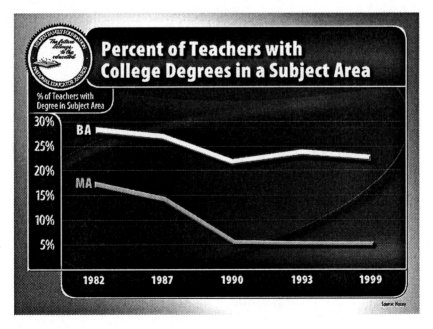

Chart 1.14

Further, studies show that schools with 20% or more students scoring at the lowest levels have consistently less qualified, less experienced teachers. Yet, very few states focus their efforts on programs targeted at hiring teachers for high needs schools.

Even though these numbers tell us that we have a great deal of work to do, the current state of affairs does not exist from a lack of effort to reform the system. Quite the contrary, over the past 4 decades, there have been literally hundreds and hundreds of reforms, in every shape and size, ranging from national initiatives to state, district, school, and classroom reforms. For example, in 1983, the National Commission on Excellence refocused the public's attention back to the basics of math, reading, and science with the release of the report *A Nation at Risk*. The report received unprecedented attention in the media and within the education community. The key issues raised by that report were the fact that we needed to improve academic content and expectations, that students were not spending enough time in academic study but rather in nonacademic courses for which they received credit toward graduation, and that teachers lacked subject matter knowledge and preparation. There were many recommendations that stemmed from this report. These recommendations included strengthening the content, adopting more rigorous standards, devoting more time to learning the basics, and improving teacher preparation courses.

So what was the impact of this major educational reform report? Some progress was made, as was noted earlier, in terms of the number of units of academic subjects taken, narrowing some resource gaps and augmenting the system's resources. But for the most part, achievement gaps remain as wide as ever, and the education system still cannot attract talented college graduates in sufficient numbers to meet the needs of our nation's public schools. More often than not, bold reform attempts have proved ineffective for reasons such as lack of continuity, poor design, and not being school-centered.

Nearly a decade after *A Nation at Risk*, Congress authorized the Educate America Act, which set in motion Goals 2000. These were a series of educational goals that the nation's leaders expected public K-12 students to meet by the year 2000. However, despite good intentions, none of the major goals on K-12 education were met. All too many students still come to school not ready to learn, high school graduation rates remain around 70%, significant numbers of students perform at below basic levels in math and science at all grade levels, the teaching force does not have access to high-quality programs to improve their professional skills, U.S. students are not first in the world in math and science, and every American adult is not literate, nor do enough American adults possess the knowledge and skills necessary to compete in a global economy.

In addition to national education reforms, there have been literally hundreds of other school reform initiatives. We have examined at the Foundation more than 300 school reforms ranging from those based in distinct educational philosophies to those focused on specific subject matter to others on instructional tools, and still others on the structure and management of schools. The fact is that the system of K-12 education has been constantly reforming, but with little success. Former President Carter once characterized the nation's bureaucracy not as a source of fierce resistance, but as a "giant Washington marshmallow" that absorbed changes without ever really changing.

When we look at the system overall, we see little progress in the way of achieving growth, which brings me to the following questions. Is the K-12 system so resistant to change that it is not possible, under present circumstances, to reform the system? Does the K-12 system need competition to jump start significant improvements? If so, what are the most effective ways to introduce competition to the system in order to yield student achievement gains?

Ted Sanders

I think the answer is *yes*, but it will be extremely difficult to do so for several reasons. The marshmallow metaphor is a good one. I would use a principle of physics in describing the education system and why it is so difficult to change or modify. The principle of inertia that all of us studied in Physics 101 says that a body at rest tends to stay at rest, but if it is in motion, it tends to stay in motion and in the direction that it's moving. The education system is a significant mass that we're talking about, and the force required to impact any kind of change is extremely significant. So, inertia is one of the major reasons why the system is so unsusceptible to change.

The second reason is that we are victims in many ways of our own success. The reality is that the fundamental structure of American education has actually served the nation pretty well up until the transition into a knowledge-based economy, where now we have to educate every child to high levels. The fact that we spend so little on research and development and data management conveys a very powerful message and it explains why the system is not susceptible to change. There may be lots of innovation, but very little science in reality. Indeed, we do not do research and development. We do not test or measure whether ideas are actually successful when we do try to innovate. However, there is a lot of churning and innovation, but we have no science to create systematic change.

Politics factor into the discussion as well. Not partisan politics, but the politics of community that requires redistribution of both human and fiscal resources. Anyone that is working in a state with an adequacy lawsuit understands how difficult the politics are in moving resources to affluent communities.

We have heard a nice description of what happens in the beginning of a teaching career. When I began in the profession, I started teaching in Idaho, but then moved to New Mexico. In Albuquerque, a large urban district, you started in one of the *barrios* with the most difficult-to-teach environments. If you were successful, you moved up to Northeast Heights to the more affluent, attractive places to teach. So the best teaching resources actually were systematically moved away from the schools and the children that needed them most.

Culture, too, went inside of those politics. We have not had the will even to adapt in some of the fundamental ways that one would expect. For example, we refuse to think differently about time. We are still caught in the old agrarian calendar, which does not make sense today. Especially now with graded instruction and the technology to create virtual schools and other kinds of experiences that could move children at their own rate through the system.

Lowell Milken

Congressman Boehner, is No Child Left Behind an answer to improving student achievement? Why should we have confidence that No Child Left Behind will yield different results than other major federal reform initiatives that we have seen over the past 3 decades?

John Boehner

There have been many efforts at improving our schools over the last 20 to 30 years. What we lacked in each of these major reforms was the will to stick with it. What will it take to be able to change our schools? I can tell you that sitting here in Washington, I've worked with many people in the educational establishment who have done everything humanly possible to stand in the way of this bill, No Child Left Behind, becoming a law and its implementation.

I hate to say it, but I call it the blob. I think that Ted's analogy of inertia mass at rest largely covers the educational establishment that represents teachers, the school boards, and PTAs here in Washington, D.C. If we are really going to succeed, those of us who are interested in ensuring that every child gets a chance at a good education, it's going to require vigilance on all of our parts. I mean, every day in the trenches taking punches. I have done it for 10 years now. Every day, I'm in this fight, and every day that I'm on this earth, I will be in this fight. Because that's what it's going to take if we're going to move the system to one that really does give all of our kids a chance.

Another thing is the issue of competition. I happen to have 11 brothers and sisters. Having so many siblings was great training for what I do here every day. But I also was in a business world, and competition was a key element. As much as we hated our competitors, because they were always driving the price down, they also were driving the quality up. It was always hard to compete, but it made all of us better. Indeed, I'm a big believer in competition. Whether it's charter schools, or whether it's the D.C. School Choice Initiative that I worked on with Kevin Chavous, I believe that competition is a good thing.

When it's all said and done, 80% of our kids are educated in public schools. If we're serious about giving every kid a chance, we're going to have to stick to it. I can tell you that, regardless of all the noise you hear about NCLB, there is no real effort among legislators in this town—Democrat or Republican—to change it. George Miller, a liberal Democrat from California who was the ranking Democrat on my committee and I have our arms locked. There is nobody that feels as strongly about No Child Left Behind as the two of us. For that matter, put the president and the secretary of education, put Senator Kennedy and others, and you will see that there's no real interest here changing the law. We understand what's happened over the last 20 years and why those efforts failed. I would suggest to you that they're not going to fail again.

Kevin Chavous

I want to answer your first question of whether or not our current system can be reformed. I think we have to be intellectually and practically honest. This current system, the way it's structured, the way it's been structured for 150 years, cannot reform itself. I think we need to be honest about that. It is a system that was put in place during the Industrial Revolution. It doesn't relate to today's children or the technological advances we have seen over the past 10 years. It is built on the premise that the bureaucracy that supports it ranks ahead of the children. It is self-protecting. It will survive where no one else survives. If your review of reforms over the past 40 or 50 years is any indication of what's yet to come with the marginal increases or gains that we have seen, then I think we're fooling ourselves to believe that it's going to get any better over time.

I do believe the competition works. We need to stop thinking in terms of the 9:00 a.m. to 3:00 p.m. models and everyone learning the same thing at the same pace at the same time. One size does not fit all. I strongly believe in choice in all forms because competition does make a difference. When you have charter schools in and around public schools, there is some improvement.

Lowell Milken

Let's look at some data with respect to the issues Kevin has raised. Chart 1.15 shows fourth-grade test scores in public schools faced with more competition, less competition, or no competition from the vouchers program in Wisconsin. Public schools faced with more competition showed improvement. This also occurred in Arizona where the public schools had to compete for students with neighboring charter schools.

Kevin Chavous

This is important because it is totally un-American to allow a failing monopoly to continue to exist. That is why we really have to focus on com-

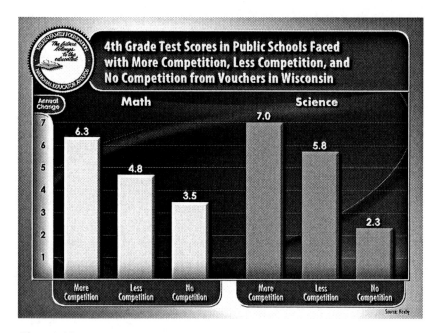

Chart 1.15

petition in all forms; and if a school is failing and educators are not meeting their goals, then the school must be held accountable. That is what I like about charter schools. They have 5 years to demonstrate their methods are working, and if they do not work, they close.

I would love to close some of our failing schools in Washington D.C. But the political reality suggests we cannot, and I think we need to be honest about that.

Mary Landrieu

I would like to jump in here. Perhaps every garden party needs a skunk! I'm not sure how big of a skunk I'm going to be, because I agree with so much of what has been said. But I also disagree with several things. I recognize we are a marshmallow today, but we don't have to stay a marshmallow. We can be something different and something better.

This presentation is a clear beginning of the realization of the truth that everyone in this room recognizes. If the American people come to know the truth, then they can mobilize for change. They have done it before. We mobilized for World War I, we mobilized for the Space Program and we mobilized for the Civil Rights Movement. All were efforts where there were fundamental, enormous, unprecedented changes that this country adopted; and in turn, we were able to progress. To those who think that we cannot get from where we are to where we need to go, they are wrong. We've done it before and we can do it again, given the right information, the will, and effective leadership.

Without a vision, people will perish. Right now, there is no clear vision. However, as the vision becomes clearer, as the options become clearer, and as much of what Kevin says becomes a reality, we're going to believe that the system can change. I'll agree with Congressman Boehner, No Child Left Behind is not perfect, but there is a very strong coalition of the Left and the Right, agreeing for maybe different reasons, but with the same goal, to keep this legislation in place. It is very different from anything we have done before because its tenets provide real consequences for failure. Neither *A Nation at Risk* nor President Clinton's vision of Goals 2000 mandated this type of accountability. No Child Left Behind is about setting measurable goals and imposing real consequences, such as closing the school, for failing to meet these goals.

In conclusion, I believe that the people in this room are some of the best and brightest. Because of your passion and commitment, we are one step closer to creating a public education system that's not a marshmallow. I think we can do it if we continue to work hard and set our minds to it.

Eugene Hickok

My hope for *No Child Left Behind* is that years from now, they'll look back and argue that this is when the reformation in American education began to take place. What we need is to think differently about what education in America should look like. Frankly, this law creates information, it creates data, and hopefully, it will free up the genius of teachers, faculty, and students who will look back and find out if this is, in essence, a human enterprise.

We have allowed teaching to become so bureaucratized that the very best and brightest, who were once attracted to the classroom, choose to leave. The goal of NCLB is to transform this enterprise into what it could be.

We have talked about the calendar. We have an agricultural calendar, an industrial model, and yet we live in a digital age. This just does not make much sense. Therefore, we start with No Child Left Behind in the hope that through a combination of smart investments and getting the truth out, people will recognize the need for fundamental change. The data about competition speaks to the human aspect of this enterprise. It's human nature. I think the American people want to do better. I think the American people want to expect more of their kids, of their teachers, and, frankly, want them to expect more of America. I think No Child Left Behind plants that seed of opportunity.

Frank Brogan

The good news for everybody gathered here today is the fact that I am now a university president. For the first time I see everything so much clearer. There is an amazing capacity that children have. If you took a group of children and put them out in the middle of a field, no balls, no bats, no gloves, no equipment of any kind, they would: (A) begin to play a game, but (B) they wouldn't begin to play it until they set some ground rules—it's a remarkable capacity that they have—(C) regardless of the game and the rules, fairness would rule the day.

The amazing thing about education is the fact that we are, for the first time, on a national scale, beginning to set the rules. I think No Child Left Behind, is, for the first time, setting the ground rules. Think about it. Should there not be, in every state, clear, concise, and rigorous standards for what children are expected to know and be able to do as they move from grade to grade? I think everybody agrees with that. That's a basic rule, a basic premise. Should there then not be, as we have in our classrooms every day, a fair, consistent assessment to determine in benchmark fashion whether children, to the greatest degree possible, are meeting up to those standards along the way? Remember, those standards are what they need to know if they're going to be competitive in the most competitive global economy the planet has ever known.

No test, no assessment, is perfect. But should there not be an assessment? Not just one assessment, but shouldn't we continue to assess children on a regular basis? Should there not be a clear definition of what a quality teacher is?

We've grappled with that issue for centuries. What is a quality teacher? Shouldn't we, in the twenty-first century, finally be able to see and know what a great teacher is all about? We have them here today. Shouldn't there be transparent reporting to teachers, to parents, to the students themselves? Transparent in that people can see it and understand it. Should there not be, as Senator Landrieu mentioned, rewards and incentives for those who are doing a great job—individual teachers who are out-performing their peers? Shouldn't they be rewarded in a way that is special, or should we lock them into an industrial model that rewards them for two things, the degrees they hold and the number of years that they've had on the job? Shouldn't there be actions? I've stayed away from the word *sanctions*, because I believe in action when there's failure present—action to remediate, action to change, and action to see something better at the end of the day—not to punish.

If you stop and think about it, those are the new rules of the game. Now, at the end of the day, we allow the creativity, the innovation and the pure genius of people like those in this room to determine how they are going to satisfy the rules of the game. I think for the first time we have the will to sustain this effort. We've been at it for 12 years in Florida with our hybrid of the A+ plan, which is a hybrid of No Child Left Behind; and at the end of the day, we have to ask ourselves, is it working? We're seeing rising student achievement. Not only generally, but we're seeing it among children of color. We're seeing it among children of low socioeconomic status, different backgrounds, and different cultures. They're leading the way and proving what we all know in this room—that color of skin, native tongue, socioeconomics, and family structure have not the first thing to do with a child's innate capacity to learn.

Mary Landrieu

I agree with so much of what's been said, but wish to add a caveat regarding No Child Left Behind. I think the goals of it are important, and it was something that I and many other members of Congress supported.

However, the commitment to fund it is also very important. Without the funding that was promised, none of what was just said is going to happen.

Let me explain some of these numbers. It is important to understand that in the administration prior to Clinton, we were running record deficits. When we got to a surplus in the last 2 years of the Clinton administration, we put a 19% increase, followed by an 18% increase in funding, into education. When President Bush took office, I, along with many Democrats, helped pass No Child Left Behind. The next year's increase was 16%, but this is the tragedy: in 2004, the increase is only 5%, and it is decreasing. Next year, it's only 3.8%. The next year, based on the projections of the budget currently in debate, it goes down to 1.9%.

All the wishes, goals and good intentions in the world are not going to be able to be sustained if the federal government's commitment goes down. Further, one of the principal goals, or obligations, of the federal government is to try to equalize the playing field. We know that the disparity and inequity in funding is in large measure the problem. Some of our wealthier students, in better or stronger counties, do okay. It's in the poor minority communities that children need the help and are not getting it. It is not always the case, but most of the time the more resources you have, the better results you get, if you're spending them in the right way.

Sometimes, in the poorer areas, people are doing their very best and trying their hardest, but they are starving for resources. The federal government's job is to come in and say that in this great nation we recognize there are wealthier counties and poorer counties. Our commitment is to give every child an equal chance, not a guarantee, but a chance to succeed. If the federal government's percentage, which you can see on some of the charts, is just slightly increasing, it's only by 8%. If we don't get that number up to about 20% of the total, we won't have enough money to spread on the top of the cake to make it even. Title I, while it should be going to equalize the playing field, in large measure has been siphoned off in an equal manner to all districts, regardless of need. So the final conclusion is, the federal government must step up to the funding challenge, and we must be committed to match dollars with our words. We must be committed to recognize our role as one of trying to equalize opportunity.

Eugene Hickok

With all due respect, you point out increases in the budget, and then you refer to them as decreases. But there have been increases. The American taxpayers passed a milestone this past year on K-12 spending: over $500 billion, $125 billion more than national defense in a time of war, and this is as it should be. The goal here should not just be money, because as the charts have demonstrated, we spend a lot of money and we will continue to spend more money. When you focus on spending, you never will be able to spend enough. I've never met a school board member, state chief, or superintendent who said, "Please, no more money."

You need to think about investing. When you think about spending, it's all about more. When you think about investing, it's "What's the yield on the investment?" As the charts demonstrate, and as the American people are beginning to realize, we have not invested smartly. We have not invested in a way that yields tremendous results. In the wealthiest nation on earth, we need to do a much better job of how we invest, whether it's at the state level, the local level, or the national level. So, the money issue can be debated, but if we don't start talking about the yield on our investment, we'll never spend enough money.

Lowell Milken

Certainly, if No Child Left Behind is the "answer," we need to ensure that it is properly funded to enable it to succeed. But funding levels have increased over the past 2 decades; and as you can see on Chart 1.16, little progress was made in reducing the percentage of fourth-grade students

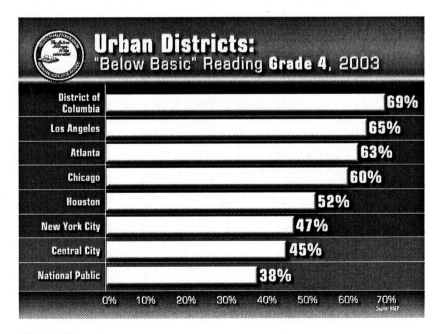

Chart 1.16

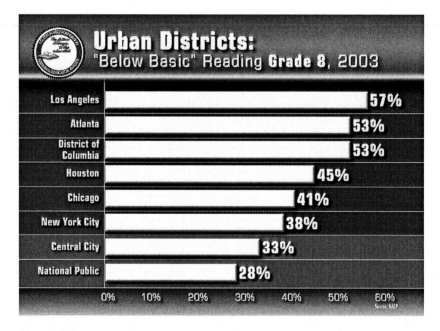

Chart 1.17

and eighth-grade students, respectively, in urban areas who score at below basic in reading levels (Chart 1.17).

It is always easy to say that if we only had more money, we could do the job. The problem, however, is not just about money. Aren't families and students themselves responsible for the poor results? If inequality in education represents the most serious civil rights issue in America today, why are those families and communities with large numbers of students performing poorly not in an uproar about their children's education? Why do families protest an opening of a Wal-Mart store in their community but do not protest against the poor educational opportunities afforded their children?

How do we change a system where there doesn't seem to be the political constituency to do so?

Kevin Chavous

I am hopeful for change, but when I initially said that we couldn't expect this system in its current form to work, I really meant that. With all the reform we have put in place, the sameness of what we do is what is getting us in trouble. You are absolutely right about this issue about the political constituency. In business, you focus on the end user. The end users—in terms of education, particularly when we look at the charts that relate to the reading and math scores in urban America—are low-income and, most notably, folks of color who aren't getting the end result. Many times they don't know what they know, and the problem is that the agenda is controlled.

We have deferred the issue of schools and school reform to the status quo, to folks who either, as you indicated, are benefactors of the system or the problems in the system don't directly impact them or their children. There needs to be a call for action. I have taken a lot of heat here in D.C. for my views on choice. When I talk to real parents in my ward, east of the Anacostia River from Deanwood to Anacostia, most of the people who are strongly against change no longer have young children in the school system or they are otherwise disengaged in terms of what's going on in schools. However, when you talk to real parents, they're crying out for anything, and they don't know the power that they have.

There has to be a more collective and focused effort to educate people about the realities of what's going on in our school system. I think we need more federal money, but we need to make sure that money is applied the right way. We have added 400 million new dollars to public education here in D.C. We have had 10,000 fewer kids in D.C. public school, and we have not seen the results. If you talk to some of our best teachers—and I applaud the teachers from D.C.—they know this. We talk to the best teachers in D.C. and they say sometimes their biggest challenge is dealing with that bureaucracy.

Mary Landrieu

Kevin is correct about that. I am sure everyone in this room agrees that bureaucracies can get you in a lot of trouble, not just in the school system. Breaking up the bureaucracy, making it more entrepreneurial, being goal-oriented, allowing more flexibility, encouraging people to experiment in a variety of different ways, funding the reforms and staying the course— that is the hope of No Child Left Behind. I know it's not perfect, and I know we need to make some changes. One size doesn't fit all. The principles outlined are historic. It's not just another education reform. The big accomplishment of this law is the message it sends about our commitment to reform. It says we are no longer going to passively tolerate failure. Instead, we are willing and able to invest in success. School by school, area by area, the system as we know it will be dismantled under No Child Left Behind, and a new system will emerge if we stay the course.

Now if you want to blow it up overnight and give everybody a voucher, then that's a whole other debate, of which I am not going to be a part, because I don't think that's the answer. However, if you want to force the current system to change, then a federal law that mandates it to change within a certain period of time, and funds that change, is in place.

Eugene Hickok

First, the way you sustain it is to find those who are trying to make it happen. We need to capitalize on the sense of ownership on the part of teachers, parents, and students and the school board members. Once people realize how bad things are in their school or in the District of Columbia, then things happen. The best evidence is something that Kevin Chavous helped make happen last Friday at the D.C. Convention Center. The center was full of men and women and kids signing up to exercise an option that Congress has given them for school choice, because they recognize that in this city, the nation's capital, we have what might be the poorest performing school district in the country. Parents realize this now and want to exercise what's best for their kids. Moments like that are taking place all over the country, whether it's charter schools, No Child Left Behind, or whatever. They capitalize upon that because, in the end, it's the power of ideas and attitudes that will change American education.

Ted Sanders

No Child Left Behind will not work, and I happen to be a fan of No Child Left Behind. This chart (Chart 1.18) shows a big paradox going on here. I think it's too early to know whether there really is a constituency or not. But something is different in the country today with the passage of this legislation; it is heavily bipartisan and includes action more than exhortation this time around. We actually track which states are doing real policy action and response to the law. One of the most important levers inside of No Child Left Behind is the assessment of learning and accountability by subgroup. In March of 2003, only nine states actually had met the accountability demands for the provisions of the law. Today, 46 of them have met the requirements and three more are really close. There is action afoot in the states in response to this law unlike anything we have ever seen before.

States are doing some powerful innovations in the interventions in low-performing schools. Virginia Governor Mark Warner is trying to train spe-

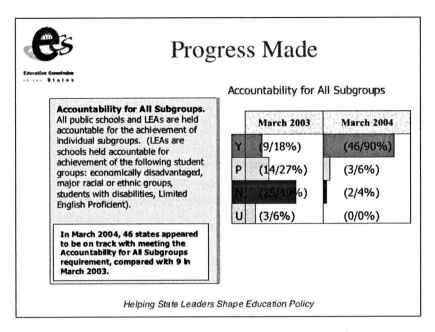

Chart 1.18

cialists to go in and service principals. Ohio State Superintendent Susan Zelman's Schools of Progress are also having an impact. There are some powerful and important ideas that are being tried. Also, underneath this implementation is some of the same old business as usual. This law really clarifies that "state certification" does not mean "highly qualified." That is an important policy realization, or realization on the part of the country. Yet when you look at the plans that people had from the states that I happen to represent, you have some really good policies in play in the states regarding highly qualified teachers in the existing workforce. However, in almost every state, with one or two exceptions, there are multiple criteria for defining highly qualified, yet there is always one option that is extremely weak for teachers in the existing workforce to get that designation. Only time will tell, because it's going to take constituent advocacy if we're going to be able to make some of these kinds of tough changes.

Frank Brogan

In all my years in education, it has always amazed me how we deal with death by anecdote. We have voluminous teacher contracts that are full of rules and regulations as to who can do what, because something happened to one person somewhere one day. To make sure that never happens again, we fill volumes with contract language that actually hamstring teachers' ability to do all kinds of things they want to do. Worse, it keeps us from being able to organize ourselves around children instead of demanding that children organize themselves around us, the adults.

In Florida, we now have a class size initiative. I told my friends that requirement was actually something we did long before it was put into the constitution. What would happen at the beginning is that Mrs. Smith and Mrs. Jones would each have an equal number of children in their first-grade classes. Mrs. Smith, because she was a weak teacher, would have a torrent of parents coming into the principal's office saying, "Not to my child, you don't. I want my child out of her class." By the end of the year, Mrs. Jones, an outstanding teacher, would end up having the children with whom she started and half of Mrs. Smith's class. Therefore, we rewarded Mrs. Jones by doubling her class size. We actually punished the other one by cutting her class load in half.

Guts is the answer to your question. At what point do we stop putting in trap doors to allow people who are failing to fall through it? At what point do we raise standards for my profession? I'm still a certificated member of the professional teaching ranks, and I'm proud of it. At what point do we, the teachers, stand up and say, I want to be paid for what I do? I don't want to be paid for what she does, or what he does. A friend of mine who is a businessman said it best. He said the difference between private sector and education is this: In the private sector, when a business doesn't work, it's gone. It goes bankrupt, belly-up. In education, we don't ever go belly-up or bankrupt. We simply become less relevant.

Audience Question

We all know that we can't turn out enough teachers from colleges right now because teachers are not respected, and we're in a society that respects money and salaries. So what I'd like to know is, how can we raise the teacher salary by some kind of mandate that directs the funds from the state, so that it doesn't go to the bureaucracy first?

Frank Brogan

First of all, we have to start from the basic premise that your dream will never become a reality if we maintain the same industrial-model pay schedule that we have used forever in education that, as I mentioned earlier, this system rewards two things: time and service.

Experience is a great contributor to someone's success, but it's not the only one. Neither is the degree that a person holds. Oftentimes, we give people more money for getting an advanced degree in an area that has absolutely nothing to do with what they're doing for a living—but they got the time, the energy, paid the money, so we give them more money as a reward for doing it. I am convinced that until we break from the shackles of that industrial model and begin to reward people for the job that they are doing—not the job that everybody on their step is doing—putting more money into the same system just isn't going to give us the return on investment that we expect.

So, it's not only a matter of more money, that's always an issue, but it's a matter of what are you going to do with the new money you get? As a great man once said, "If you always do what you always did, you'll always get what you always got." That's the bottom line.

Eugene Hickok

I think you're talking about symptoms of a larger problem, and you're exactly right. It is almost naïve to think that it is possible, through a mandate, to create a better profession without changing the world in which that profession operates. That's the problem. The mandate will not lead to change, and I think we have to recognize that students and teachers, not bureaucracy, should drive it.

Frank Brogan

At the university level, we are not the keepers of all wisdom and light, but I will tell you that we certainly don't use a standard salary schedule. When we go to hire a new professor, we don't hire that professor and pay that individual what we pay everybody else. If we want a great professor, we pay them a competitive market salary. That means from time to time we have to go back and adjust the salaries of our best and brightest, or they may leave. That's the expected and accepted protocol at the university level. It's not an aberration; that's how professors understand it's done at the university level to always attract and maintain the very best and brightest. If we can create a system like that at the university, why can't we create a system like that in K-12 education?

Ted Sanders

You probably pay some your faculty more than you pay yourself.

Frank Brogan

Oh, a few of them are doing very well.

Lowell Milken

If you were to pay every teacher $5,000 more, it would cost approximately $15 billion each year. Will the American public today support an across-the-board increase in teachers' salaries? I do not believe it will. However, I do believe that the American public will support programs to pay talented teachers more—those who exhibit the skills and behaviors that are conducive to student learning and who perform at high levels. Senator, what is your feeling on this?

Mary Landrieu

I agree, and one of the reasons there is not a bill to give every teacher a raise is because it would never pass. There are ways to determine which teachers are excelling and recognize that achievement. You could give those teachers who get national board certification a certain tax credit. Not only do you get an automatic $5,000 or $10,000 increase in your salary, but also there is a tax credit so you don't have to pay taxes on that increase. Some states are beginning with extra certification to recognize that some teachers deserve more pay than others do.

Again, what do you do in a county that is basically poor with a school system funded by property taxes? Nobody wants to raise property taxes, so where does the money come from? Where do we get the money for even an increase for good teachers in that county, or for differentiated pay? As we move through this transformation, I think the answer is the federal government, at least for the next 5 to 10 years.

When we passed the Welfare Reform Act, the federal government had to increase spending significantly to change the welfare system as we knew it. I think the federal government is going to have to step up and stay that way as we move through this transition. At the same time, we are asking states to find new and better ways to pay teachers in a more exciting way. We have flatlined the federal funding for teacher quality. I don't think we're going to make it when we require one thing and can't fund it at the federal level.

Audience Question

Hi, I'm from the great state of Louisiana, and I am a National Board certified teacher in English/language arts and mathematics. For every dollar that the federal government spends on education, what percentage actually gets to my classroom? I suspect it's probably less than a nickel. You see, when you send the money, and we believe you are sending it, it does not seem to get there.

I believe that everybody loves children and wants the best. What happens is, as it trickles down to local school boards, you have people who have never been in education. In some cases, their children have never been in a public school. As you vote on the spending limits, how can you guarantee me, the taxpayer, that you are going to watch that money closely and make sure it goes to where it was intended?

Mary Landrieu

Let's look at (Chart 1.19) which shows the percentage of education funding that comes from the federal government because it's very important. Even though we talk about it in billions of dollars, it's still only 8%. So, if every single dollar the federal government spent went to your classroom, it would only be eight cents of every dollar.

The question is, how much of your local and state dollars are getting to your classrooms? This is a very legitimate question. We've tried over the last 50 years to ask that question, and it's very difficult to get to an answer.

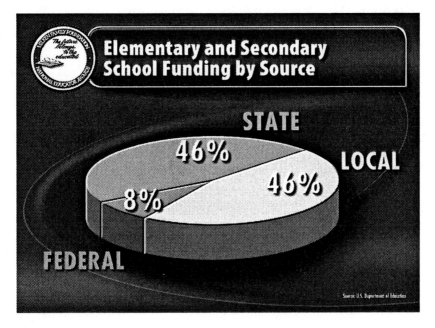

Chart 1.19

Therefore, instead of doing the same thing that we do, we changed; we stopped looking at funding and tracing those dollars and just expected results.

Now we try to measure results, and we look at a school or the classroom and say, "This school is not doing its job." Then we look further and ask, "How is the money being spent in that school?" In the transformation of that school, if the process works and we stay on the course, that question that you asked will become more apparent because for 4 years we have been trying it the old way, which doesn't seem to be working.

Kevin Chavous

I didn't believe in the trickle-down theory during the Reagan years, and I don't believe it in education. It just doesn't work. One of the big problems we have on the local level is that the bureaucracy does gobble up the money. In addition, I think that we have allowed our local school districts to evolve into being all things to all people.

Here in the District, I've proposed that we narrow the scope and put the focus where it should be. Frankly, I don't think a superintendent of schools should be in charge of procurement or food service or bus transportation or facilities. I mean, with all due respect, educators aren't always the best business folks, and I don't necessarily trust someone who was a teacher and then a principal and then in central administration to deal with the architectural designs for a new school. School districts are involved in so many things that gobble up so much money, that's why it doesn't trickle down to the classroom. We need to narrow that focus so that a superintendent of schools is primarily responsible for instruction, academic achievement and providing support for teachers. Then we get some experts in other areas to be responsible for those other areas. That's where I think the push has to come when you talk about change in the system, so that we have a better synergy created as a result of the dollars that we use.

Eugene Hickok

We know that more federal dollars are going to the school, or at least to the district, more than ever before. To build on Kevin's point, why do we have to continue to think we have to have districts? Why do we confuse schooling with education? Education starts long before a child enters a classroom; it goes on forever. Schooling is an institutional apparatus. Why aren't we willing to begin to think and talk about money going to a classroom, money going directly to instruction?

We tend to buy into the structures, the governance, the institutional paraphernalia we have always had, because we have always had it. I long for the day we begin to think that maybe we could try something dramatically different.

Ted Sanders

I spent 2 weeks last year in Australia. Australia in 1901 plagiarized the U.S. Constitution for its constitution. Therefore, its legal construct for education is precisely the same as ours. Every school is a public school. However, the reason why you may not actually see any of the federal money is the elementary and secondary education act is more elementary than secondary.

Second, the money does not go to every school. It actually was intended from the very beginning to be a rival shot into the most disadvantaged because it was intended to start equalizing opportunity for our most disadvantaged kids. The bulk of the money goes into Title I eligible schools, not all schools. Even if the money made it down, without any drag at all from the bureaucracy, you probably wouldn't see any of it in your school just because of those two features of the act itself.

Audience Question

I am unlike most of the other teachers here; I teach a career and technical course. Most of my students are disadvantaged, and a full 60% said that they would leave high school if the career and technical center was not there and operating. The 60% stayed in school and graduated, and many did find careers. This year's budget is discussing cutting Perkins funding, which is our lifeblood of funding, from $1.5 billion to $1 billion. This would have a dramatic effect on the children at this school. They get through high school, they become doctors, they become nurses, and they become teachers.

Frank Brogan

We made an interesting mistake some years ago in education relative to vocational and technical education. We started to track students. Vocational or technical was an acknowledgement that not all students needed to go to college. However, there are wonderful high-wage, high-tech, job opportunities out there in the trades, in the professions that require an advanced vocational or technical education. Unfortunately, we began to use vocational courses as a dumping ground for some students that were not successful in the academic program. The teachers knew it; they saw that it negatively affected the whole world of vocational and technical education. Instead of recognizing the mistake we were making and fixing it, we stopped tracking students.

Therefore, we eliminated the emphasis on a powerfully important part of the educational program—such that we still see too many students walk across that high school graduation stage and receive a diploma yet they cannot get into a college, even in an open enrollment community college, and do not have the skills to go on to advanced vocational technical course work. Where do they go, and what do they do? It is time to acknowledge that college is great and more important than ever before. There is still an important world out there. Try to get somebody to come to your house to lay tile; they do not exist.

Eugene Hickok

One of the reasons that more hasn't been done is the budget. Every budget is an attempt on the part of a president, regardless of who the president is, to engage Congress in a conversation about where to go next. I think the idea behind this budget proposal is basically to ask that question. Carl T. Perkins, the oldest federal vocational education program, has been around forever, and it hasn't really changed very much. In large part, we recognize, as an administration, that we need to think about it differently than our past mistakes.

In addition, we need to talk about high schools a bit differently. In far too many places, the high school experience is not what it needs to be and we have allowed ourselves to develop this way of thinking—that you have academic students on one side and vocational students on the other, and never the twain shall meet. Yet, everyone needs academics and everyone needs some hands-on experience. Therefore, part of our job through budgets, through programs, and through policy is to try to reengineer the high school vocational division and talk not just about what takes place, but how to prepare for what comes next. Preparing for change is essential because we have not done that very well in this country.

Mary Landrieu

One good way the federal government can help, which has been a traditional way the federal government has helped, is by identifying the models that are working. Across the country there are districts that are experimenting with new and exciting reform models. Many of these models allow options and choices and really support both tracks. I am not sure even you would call it two tracks, but just different options and choices.

Furthermore, instead of cutting funding, the federal government should readjust it instead. For example, say we have been spending X amount on a certain program or reform that has not made much progress. Why don't we take that funding and instead seek out and support the exemplary programs with research-based results all over the nation? Similar to the Milken Family Foundation finding exemplary teachers, highlighting them, and rewarding them financially for their hard work and proven skill, the federal government should do the same. By rewarding and highlighting the successful reforms, we can then scale those models up and implement them on a wider scale.

Audience Question

The panel has talked about the problems with bureaucracy. I think it has been referred to as a marshmallow and an inert object. Why then hasn't a piece of the No Child Left Behind legislation actually dealt with failing bureaucracies? If you had 20 schools in your district and 20% of them were failing, would you actually close down the district?

Frank Brogan

We have had something comparable in Florida, the A+ Plan, and have been working on it for 12 years. It does not necessarily have the bureaucratic provision in it; however, what it does have, and what I'm convinced the No Child Left Behind plan will do if we can sustain the momentum, is that it uncovers failing bureaucracies and identifies them for everyone to see.

In Florida, what we began to see is that people rally around the concept, "somebody had better do something in this system to change the way you do business." There was a mass outcry in the systems where there was chronic and sustained failure because we finally exposed the bureaucratic failure for what it was. We began transparent reporting.

In Florida we grade schools A through F. You want to see uproar? Wait until you assign an F to a school where two thirds of the children can't read, write, or count on grade level. We use the grading scale because everybody understands it. They do not know one through five. They do not understand sustained growth. However, they do understand A through F, and the uproar that we have heard from parents and teachers who will not tolerate a school with an F is astounding. It reinvested that ire back into the school by demanding more and ensuring new opportunities for children.

Audience Question

One of the things you talk about—investing and getting the best yield on the investment—is teachers who get together and talk about what they are doing. I was talking with my new friend from Louisiana about what's made us better teachers. I went to what I thought was a great university in Ohio with an excellent teacher education program. When I look back at it now, when I first started teaching, I wasn't very good those first couple of years. I got better as the years went on. Growth occurred when I started talking to other teachers, when I really started reflecting on what I was doing, in terms of what students were learning. We have teachers doing great things—often in isolation, for one thing. How do we see policy affecting that, rather than just talking about it? How do you see at all the policy affecting the culture of teaching?

Mary Landrieu

One of the finest examples is the Teacher Advancement Program (TAP) that the Milken Family Foundation supports. TAP's model is one of the best. The schools have master teachers helping all of the other teachers within a school.

Again, the federal government can help, but so could states by highlighting and identifying effective programs and scaling up the funding. However, without the extra funding or without taking funding away from other education programs or increasing the overall amount, you just cannot get the scale. TAP is certainly one example, and maybe some of our panelists know others.

Eugene Hickok

Teaching is a human profession. It is all about people. In far too many places, I have seen teachers almost in a solitary profession. They are so busy doing whatever they have been assigned to do that their interaction with their colleagues and their interaction with the district at large is cut short. To me, it's almost the bureaucratization of the American mind. A great teacher is the exact opposite of a bureaucrat. Yet, in far too many places, they've been asked to do bureaucratic things. We need to rethink the profession and rethink the world in which that profession operates.

Frank Brogan

We have talked an awful lot about what we can do for teachers, but it is very difficult to attract a young, aspiring teacher to the profession when they talk to teachers who run down their own profession in horrific ways. There are teachers on your campus whom it is hard to believe come to work every day, because they are so miserable about what they do and how they do it. The worst thing I hear is when a teacher says, "My daughter talked about becoming a teacher and the first thing I did was tell her, 'Over my dead body.'"

Teaching is tough, like every job, maybe tougher than most. However, if we as teachers don't start talking more proudly about the profession and all the wonderful things about teaching, why would anybody want to get into our business if they listen to the lounge lizards that run it down every single day?

Ted Sanders

If the structure and the culture are going to change, it's going to be because of teachers like those here today that actually cause that change to take place. When I was a state superintendent, I used to come to this conference and spend a couple of days with the very best of the teachers from either Illinois or Ohio. I'd go back home, really pumped up about what could be possible, just based on getting to know and interacting with a handful of teachers from my own state who really were at the top of the game. I am convinced that if it's going to happen, this is one of the two constituencies that can possibly make it happen.

Lowell Milken

We do need strong leadership in districts and in states to create an environment so teachers have the time to interact on a daily basis. Can you imagine if you are the CEO of a business, and during the day you do not have time to interact with other members of management? Teachers need time to focus on instructional strategies with one another to improve, for example, Billy's reading skills or Sue's math comprehension.

Audience Question

I am the superintendent of the Woodland School District in Illinois. Politically, it seems that for a number of years we have had mandatory education. We have had ESEA, we had *Brown v. Board of Education* and Public Law 94-142 (Education of All Handicapped Children Act), which all gave more opportunity to students. These programs were meant to affect participation of children within the system who were excluded in some way, shape or form by race or by handicap. Suddenly we have this program, No Child Left Behind, which doesn't deal with participation, but deals with performance. It has taken something like 50 to 75 years to get everybody involved in the system. Do you think it's realistic to expect 100% proficiency from all students within the next 12 years?

Eugene Hickok

In this nation, if it is going to happen anywhere (and it'll be the first place it ever happens, by the way) we should set as an aspiration the idea that every child can be on grade level. That is what proficiency means: grade level. If we believe in the promise of *Brown v. the Board of Education*, which is 50 years old week after next, that created the idea that in this nation, the very American idea that everyone should have access, then it seems to me that the next logical step in the promise of this nation is that everyone should have success. We will probably fall short. But we as a nation have always fallen short of our ideals. What makes us different is that we pursue our ideals. That's why I think this is a very important ideal.

PANEL CONTRIBUTIONS

CHAPTER 2

A SMART START STRATEGY
FOR SCHOOL REFORM

Kevin P. Chavous

No democratic responsibility is more sacred than the care of the young. The nurturing, protection and education of our youth has been advocated by every serious American thinker from Thomas Jefferson to Frederick Douglas to Horace Mann to W.E.B. Dubois to John Dewey to Mary McLeod Bethune to John Gardner to James Nabrit. All who fought in the civil rights movement agreed that better education for all American children was the key to a far better American future. When I sought the chairmanship of the DC City Council Education Committee, I did so because I knew that in our city we had betrayed the best hopes of those who had struggled for that American future. My visits to schools and growing understanding of the realities of public education led me to one stark conclusion: That our current system is not just dysfunctional, it is utterly broken. Yes, many parts excel. Many of its teachers and professionals are deeply committed. But as a system, public education is not working in America.

How did this happen? Incredibly, for a century and a half, there has been little substantive change in public education. In America's public classrooms, the classic approach remains essentially the same as it was years ago: one-size-fits-all with a core curriculum of subjects presented to

Improving Student Achievement: Reforms that Work, 45–52
Copyright © 2005 by Information Age Publishing
All rights of reproduction in any form reserved.

all students in largely the same manner. Students are divided by age and taught according to this curriculum. And they are promoted based on their perceived mastery of subjects. Or worse, they are advanced as part of a tacit social promotion system that serves no one—and particularly not the children themselves.

The result has been a system ill equipped to address the diverse needs of today's students within the realities of today's social dynamics.

The best way for public education to right size itself is to allow innovation and creativity to flourish. The traditional one-size-fits-all model must be exploded. Children and parents deserve classroom rigor and educational options that far too few students receive in today's classrooms.

Giving parents a choice is a critical factor in the future success of public education. Parental school choice allows each parent to find the right educational fit for their child. But choice is also important because it forces the traditional public education to keep pace with school programs that work. Unfortunately, our traditional public education system will never reform itself internally. No monopoly ever has. True reform will only take place through external pressure. The most effective form of external pressure comes by way of parental choice.

Charter schools, in particular, provide a model for reform that offer hope. Charter schools are, in fact, public schools: They receive public funding, are open to any students, and are overseen by a public agency, which holds them accountable to the academic and fiscal management goals outlined in their charter. Although they enjoy greater flexibility than traditional public schools, charter schools are highly accountable to both the public who must choose them and the sponsor who approves their charter. Significantly, the best charters are allowing for the coordination in one central location of desperately needed services for students parents and community members. They are providing a system malleable enough to respond to children's needs. Charters are, in short, filling a void left by the traditional public school system.

A review of the best practices found in many successful charters and traditional schools suggest that eight core components should be applied forcefully and consistently as guiding principles for sustained, systemic education reform.

1. PROVIDE CHILD LEARNING AT A MUCH EARLIER AGE

A core challenge is to support early learning for our children from age 3. This is where we will start. If we can begin on this premise, and work persistently and consistently, every goal we have for our children, our economy, and our culture will fall into place.

The latest scientific research on how the brain works informs us that a child's brain is at its most active stage of growth from birth to age 3. For example, a child learns a language by age 2. An adult's potential vocabulary is shaped by words learned before age 5. The neurological foundations for later learning of math and logic are set before age 4. Moreover, the experience of the child in the first 2 years of life largely determines how the brain develops into adulthood, along with its overall level of emotional stability.

Waiting until age 5 to begin learning is a dinosaur-like practice that should be eliminated. Age 5 is too late! We must focus on providing a good basic foundation in the early years of life.

To succeed, we will have to start early and drive slowly, but we will get there safely and on time. All families, particularly those with limited incomes, must have access to this early public learning opportunity for their children. This early start will decrease the cost of successfully educating a student, since the recurring costs for failure would be eliminated. We spend millions of dollars on remediation, compensatory education, security, special education, retaining students, summer school, and incarcerating those who enter the juvenile justice system. Funding early learning will cost taxpayers much less than funding the incarceration of so may of these children in later years.

2. PROVIDE MORE TIME TO LEARN: LONGER SCHOOL DAY, LONGER SCHOOL YEAR

The current school day does not match the 9-to-5 workforce realities faced by most parents, who now work out of the home for longer and longer hours. Most juvenile crimes are committed between the hours of 3 and 6 pm. The phenomenon of the latchkey child is a reality that requires the rethinking of the time of day that our public education system provides its services. In the information age, learning is not limited to the schoolhouse walls, the time of day or the yearly season traditionally designated as the *school day* or the *school year*. Our children need more time in school. The current school year does not provide our students with enough time to learn what it takes to succeed in this world.

By way of illustration, the school year in the District of Columbia is 180 days long. In Europe and Japan, students spend as much as 220 to 240 days in school per year. When our students are shortchanged by up to 33% of the *time to learn* in their school year, they will suffer during their entire life trying to meet international standards of performance.

3. IMPLEMENT A RIGOROUS
CURRICULUM AT ELEMENTARY LEVELS

Public school students can achieve at much higher levels if the curriculum content provided were of a higher level, taught by teachers who know the subject matter, and engage students in active learning. Higher-level content must be taught in the elementary grades. For example, many public school students in the District begin the study of geometry in the 10th grade, after completing a course in algebra in the ninth grade. Geometry is taught in the sixth grade in many American private schools, and in the more successful public schools. It is considered standard for elementary students in Japan and Europe. When the opportunity to engage in higher-level content is denied in the early grades, we place limitations on a student's ability to learn.

In essence, America's public schools must become flexible enough to implement a rigorous elementary curriculum, particularly in the areas of math and science.

4. IMPLEMENT RIGOROUS CURRICULUM FOR
ALL HIGH SCHOOL STUDENTS

The mismatch in our public education system is threatening the ability of the next generation of our children to compete effectively in a global economy. That disparity becomes tragic later in high schools where the curriculum taught is far more advanced than the knowledge and skills needed. And most of all, there is a mismatch in the level of excellence our children achieve and the level of excellence achieved regularly by students in other industrialized nations. Only 6% of America's high school students study calculus. In Germany, that figure is 40%. In Japan, 90%!

When our students have the opportunity to compete in advanced public and private schools, they do well. It is in our collective self-interest to give every American child such an opportunity.

I propose to provide a high school education for every student that is competitive with the best in education nationwide—in content, quality, and excellence. But every student need not complete 4 years of college. Today's high-tech job market requires training and excellence, but not always through a full college degree. Our school system must match the career opportunities that are emerging nationwide. Every high technology center in America was accompanied by a sustained commitment to creating education excellence at the grade school, high school, technical training, and college education levels. North Carolina's Research Triangle, California's Silicon Valley, Massachusetts' Route 128 Corridor, Maryland's 270 Corridor, and Fairfax County's Dulles complex are all the result of serious sustained public investments in quality education.

If we are to participate in the world-class economy growing at our doorstep, we must do what others have done: We must demand, pay for, and manage a sweeping reconstruction of our public school system. It is not a matter of running our current system more efficiently. We cannot take pride in our children becoming dropouts more quickly.

Immediate actions should include the implementation of a solid core curriculum that all students must complete by age 16. These high school curriculums must be designed to offer more rigor in math, science, and the arts. The curriculum must also provide compatibility with the best school-to-career practices.

5. CREATE SMALLER SCHOOLS

All school districts should embargo disposing of school properties until plans for smaller schools are finalized. Construction cannot lead instruction. The trend toward building larger school buildings has been determined by architects, not educators. Large construction does not provide real economies of scale. Dollars that are saved by constructing large school buildings are almost immediately lost through additional staffing for administration, security and the academic and social failure that is so often the result of the isolation and impersonal nature of the large school. Appropriate capital funding must be structured and remain consistently directed toward the construction of smaller school buildings. The recent trend toward creating smaller schools within schools is a step in the right direction.

Students are alienated and anonymous in large schools. Students are lost in an impersonal setting where very few adults, if any, know their name.

A sense of ownership or belonging is not fostered in a school of a thousand or more students. Students do not know their own classmates, and teachers do not know them. Appropriate sized schools are much more likely to become key elements of their neighborhoods and communities.

Parents, employers, and other stakeholders can become players in the school's support network, providing tangible contributions and visible models and mentors for students.

Where possible, smaller schools should be designed and constructed across the country.

6. MANAGE SPECIAL EDUCATION FOR POSITIVE RESULTS

Special education has become a sinkhole for tax money and troubled children. Spending has skyrocketed while the number of students served remains constant. The whole concept of student re-entry from special education back into mainstream learning has been lost in the shuffle. Management of special education for the seriously impaired is a serious challenge for the public school system. Children seriously inhibited by learning disabilities should receive appropriate guidance from teachers or counselors. Too many children with advanced levels of difficulty are in expensive and stigmatized care because our system skills for dealing with problem children are poor.

Rebuilding our school system must include rigorous professional training to spot and deal with troubled children, timely contact and referral services with parents, and strong, consistent collaboration with community resources, including the faith community. This effort cannot occur without facing the backlog of thousands of children awaiting professional evaluation. Reliance on regular system staffing for assessments will never resolve this problem.

I strongly support authorizing payment to assessment resources outside the system, using a competitive case rate by any qualified professional. State governments pay for an enormous amount of specialized education services, including separate classrooms, private schools, and residential facilities out of the city. Lack of appropriate management, outdated legal mandates, and failure to coordinate information and care between all child service agencies has led to exorbitant costs as well as poor outcomes.

Appropriate and effective care for troubled children can only occur by accepting a system view of public and private services and resources. Child resources must be brought under a coordinated philosophy and strategy. That strategy centers around collaboration with public and private stakeholders in child, youth, and family services to produce a seamless and caring service delivery system for troubled children. Such collaboration includes managing special education dollars to assure appropriate care and eliminate waste and duplication as well as instituting fixed rate assessment payments to private sector assessment professionals for children at risk for learning disabilities.

7. RESPECT, TRAIN, AND REWARD PROFESSIONAL TEACHERS

If the job of teaching is to be more than providing custodial care for children, educators must be helped to educate themselves and to create communities of professionals. Incentives must be implemented to encourage accountability, professionalism, and performance.

Performance measurements that simply measure inputs, such as time clocks, demean professionalism and do not ensure better outcomes. Businesses that succeed in "high labor" industries facing global competition must pay well, invest heavily in continuing professional development and make sure working environments enhance entrepreneurial attitudes and performance.

We must increase spending on professional development for teachers. Personnel costs represent hundreds of millions of dollars, which may be a wasted expenditure if we do not continually invest in the renewal of this human capital. Professional development must be viewed as mandatory, necessary for protecting our investments paid out as teacher salaries. Our schools must demand excellence. School leaders must rid the system of unqualified teachers. More importantly, all school districts should provide ongoing professional development for teachers and facilitate the development of a community of professionals in schools.

8. COLLABORATE ACROSS AGENCY LINES TO REDUCE TRUANCY, DRUG ABUSE, CRIME, AND VIOLENCE

It is a sad reality of our times that school-aged children use illicit drugs and alcohol. This impacts their ability or willingness to learn and the level of crime and violence among juveniles. There is, however, a relationship between a student's school experience and his or her involvement in drugs, alcohol, and crime. Students who are not successful in school are more likely to cut class, be truant, or drop out all together. Students who are not successfully engaged in school are at greater risk for illicit drug use, crime, and violence. Young women who are academically challenged and engaged in schools are less likely to become teenage mothers and/or enter the juvenile justice system.

Over 80 to 90% of our incarcerated juveniles did not have a positive school experience, and most dropped out of school. These students are in our schools for most of the day, and we will have to address their needs during the time that they are with us. It serves no useful purpose to blame parents, blame society, or blame anyone else, while continuing to maintain the obsolete practices now offered in our public schools, and which these young people reject as other consumers reject a product that does not meet their needs.

Public education must join forces and collaborate with all other agencies and community-based organizations addressing the problem of illicit drug use by children. Dollars must be put into re-engineering schools so that they become places where young people want to be, where they can learn, and become productive citizens.

Re-engineering our schools is essential. But we must go further. We must fit school services into a community. School is the largest piece of life for a growing child, but it cannot be all of life. We must integrate our work with the work of parents, churches, businesses, and community organizations. We must also collaborate proactively with all agencies charged with responsibilities toward children.

Schools must link with the police, parole officers, youth agencies, health agencies, housing agencies, employment agencies, and welfare agencies. This linkage will substantially reduce confusion, reduce costs down the road, and rescue countless young people.

In spite of all the problems found in the American public education system, hope does spring eternal for one primary reason: the resiliency of our children. I have run into countless examples of children who come from dysfunctional home settings and who have received limited, if any, nurturing along the way and they still have an inner drive to excel and succeed. These children demonstrate daily an indomitable spirit that guides them through hardships. Oftentimes the determining factor about their eventual ability to succeed or fail is reduced to one or more positive influences in their life.

Our traditional public education system must recognize that the new realities of our society dictate a dynamic, diversified approach to the way children are taught and treated in our schools. One approach no longer works with children. Just as diversity of population is one of the greatest strengths of this country, diversity of educational options and experience will help start meaningful change in public education.

Once education reform is truly depoliticalized and policymakers become open to change, all of America's children will benefit.

PART II

STATE CHALLENGES

CHAPTER 3

CRITICAL CHALLENGES
FACING STATE LEADERS

Governor Mark Warner and Governor Tim Pawlenty

Introduction by Lowell Milken

I have the distinct honor to introduce the governor of the great state of
Virginia, Mark Warner. It is always enjoyable to introduce someone who
has become a good friend. Prior to being elected governor of Virginia in
2001, Mark Warner pursued a successful business career in venture capital, funding innovative ideas and creating jobs for Virginia and the
nation.

As governor he has used his business knowledge to make state government more effective and accountable to taxpayers in the face of what we
know is all too prevalent today, record budget shortfalls. Working with the
legislature, he reduced the size of state government while actually increasing support for K-12 education. Governor Warner's "Education for a Life-
time" initiative, introduced in 2003, offer a series of reforms from
preschool to graduate school and beyond, including a wholesale rethinking of the high school senior year.

His nationally recognized partnership for building successful schools
brings extra resources to Virginia's more academically challenged schools.
I trust we will hear more about these programs and others like his new ini-

Improving Student Achievement: Reforms that Work, 55–72
Copyright © 2005 by Information Age Publishing
All rights of reproduction in any form reserved.

tiative, "Project Graduation." As chairman of the Education Commission of the States (ECS), Governor Warner provides strong leadership in the organization's efforts to recruit and prepare high quality teachers to work in hard-to-staff schools, a great priority in states and districts nationwide.

I first met Governor Warner while touring Virginia with State Superintendent Jo Lynne DeMary during our Milken Educator Awards national notifications week. On that day, the governor told me he is as concerned about quality education for all children as he is for the education of his own three daughters. When we arrived at Roberts Park Elementary School in Norfolk, the local high school band marched while we were led by unsuspecting principal, and soon to be Milken Educator, Doreatha White.

Roberts Park Elementary may be a high-poverty school, but I can tell you that the respect and the spirit for education demonstrated by its students and staff could not have been richer. Inside, Governor Warner asked his constituents for their views on the issues and he marveled with the rest of us as two third-grade boys recited a lengthy passage from Shakespeare by heart. When it was time to reveal the event's ultimate guest of honor and newest Milken Educator, Governor Warner offered his congratulations and a belief that successful education programs begin with great educators. Now it is my pleasure to welcome Mark Warner, Governor of the Commonwealth of Virginia.

Mark Warner

Thank you for that kind introduction, but more importantly, thank you for all that you and the Milken Family Foundation do for education across this nation. It's your passion that drives this Foundation, and recognizes and rewards great educators like Doreatha and others who are in this room.

I spent 20 years in business and I've now spent 2 years in politics, although sometimes the 2 years in politics feels like 20 years in business. Trying to make meaningful change in education is a little bit like being Sisyphus; you keep pushing the rock up the hill and it keeps rolling back down and then you just push it up again. In this challenging undertaking, I've had a partner by my side who provides the expertise, the counseling, and continues to spur us on toward making our schools better. That person is our State Superintendent, Dr. Jo Lynne DeMary.

What I want to do in my few minutes that I have today is talk about what I believe, and I imagine most of us in this room would agree, is one of the most critical challenges facing public education in America. That question is how to provide quality teachers in hard-to-staff schools? It's a question we've been trying to grapple with in Virginia and it's a question that I've taken on as chairman of ECS in terms of the chairman's initiative. I hope today I can lay out some specific strategies that could be useful in your community in addressing this question.

How we answer this question will have a lot to do with not only effectively meeting the goals of No Child Left Behind, but also making sure that every American is prepared to compete in a knowledge-based economy. Before I get into some specific suggestions, let me give you some background about what we're doing in Virginia. We were one of the first states in the nation to take on the issue of trying to deal with high standards and accountability. Governor George Allen began the effort 7 years ago and it will come to fruition in a little over a month. For the first time ever, students who graduate from high school in Virginia will have to pass at least two of our standards of learning (SOL) exams in English and reading, as well as other verified credits in courses including algebra. Now, with this deadline, the consequences component of our accountability movement is going to be put to the test.

What I saw over the last couple years as governor is that in too many of the states where they have talked tough about accountability and standards, when the rubber actually hit the road they retreated. I believe in a most recent count of the 13 states that had high standards and high consequences components, nine of those states have retreated from the consequences components of their accountability standards. In Virginia we're not going to retreat.

We believe it is very important to honor our commitment to the educators, and more importantly to the students. We are going to stick to the expectations that we laid out years ago, but we also hope that Virginia can provide a model to the rest of the nation about how standards and accountability can be implemented both effectively and with compassion. Because once we have high standards, once we ask more of our students, we owe it to those students to make sure that we are willing to go the extra mile to help them succeed.

That's why last year, before the consequences component of the high standards was going to kick in, we initiated something called Project Graduation. It includes online tutorials developed specifically for students who'd been unsuccessful on SOL exams. It included a series of 3-week intensive courses over the summer for students who had failed previously. During the sessions the students received the extra help they needed. This spring the initiative includes remediation efforts after school, on weekends, and again in this academy model.

Currently, there are over 2,400 students in Virginia either working with the online tutorial or enrolled in a remediation academy. What is perhaps most remarkable is that with this little extra concentrated help, over 75% of the students who had previously failed their SOLs have now passed their SOLs. We believe those percentages will increase further as we approach our June deadline. By expanding opportunities and providing flexibility, Virginia has maintained its academic standards and by offering alternatives to students who need extra help, Virginia has maintained the public's support for accountability.

In Virginia, accountability has been given time to take hold and our reforms that long predate No Child Left Behind have produced results. Specifically, nearly 80% of our schools now meet Virginia's achievement-based accreditation standards. The reading and math skills of our elementary and middle school students are improving. Our NAEP scores, which plunged in the early 1990s, have rebounded and Virginia students are again among the nation's strongest students in those subjects.

In addition, more of our students are taking the SATs and more Virginia students are earning college credit through advanced placement tests than in virtually any of our neighboring states. While we have to deal with the consequences component for high school graduation, there still remains a lot of hard work in front of us. Most of our schools have dramatically increased student achievement, but there are still schools and even whole school districts where achievement remains low. In Virginia, as elsewhere, these schools and districts tend to be those where a majority of the students are minority and economically disadvantaged.

We faced this problem head-on in Virginia by targeting 34 Title I schools and with our Pass Initiative. We brought in academic intervention teams, made gubernatorial visits, and built community partnerships to try to improve the scores in those schools. Our board of education has taken action as well. The state board has the authority to take failing school districts to court in order to compel institutional reform. Even these kinds of steps, whether it's a pass initiative with the carrot, or the state board action with the stick, won't be enough unless we can insure that our most academically needy students have teachers and principals who are as effective as their colleagues in the more affluent schools.

As I mentioned earlier, trying to take on this question of staffing hard-to-staff schools in economically disadvantaged areas has been my focus as chairman of ECS. By no means are we saying that in Virginia, or in any other state in the nation, there aren't examples of extraordinary principals and teachers in hard-to-staff schools. The Milken Family Foundation has recognized Doreatha White of Norfolk. She is the principal of Roberts Park Elementary School, a school that is surrounded by housing projects. When I was talking with Ms. White about what her real secret of success was, she told me it was good teachers, because without teachers who are up to the challenge of educating children who come to school with appalling academic and social deficiencies, the likelihood of success is slim.

In celebrating the extraordinary success of educators like Doreatha White, I think we have got to be honest. We must acknowledge that while we're equipped to hand out awards and blue ribbons to educators in schools that beat the odds, we are also unfortunately equally reluctant to make a systematic challenge to the antiquated system of recruiting, preparing, assigning, and rewarding teachers. Our failure to take on these challenges decreases the odds for too many students in poor, urban, and rural communities. Our failure to confront these issues more aggressively is costing our most vulnerable students dearly, and the price of inaction rises as our schools move more deeply into the realm of accountability. While it is clear that teaching in a standards-based system is intellectually demanding work, we don't do a very good job or put very much effort into recruiting the very best and brightest into the teaching profession. Rather than investing and understanding what the best teachers do, and using this knowledge to reshape teacher preparation programs, in too many places we are simply maintaining the status quo.

I know I'm preaching to the choir here, but every day in America, children who attend high-poverty and high-minority schools are far more likely than other children to be taught by under-qualified teachers. Kids in these schools are twice as likely as other children to be taught by an inexperienced teacher. Kids in these schools are more than twice as likely to be taught by a teacher who was a low achiever in college. These kids are more likely to be taught by noncertified teachers and often teachers without a major or even a minor in the subject matter they are teaching. Moreover, even when we get those great teachers in these hard-to-staff schools, often we make it too easy for those teachers to flee into more affluent schools and more comfortable teaching positions. The bottom line is that this situation is a national embarrassment.

We all know that students who have enjoyed several good teachers in a row have test scores soar, regardless of their family background, economic status, race, or any of the other criteria we usually look at to qualify a student as disadvantaged. For that matter, we know that a student from either a disadvantaged background or an affluent background, who has up to 3 years of poor teachers in a row, may never recover. When students in hard-to-staff schools are given these poor teachers, we often doom these children to the margins of society. One of our great hallmarks in this country is that we place a very high value on fairness. However, the way we deploy our most important resource in education—our teachers—simply isn't very fair.

Students who could succeed on state exams, and go on to higher education, often never get there because we have not put good teachers within their grasp. Not only is this unfair, but again, as somebody who spent 20 years in business, it is economically and socially counterproductive. You don't have to be an economist to see how much more sense it makes to provide effective instruction for young people in the first place than it does to pay downstream in remediation, intervention and dependence.

I think we too often have the notion that the achievement gap is an inevitable result of poverty, poor family structure, and social problems. Indeed, those are frequently contributing factors, but in schools like Doreatha's, and others across Virginia and the country, we see students from those backgrounds achieve remarkable results because of great leadership, principals, and teachers.

I believe that a nation that has planted a flag on the moon and can send robots to Mars should be able to figure out a way to get the best teachers into the schools that need them the most. In Virginia we're starting to try to do that. I am personally committed to an all-out comprehensive strategy to put high-quality teachers in the classrooms of children who need them the most. We have begun this effort knowing that the road leading from diagnosis, to effective action, to producing good results, will be difficult.

Let me briefly outline seven specific strategies that we're implementing in Virginia. First, we have to expand the pool from which we recruit new teachers. We all talk about easing the shortage of quality teachers throughout our public school system, but if we do this in creative ways, we can also address the needs in hard-to-staff schools. There are talented professionals in other walks of life with a depth of content knowledge and real-world experience to make subjects, particularly math and science, come alive for young people. We must remove the obstacles that prevent idealistic professionals from making teaching a second career. We must insure that once they enter the classroom, these second-career teachers are welcomed and respected. We are trying to do that in Virginia through our career switchers program that has put hundreds of engineers, lawyers, and retired service men and women into the classroom. In addition, our administration is expanding this effort through our participation in the New Teacher Project, which has already seen great success in states like Arkansas and Louisiana in recruiting high quality teachers from other professions into urban and rural schools.

Second, we must have rigorous preparation and in-service training programs that are customized to the needs of teachers in hard-to-staff schools. Oftentimes the in-service program for those teachers in middle class communities may not be the same type of in-service preparation needed for those teachers in hard-to-staff schools. We need to provide appropriate trainings for teachers entering these more challenging environments. Successful teachers in these hard-to-staff schools should provide more of that in-service training.

We also need to do a better job of mentoring. In Virginia we have started the Teacher Quality Enhancement Initiative, which I launched during the first year of my administration. We distributed more than $1 million in grants to rural and urban schools to fund structured mentoring programs, and I emphasize *structure*. Every school system in Virginia is supposed to have a mentoring program; however, too many of them are buddy systems that don't really have accountability or proven results. If we're going to invest in these types of mentoring initiatives—and my recent legislative agenda has increased funding for our mentoring effort—it must be geared toward proven, data-driven mentoring programs.

Third, states and school divisions must replace salary schedules that reward years of employment and units completed with new schedules that also reward teachers for taking on challenges and producing results. I know that may sound strange coming from a Democratic governor, but we have to engage our teachers and the organizations that represent them in an honest conversation about how to strengthen the present system of rewarding teachers. We cannot put off that conversation any longer.

On this front, we have formed the Virginia Middle School Teacher Corps to focus on schools with chronically low achievement in mathematics. Teachers are selected for this program on the basis of their content knowledge, teaching skills, and ability to raise student achievement. We're encouraging these teachers to go into hard-to-staff schools for a minimum of 3 years, by providing extra incentives, such as double retirement benefits and increased pay for teachers who are willing to take this plunge. Other states are trying other types of efforts and many of these initiatives hold great potential. The bottom line is we need to look at how we pay and compensate teachers differently. We need to make sure we have the right mix of incentives to attract teachers to hard-to-staff schools and we must find a way to tangibly reward good performance.

Fourth, we must improve the working conditions in our high poverty schools by providing more support and otherwise balancing the challenge between these schools and those schools in affluent neighborhoods. It's an awful lot to ask an expert teacher to exchange a school full of children who come to school ready to learn every day, for a school filled with kids who come from homes where learning and literacy are not modeled or appreciated, or where a parent or a grandparent is not able to help that student with their homework.

Despite this, recent studies conducted by Harvard University show that there are talented teachers who are willing to accept this challenge. However, their willingness is contingent upon assurances, like additional support and a school climate that promotes effectiveness. We know what kind of support that means. I think I've visited more schools in Virginia than any recent governor and the majority of the schools I visited are not the high achieving schools or the governor's schools or the schools that are most in jeopardy of losing their accreditation. Upon entering a school, before you even talk to the principal or a teacher, or walk into a classroom, you can almost tell which schools are going to be successful or are turning the corner. You can tell by whether the students treat each other with respect, the halls are orderly, and whether teachers are well groomed and are making sure that the school is operating efficiently. Those schools that are still struggling are often the ones that lack those characteristics.

I mentioned that I spent 20 years in business; well, we are trying in Virginia to incorporate a business notion into how we change the support system for these hard-to-staff schools. As a venture capitalist, I spent a lot of time with companies that were not doing that well. When we had a company that was not doing well, we would bring in a turnaround specialist to help improve it. In Virginia we want to introduce the concept of turnaround specialists in hard-to-staff schools. We've already recruited some of our best education schools and business schools across the commonwealth to create an initial cadre of 10 principals for this purpose. These individuals will go back to school to get turnaround specialist training so that they can go into these hard-to-staff schools with enhanced powers and compensation. In effect, their presence will be like adding a free hand to make that turnaround take place. If you've got that kind of leadership, the ability to attract teachers and keep them at the hard-to-staff schools goes up exponentially.

We also have to recognize that not only does it take leadership, not only does it take the orderly organization of the school, but in these hard-to-staff schools there are extra steps we need to take. We have to reduce class size and we've provided Virginia incentives to reduce class sizes, particularly in the early grades. We also have to recognize that the teachers must have enough time for individualized instruction time. Many of these kids who come from disadvantaged backgrounds need that extra help if they're going to be successful. If we provide those kinds of incentives, like small class sizes, individualized instruction time and turnaround specialists to assist schools in turning the corner, I think our ability to keep teachers in those hard-to-staff schools will go up dramatically.

Fifth, we have been grappling with a budget and our state's finances and we're about to do the right thing and make a sizeable monetary investment toward supporting our schools. Coupled with this, I'm going to be asking the legislature to make sure that while we ask for this increased investment, we also obtain an increased focus on accountability. Most of the focus has been on academic accountability, but there must also be financial accountability. In Virginia we are launching a level of financial accountability and conducting reviews so that we can make sure that when we invest these dollars they end up in the classrooms and particularly in our hard-to-staff schools.

In terms of reform, smart decisions are informed by meaningful data and states must build data systems to track and monitor teacher effectiveness. One of my greatest frustrations as chair of ECS has been that, despite wonderful studies on what makes a great teacher, the results are inconclusive because there was not enough data. When we talk about our most important resource, educating our kids, and what makes a good teacher and how we follow a teacher's progress, the abysmal lack of data to be able to do that is holding us back in terms of making meaningful remediation efforts.

Current academic and accurate data on teacher quality are essential if states are to develop strategic and effective strategies for recruiting, preparing and retaining highly qualified teachers. States need good data on the value of every individual teacher. Without data, there can be no accountability. In Virginia we are developing a data system that will allow us to trace the academic deficits of students back to the teacher preparation programs. Now think about that for a moment. If we can monitor how students are doing and trace it back not only to the teachers, but to where those teachers were prepared, you layer in a whole level of accountability that has so far been unknown. Our intent here is not to identify scapegoats, and clearly there are privacy concerns that must be addressed; but to simply have those kind of concerns should not scare us from effectively using data.

The sixth strategy is that states must begin evaluating colleges and universities that prepare teachers based on their graduates' abilities in raising student achievement, and on the proportion of their graduates who teach in settings where we need them the most. Too many of our education schools, while they talk about reform, are often reluctant to be partners in true reform. When I talk about reform, I talk about reform that is based on measurable results. Some colleges have made efforts to refocus their teacher preparation programs; however, too many education schools are simply continuing the same old ways. We must focus on and monitor the results that teachers provide and also spend more time with our teaching colleges and universities, encouraging them to prepare specialized teachers for hard-to-staff schools.

We are asking them to do this while they also have to deal with a standards-based system of accountability. We are asking a lot of them, but in Virginia we're going to be making some new investments in our higher education system. If we're going to provide additional resources, I want to see the results. One of the ways that we can see these results is by urging our universities to change the way they prepare teachers for hard-to-staff schools and to be willing to have those teachers' performances monitored on an ongoing basis. We have to challenge some of our colleges and universities to recognize that their commitment to their graduates ought not to end when that teacher walks across the stage and receives his or her degree.

Finally, the seventh strategy is to engage in a broad cross-section of citizens, community organizations, churches, other religious organizations, and business groups to help restore honor to those who are doing our most important work, our teachers. I think all of us who are my age or older remember back when we were growing up, teachers had a lot more respect than they do now. I don't know what the silver bullet is to return that respect, but it is going to take more than lip service from elected officials. It is going to take increased compensation. It is going to take buy-in from the whole community.

I spoke earlier about our Project Graduation efforts. I remember last summer, we were down in south-side Virginia where some of our state's most rural and poorest areas are. This is the area that's been hard hit from tobacco losses, from manufacturing losses. It was the second week of Project Graduation and the kids were taking their SOL exams. These were students who had failed. These were kids who for the most part had been told, subtly and not so subtly, "You're probably not going to amount to much." Well, 76% of the kids who took those exams with simply 2 weeks of additional remediation passed their SOLs. The joy on those kids' faces made up for a lot of the crummy days as governor. At the same time the joy was on the teachers' faces; and the fact is that we were there to celebrate not only the students' accomplishments, but also those of the teachers.

Perhaps in a small way, this was the kind of restoration of honor to teachers that is lacking in so many communities. We have got to make sure, whether it's with these seven specific strategies or others, that we understand that finding quality teachers, recruiting, mentoring, rewarding teachers appropriately, providing leadership at the school and district level, and making sure the teacher preparation courses are appropriate, and then ultimately providing honor to these teachers who are willing to go into the hard-to-staff schools, can make a difference. There is no better investment we can make as a society. Ultimately, in Virginia we're going to take great pride in exhibiting ways to deal with accountability with consequences that incorporate both efficiency and compassion.

It is also our goal to be the place to try to make sure that teachers in these hard-to-staff schools recover the honor and respect they deserve. Most importantly, it is key that we, as Virginians, see results that will allow our young people to compete in this knowledge-based economy. It is an enormous challenge, but I can think of no challenge more important in

Virginia and for that matter, anywhere across the nation. Thank you all very much.

Lowell Milken

Thank you governor for those inspiring remarks. Now it gives me great pleasure to introduce Governor Tim Pawlenty. This past October, newly elected Minnesota Governor Tim Pawlenty participated in his first Milken Educator Award Notification, surprising English teacher Susan Henke-meyer at Sauk Rapids-Rice Senior High School; and from all reports you communicated a powerful message to the assembled. You conveyed the critical role that teachers play and the need to reward and honor those who truly excel. You let the audience know that the Educator Award means much more than merely money. It's a symbol of the importance of teaching, of the nobility and dignity of the teaching profession.

The Governor also urged the students to consider a career in education. When he was elected governor of Minnesota in 2002, the state faced a $4.5 billion budget deficit. Immediately he set a goal to balance the budget, and the legislature where he had spent 10 years as the elected house majority leader adopted his plan to eliminate the budget deficit. He accomplished this without raising taxes or harming K-12 education.

Governor Pawlenty has also fought for and passed a dramatic overhaul in Minnesota's education standards, measuring performance and increasing opportunities for every child. His "Excellence and Accountability" initiative boldly links teacher pay to performance. He has also received support in the form of a $7.8 million grant from the U.S. Department of Education to implement a professional pay program.This includes, I'm pleased to say, the Teacher Advancement Program. The end result, as the *Saint Paul Pioneer Press* editorialized about the governor's plan, should be the creation of a core of well-paid, professional teachers with a demonstrated track record of classroom success. I'm sure you join me in wanting to hear more about the governor's education programs for improving teacher quality, so please welcome Minnesota's Governor, Tim Pawlenty.

Tim Pawlenty

It's a pleasure to come share a few thoughts with you about public education in Minnesota. However, before I do that, I do need to share with you a Minnesota-based story about a freshman in college. This happened some years ago at one of our local colleges outside of the Twin Cities in a class that had something to do with science relating to animals and there was an aviary section.

In this class they were studying birds, bird names and bird identifications. At the end of the semester there was a test. This class used an anonymous testing system where you turn in your bluebook, but you don't put your name on it, so the professor doesn't know whose test it is. The test was distributed and, lo and behold, a significant part of the test was simply illustrations of bird's legs without their bodies.

The challenge to the students was to identify each species of bird based on a depiction of only their legs. Apparently, one particular student who was somewhat astonished by this test wrote on the cover of his test booklet, "This is a stupid test and I'm not going to take it!" He then got up during the middle of the testing period, walked down to the front of the room and slapped down the testing booklet on the professor's desk.

The professor was seated there looking down and the student started to make his way towards the exit. The professor looked at the booklet and saw the note from the student and said, "Wait a minute, young man, just who do you think you are?" At this, the student bent over and pulled up his pants leg and said, "I don't know. You tell me who you think I am!"

That's a little story about matching expectations. We have a great deal of discussion and debate, appropriately so in America, about education and education reform. In this conversation, the buzzword is *accountability* and all that it implies. I think we need to start by just stepping back from that, particularly on an occasion like this, with a room filled with accomplished, successful, and dedicated people.

I have an 11-year-old daughter and a 7-year-old daughter, and when I have a sleep over of just 10 or 11 kids for one night, I can hardly take it. I can only imagine what it would be like to be a teacher and have 30 rambunctious kids in a classroom every day. It is a hard job. I don't think teachers make too much money. I don't think this is a profession that we overcompensate. I believe the primary motivation of people who go into teaching is that they have a heart for children. They have a heart for public service, and they have a heart for learning.

There is great change sweeping across America and the world. We see change happening demographically, technologically, culturally, socially, and economically. Many observers have said that there is more change happening more rapidly across the globe in these times than in any other time in human history. So it is not an option for our schools not to change. It is not an option for the teaching profession not to change. It's not an option for policymakers not to change. If the world is changing 100 miles an hour and we have institutions or people who say, "I choose to stand still," you will be passed by. Together, policymakers, teachers, educators, encouragers, and thinkers need to constructively join hands and say, "Let's increase our appetite for change and innovation and experimentation."

I'm a Republican, so I have a little different approach to some of these issues than many of my colleagues; but people, on a bipartisan, nonpartisan basis, should be able to agree that there are certain things and concepts worth trying. Let's not be afraid not all of it's going to work. Some of it will work really well, and some of it will fail; but in a changing world, let's try something. That is the kind of spirit and attitude we're trying to bring to Minnesota.

The traditional measure of whether policymakers and leaders were committed to education was simply, how much are you willing to spend? The debate was, well, if we get a 2% increase, it's kind of a meager year; and if it's a 5% or 7% increase, it's a particularly good year for education. If that's the range of the debate, if that's the range of the measurement of our commitment to education, if that is the only sophistication we can bring to the discussion, then we're going nowhere. Obviously, there's much more to it. While financing is one important measure of our commitment to education, and should remain so, the debate has now appropriately broadened to many, many other issues.

The current mantra, as we have heard many times over, is *accountability*. There are well-worn arguments about where we go from here, but before we get to the issue of how we improve teachers, I always like to remind people that we should start the accountability discussion with parents. If you go down the hierarchy of things that matter with respect to influencers in a child's education, first and foremost is their parents. Guess what? We've got a lot of parents who aren't doing their job with respect to the education of their children. I don't mean that disrespectfully because they face a lot of challenges, but we need to make sure every discussion about accountability involves the question: What are parents doing to hold up their end of the bargain?

I know times have changed, but when I was in third grade, there was a teacher who thought I was misbehaving. I think her name was Mrs. Johnson. One time she called me in with my dad. My dad showed up during the work day, and Mrs. Johnson got about halfway into her presentation about my misbehavior when my father interrupted her and said, "Mrs. Johnson, you can be assured this will never happen again, and this problem will be corrected." It was.

I think most of you would agree that if you look at standardized, objective measures of public education performance in the great state of Minnesota, we do really well. Some would argue that we have the best public education system in the country, and I think almost everybody can see we're certainly near the top in most measures. We're lucky. If you aggregate the data and you take averages and look at the system as a whole, it's a good system. We are really proud of it and it serves us well. However, if you disaggregate the data, you'll also see the story that you see in so many other places, and that is the story of so many children not succeeding in our system.

I remember very vividly, before I became governor, visiting a classroom as part of a mentor program that I was involved in, in a very challenged neighborhood. I was standing there in front of this eighth grade class and the teacher said, "Look out at this class and tell me what you see." "I don't know," I replied, "I see 30 eighth-graders."

She said, "Let me tell you a little bit about this class. Over half the children in this class are recent immigrants from underdeveloped countries and they don't speak English. They speak nine different languages; I as the teacher speak one. Many of these same children perform as kindergarteners or first graders, while by age they're eighth graders, so they get put in my eighth grade class."

She also said that over half the children in her class are labeled special education and that most of them have emotional behavioral disabilities. Over half the class is from impoverished situations, broken homes featuring abuse, violence, neglect, chemical dependency, and many other social challenges. One of the other things she added was that half the kids in the class who are there in September wouldn't be there in May. Instead, the kids cycle in and out of the class all year long because of instability in their housing patterns. Finally, at the end of this litany of what this class consists of, she turns to me—this is a teacher who is 5 years out of college, energetic, bright, and committed—she turns to me and says, "And it's my fault that I don't turn these kids into A or B students by spring? It's my fault?"

That's a bright teacher, a hard-working teacher in a very challenging situation. The pathologies of society are visited on the doorstop of that classroom at a level, pace, and magnitude that is overwhelming. We have teachers and administrators in our districts in Minnesota with their fingers in the dyke, and they're running out of fingers. They are being overwhelmed with those kinds of challenges and it raises all kinds of issues beyond how we are going to pay for teachers.

During my dad's generation you could still go make a decent living with your body, doing manual labor. Today, if you don't have a skill or an education, then you're not able to hook on to this economy. It's going to continue ahead in this direction. Therefore, the stakes are higher than ever that as many people as possible receive an education or a skill. Unfortunately, it's not happening in the current system. I say to those who want to cling to the status quo, white knuckled, afraid, and to those who are unwilling to take on the vested interests around preserving the status quo, it is a tremendous disservice to the reality that so many of our children are not getting the skills or the education they need to be part of our new economy.

After parents, the next most significant influence in a child's education is their teachers. Governor Warner summarized this and presented it well. I would remind you that the Achieve Organization, which I think is well-respected by most people, says the following about teachers:

- Of the current crop of teachers, as compared to the current generation of teachers or the ones that preceded them, a vast majority of these current teachers are in the bottom third of their ACT or SAT peer group.

- Of the teachers who enter the profession, 43% leave the profession within the first 5 years of teaching.

- Of the teachers who do leave, these individuals tend to be the more entrepreneurial and in terms of their academic performance, better credentialed.

There are major warning signs flashing on the dashboard of education in America. If we don't acknowledge them and find a way to change that, we are condemning ourselves to a crisis that is not too far down the road.

In Minnesota, what we've said is this: There are a number of things that go into motivating, retaining, and recruiting teachers. One of them is money. It's not the only thing, it's not even necessarily the main thing but, if you are at all a student of human nature, what gets paid for usually gets done. What gets measured also usually gets done. Measuring things usually helps hold people accountable.

In Minnesota we'd like to go forward with a number of programs. The first, with the help of the Milken Family Foundation, is the Teacher Advancement Program or TAP. One of our districts, and soon a few more, is going to have a performance-based compensation system. This is not a new concept, but actually deploying it is a relatively new thing. The teachers are with us and they voted in favor of the program. Our state teacher group didn't much like it, but the locals said it's worth a try. Good for them, it is worth a try.

I get a lot of debate about how we compensate teachers and a lot of the debate drifts into compensating teachers for staff development. I'm not against staff development; we should be pro-staff development. But when you get into defining what the core mission of schools is, it is student learning. Staff development is a derivative of that core, but we really need to focus in on student learning. Staff development certainly should be part of the initiative, but I'm not particularly interested in how many extra classes teachers attend. I'm interested in whether those teachers improve student learning. While these two goals can be related, the emphasis needs to be on that last piece.

We can measure student learning in a fairly sophisticated, reliable way with the measurement tools we now have. So if that's the core mission, let's focus on that. You move the needle on student learning, you get compensated for that. It does have to be done fairly. Teaching is a team sport and we can look at team-based, site-based incentives. Teachers are collaborators by nature. They are also not necessarily harsh competitors, and that's a good thing in a school site. We can design a performance-based pay system smartly. The invitation to all is to please come on board and help us design this in a fair and modern way. Help us, together, get to the future.

We have a similar program that we received some federal funding for called the Minnesota Alternative Compensation Aid Program. It's a good program, but it gets bogged down and the money is going to pay for staff development. Teachers are receiving more classes and more training.

Let me also tell you about a program I proposed in the legislature. I originally called it the Super Teacher Program, but that name offended the teachers unions, because they think all the teachers are super teachers. So we changed the name of it and we're now calling it Higher Achieving Schools.

As Mark pointed out, in addition to the fact that we have concerns about the quality of our future teachers, we also have some very major concerns about getting the best teachers to come to the most challenged sites. So what we've said in Minnesota is, we'd like to have some demonstration projects where we bust open the doors on tenure and on compensation. The principal or the school administrator can then hire whomever they want and those individuals will earn a base salary comparable to what they had in their departing district; and they can keep their tenure so that if it doesn't work out, they can go back to the district they came from.

We're looking for teachers who have a heart to serve in the challenged districts, who are highly gifted, and who will come on the following conditions: Teachers will be paid $50,000 with a chance to make $100,000. The state will give you a chance to double your salary if you move the needle on performance. I think this is a very provocative idea, one that has been written about in literature but never deployed to this extent. By the way, in Minnesota, $100,000 for a teacher is a very nice raise. With this raise comes several conditions. First, we hire and fire who we want. Next, teachers have got to be effective, and we will pay you for being effective. In fact, we're going to pay you really well for being effective. It's a program that is worth a try. It's controversial and the usual suspects don't like it, but we're working to try to at least, in the spirit of collecting data, see if it works.

There are other things we're working on as well. I think that, within appropriate limitations, we should have alternative licensure for teachers. For people who have life experiences, wisdom, and skills, there should be a pathway, short of a bunch of years of college, to help them become teachers. However, we don't want to put people in classrooms unprepared, but people like Henry Kissinger and Jimmy Carter should be able to get a teacher's license if they want to go back and teach high school social studies in a somewhat abbreviated fashion. So we think alternative pathways to licensure should be explored.

Minnesota was the first in the nation to bring charter schools forward. We are going to try to bring the next installment of that forward by having another cluster of charter schools centered around English immersion and others that will be year-round. We think these schools will demonstrate success or at least gather evidence about their effectiveness.

We have a program where we are yanking driver's licenses from kids who don't attend school. We're overhauling our school finance formula in Minnesota. We have some leadership academies for students that the business community is sponsoring on the leadership and business qualities that are needed to effectively run a school.

We are also mandating summer school for failing students and other remediation programs. I want to close by telling you, as somebody famous once said, that people begin to understand the meaning of life when they plant shade trees under which they will never sit. We have a whole series of other initiatives, but the teacher preparation initiative is most significant. I don't mean to be flip about it, but if we can't legislate good parenting, this is the next most important thing we need to do. If I were to leave you with one thought, it is that this process doesn't need to be adversarial. This is an issue we can work together on in an appropriate, thoughtful, constructive way and move it forward in the best interests of the teachers, their professional organizations, individuals who are policymakers and most importantly, the students.

What I have been talking about here are probably not things from which we are going to receive immediate benefits or that will even reveal themselves to many people in the room, but they are the seeds of the trees that are going to continue to make our country great and serve future generations very well. It's up to those of us in the room to make it happen.

Thank you for your commitment and your heart for public service. I know almost all of you in the room could be making more money doing something else, but you do it because of a sense of service. We appreciate it and you need to hear thank you as well. So I'm looking forward to moving forward with you, together. I hope we can demonstrate some good things in Minnesota and come back in a future year and report back to you on our results. Thank you very much.

Lowell Milken

Governor, thank you very much for addressing us with those motivating remarks. After having the opportunity to sit and listen to both Governor Warner and Governor Pawlenty today, I tell you I am more optimistic that we're going to finally reach our goal in providing the kind of education we want for all of our children. We really appreciate your efforts and your dedication, and just keep up the fight.

PART III

TEACHER QUALITY

CHAPTER 4

HOW STATES ARE ADDRESSING TEACHER QUALITY ISSUES

**Cheryl Fagnano, Jim Horne, Lisa Graham Keegan,
Ray Simon, and Janice Poda**

Cheryl Fagnano

Good afternoon, I want to welcome you to our panel discussion on how states are addressing teacher quality issues. My name is Cheryl Fagnano and I am senior vice president of the Milken Family Foundation and associate director of the Teacher Advancement Program (TAP). I'm joined here this afternoon by five distinguished educators: Jim Horne, Florida's commissioner of education; Lisa Graham Keegan, CEO of the Education Leaders Council (ELC); Ray Simon, U.S. assistant secretary of education; and Janice Poda, South Carolina's senior director of Teacher Quality.

At the Milken Family Foundation, ensuring a high-quality teacher for every student is the essential issue in American education. We know from research and from years of experience working with the very best, that teachers are the most important school-related factor in student learning. Therefore, in organizing this panel, we sought out the strongest and most effective teacher quality advocates working in American education today. Their records on teacher quality speak for themselves.

Improving Student Achievement: Reforms that Work, 75–105

Jim Horne's highest priorities are to improve reading and to revolutionize the teaching profession in Florida. He believes that the most important factor in student achievement is the presence of a high-performing, dedicated teacher in the classroom, and he has backed up that belief with real support—$25 million last year for the Better Educated Students and Teachers Programs (BEST), as well as support for the Florida Mentor Teacher School Pilot Program (FMTSPP), both major efforts to enhance Florida's teacher quality.

Lisa Graham Keegan is the CEO of ELC and one of the nation's most prominent and outspoken education reform advocates today. Prior to her current position, she served as state superintendent of education in Arizona where she was responsible for Proposition 301, Arizona's funding source for teacher pay-for-performance. Lisa believes that the marketplace for teachers is much broader than we currently allow for, and as head of the ELC she helped establish the American Board for Certification of Teacher Excellence (American Board), a program addressing the urgency to place more highly qualified teachers in the classroom in the most effective and efficient ways possible.

Prior to becoming assistant secretary of the Office of Elementary and Secondary Education, Ray Simon was director of the Arkansas Department of Education, where he became well-known for his state's efforts to improve teacher quality. As assistant secretary, Ray plays a pivotal role in policy and management issues affecting elementary and secondary education, including the implementation of No Child Left Behind's Highly Qualified Teacher Provision.

Janice Poda worked closely with State Superintendent Inez Tenenbaum to create the Division of Teacher Quality in South Carolina's Department of Education, the division she now heads. Their work has been outstanding and is certainly paying off because, for the second consecutive year, *Education Week Quality Counts* ranked South Carolina first in the nation for improving teacher quality.

Over the past 4 years, each member of the panel has worked closely with the Milken Family Foundation to implement the Teacher Advancement Program, or TAP, as it is widely known. TAP is a comprehensive research-based strategy aimed to attract, retain, and motivate high-quality teachers to American schools by implementing five principles:[1] multiple career paths, market-driven compensation, performance-based accountability, ongoing applied professional growth, and expanding the supply of high-quality teachers. We believe that if TAP is faithfully implemented—and we have some good results to back up our beliefs—it can have a substantial impact on enhancing teacher quality in our schools. However, this afternoon we will not be focusing on TAP, but rather on the myriad of teacher quality initiatives being developed and implemented around the country.

Most folks—left, right, and center—agree that few school factors are more important to a child's academic success than quality teachers. The president and Congress recognized this when they passed the Highly Qualified Teacher Mandate in No Child Left Behind. The National Council for Accreditation of Teacher Education (NCATE) and schools of education recognized this when they revised standards and programs for teacher preparation and certification. Even groups as divergent as the National Board of Professional Teaching Standards (NBPTS) and the American Board recognize the importance of teacher quality. Clearly, they recognize it in different ways, but they do recognize the essential role quality teachers play in a quality education.

However, now it is up to the states to become key players in promoting teacher quality. The good news is they are not new to the business. Increasingly over the last decade, states have been developing programs and regulations focusing on developing accountability mechanisms for when teacher quality falters, increasing the recruitment of highly quali-fied teachers, boosting teacher training and certification standards, tying student standards to teacher certification, and strengthening professional support and training for new and veteran teachers. Some of these states have developed or participated in instituting policies that support pay-for-performance opportunities for teachers and teacher assessment pro-grams where, in a few cases these assessments were tied to student achievement.

The bad news, however, is that the quality of these efforts can vary sub-stantially, both across states and programs within states. Yet, with the pas-sage of No Child Left Behind in 2001, all the states are subject to the Federal Teacher Quality Mandate that requires, "Each state educational agency shall develop a plan to ensure that all teachers teaching in core academic subjects within the state are highly qualified no later than the end of the 2005-2006 school year."

It is clear what needs to be done to ensure this deadline is met. No Child Left Behind provides specific guidelines for determining if a teacher is highly qualified. While these rules vary by grade level, teachers are judged as highly qualified when they meet three conditions: (1) They must possess a bachelor's degree, (2) they must attain full certification or licensure, no waivers or emergency credentials, and (3) they must demon-strate content knowledge in the subject they teach.

This demonstration can come in a variety of forms. New elementary teachers must pass a state test of literacy and numerics. New secondary teachers must either have a college major or pass a rigorous test in the subject area. Veteran teachers may pass a state test, have a college major, or demonstrate content knowledge through High, Objective, Uniform State Standards of Evaluation, or the so-called HOUSSE standards that are set by each of the states. At first glance, these conditions may appear to be straightforward, but we must remember that both certification rules and HOUSSE rules for demonstrating content knowledge are developed by each state, where local conditions mixed with a variety of regulations governing implementation can present tough challenges as states try to move forward—which brings us to our panel members.

We have asked each panelist to give a brief overview of what their state is doing to enhance teacher quality, or in the case of Ray and Lisa, what effective practices they have observed around the country, what limitations they are running into in terms of politics, money or local conditions, and how these initiatives are overcoming these limitations, or not. Finally, we have asked them to comment on whether No Child Left Behind has been a help or a hindrance. Following their comments, I will raise some questions regarding state efforts.

Jim Horne

Thank you very much, it's great to be here with you, and certainly I want to thank and congratulate all the great educators who are here, because, without your efforts, we cannot succeed. Six years ago, in 1998, I was at the Milken Conference in Los Angeles. Michael Milken gave a lunchtime keynote address that crystallized in my mind the importance of teaching. He started in an unusual way, discussing why education is important. It was unusual because, I think instinctively, intuitively, we recognize how important education is, but I don't know that we often stop and really digest why. He made the point that 77% of the gross national product is in human capital. When he first said that, I'm not really sure it resonated. Then he stopped, paused and said it again. He made sure you understood that 77% of the gross national product of this country is in human capital.

We often think of America as a great nation, with vast wealth in terms of real estate and buildings and manufacturing capacities and precious metals or whatever other resources we have. However, he said 77% of this nation is in human capital. That's knowledge. That's learning and education. So, those whom we entrust to develop that human capital and to tap the potential from that human capital are critical to the success of this great country. For the first time, it really crystallized in my mind that great teaching is important for more than just the sort of intuitive reasons such as that we care about our children and want them to have many things that we didn't have. The sustaining of our economy and the strength of our nation will depend on how we produce and expand human capital.

Oftentimes Florida is viewed as one of the more progressive education states. We're kind of like the old Mikey cereal commercials. You know, Mikey will eat anything. Well, Florida will experiment with anything and probably has the most robust choice in programs. We embrace vouchers, charter schools, and home education. We have magnet programs. We have IB, AP, and every other kind of program you want to experiment with. We certainly are capable of being able to do that—be it good or bad. I think Florida is the ultimate laboratory rat for education, and we are able to do almost anything we want.

Many of you might need to understand my background. I'm not a professional educator; I'm a CPA. I'm a businessperson who served in the legislature and who, quite honestly, had no interest in the pursuit of education being my primary life goal. I wanted to fight crime. I certainly wanted to deal with issues that I thought you could handle. Education was so complex, and it was very difficult to figure out solutions. When it became my time to chair a committee, I raised my hand for Criminal Justice, and the Senate President at the time said, "We want you to chair the Education Appropriations because you are a CPA and you understand numbers, and we think you'd be a perfect fit." I didn't really want to do that and I said, "I'd prefer to chair Criminal Justice." At that time, the Senate President said, "Let me think about it for a second;" she then said, "Here's your choice: You can chair Children and Family or Education Appropriations." In a nanosecond, I made my decision. I took that education thing and it's probably been the best decision of my life because ever since then, I have focused on how to improve education in Florida and how to find the solutions for improving education across America.

Too often we are quick to blame, always pointing the finger. Who is to blame for the problems that we have? Let me share a poem with you.

A college professor once said, "Such rawness in a student is a shame, lack of preparation in high school is to blame."

Said the high school teacher, "Good heavens that boy is a fool. The fault, of course, is with the middle school."

The middle school teacher said, "From stupidity might I be spared. They sent him in so unprepared."

The primary teacher huffed, "Kindergarten blockheads all. They call that preparation—why, it is worse than none at all."

The kindergarten teacher said, "Such lack of training never did I see. What kind of woman must that mother be?"

The mother said, "Poor, helpless child, he is not to blame. His father's people were all the same."

Said the father at the end of the line, "I doubt that rascal's even mine."

So you see, we're all too quick to point the finger. Somebody else is always to blame for the problems that we have, but the truth is that we are all to blame. If we're going to succeed in making a positive change, I think the focus has to be on the teaching profession.

Clearly, we need some changes in the profession. We have been very fortunate in the post-World War II period to have had an artificial supply of highly qualified teachers. Primarily, there were no real opportunities for women in the workforce except to teach or, in some cases to be nurses. Now, as we've sort of busted through the glass ceiling, made opportunities for women in various occupations, and given women the ability to succeed in other occupations, it's time that we take what we know in the business profession to create a teaching profession. I don't believe the teaching profession is a *profession*. You know, quite honestly it's the only profession I know where you start and end your career with one title: teacher.

Now, the profession that I came from was as a CPA (and I used to be kind of proud to use that as an analogy, but with all the WorldCom, Enron, and other scandals, I'm not so sure that we want to draw the analogy, but it's the only one I know. So it's the only one I can use). In the CPA profession, you start as a staff accountant. As you move forward in your profession, you perform at a very high level, and you then seek to assume greater responsibilities and you are promoted to senior accountant. As a senior accountant, you assume some supervision responsibilities. You're rewarded for how well you do individually. You're also rewarded for how well your unit, or your office, does. Then you move forward, in some cases. Maybe a senior accountant is all you want to be and all you want to do, but in some cases, you aspire to even greater levels of responsibility and you can be promoted to a manager. As a manager, you're compensated for how well you do individually and how well your office or your unit performs. Then you may aspire to even higher levels of responsibility, maybe as a senior manager and maybe ultimately as a partner in the firm.

In the teaching profession, you start as a teacher, and you end as a teacher. If you are to succeed financially, you leave the classroom and go into administration. You actually leave the one thing that you're called to do. The truth is, when you meet teachers like the ones who are in this room, it's very clear that you have a calling in your life. You're more like a missionary than anything I know. It clearly is a calling, it's something you desire to do, but there's also this human emotion of wanting to be successful. That human emotion oftentimes overtakes that calling, and it drives you out of the classroom to go do something that, quite honestly, you may not be gifted to do. You may not be adequately trained, nor do you really want to be an administrator. But that human emotion, to be compared with others and to be successful, forces you out of the classroom.

You know, I also find it very interesting that we take our brand-new, very passionate teachers and toss them into the most difficult environments. In the CPA profession, when we hired brand-new staff accountants, we did not send them out on our most difficult client. We assigned them certain tasks, but they were supervised, they were mentored, they were helped, they were given professional development, and they were given training before they assumed greater levels of responsibility. Yet in the teaching profession, we take these brand-new teachers, we throw them in the most difficult environment, and we actually sit back and scratch our heads and pretend we don't know why they quit. That's the most amazing thing to me. It's bizarre that we actually can't quite figure out why these teachers want to quit within the first 3 years.

Florida has experimented with TAP for a few years. (Now, like many states, I will tell you that most state legislatures believe they have to invent it all over again.) I can say that about them because I was once one of them. You all probably can't say that without getting in trouble. It has to be an original idea with legislators. That was pretty much the same in Florida, so it was not that we didn't like TAP. We basically had to take TAP and give it a different name so that we could move forward with it, so Florida created something we call the BEST Plan. For the most part, it's a lot like TAP. It has a few Florida wrinkles and looks a little different in some ways, but we created the BEST Plan. We were successful in getting $25 million appropriated so that we could go forward and implement this in a very significant way. One of the things that has been missing for a while in the TAP experimentation is the ability to do it district-wide. We've been able to pick off a school here and there in a few different places, but we haven't been able to actually implement it in a district-wide kind of environment, which we think would be very important to do.

The BEST Salary Career Ladder Pilot Program (Chart 4.1)—and that's a mouthful—is still TAP. We have five broad principles in this piece of legislation including multiple career paths, which you know certainly sounds similar to TAP; market driven-compensation, which I think is critical; performance-based accountability; ongoing applied professional development; and school leadership, which sometimes is not talked about as much in the TAP model. When I was in the legislature in charge of education policy and appropriations, I used to believe it was all about teachers. It was about what teachers knew and could do in the classroom that made the difference. As I toured the state of Florida and got an opportunity to

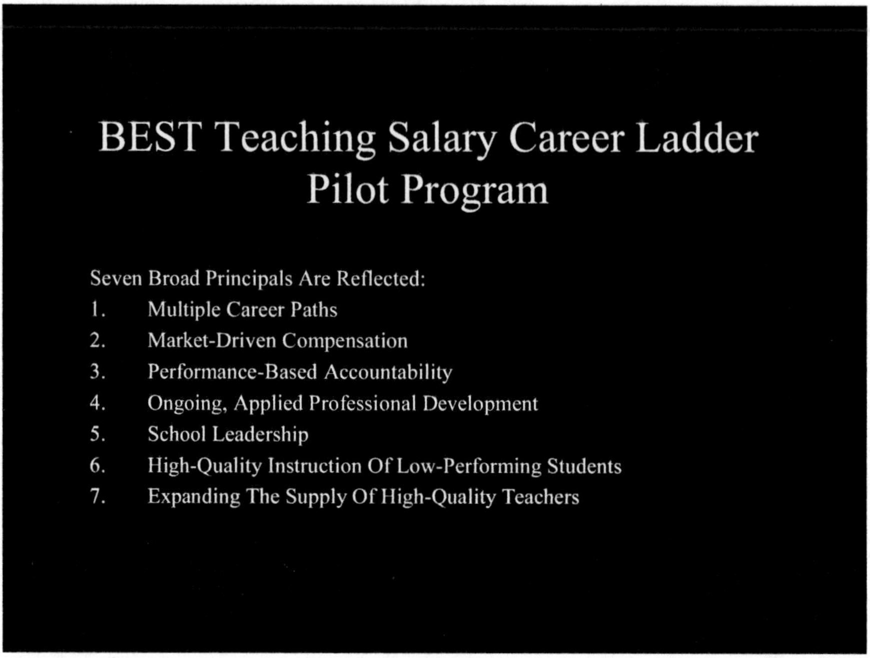

BEST Teaching Salary Career Ladder Pilot Program

Seven Broad Principals Are Reflected:
1.   Multiple Career Paths
2.   Market-Driven Compensation
3.   Performance-Based Accountability
4.   Ongoing, Applied Professional Development
5.   School Leadership
6.   High-Quality Instruction Of Low-Performing Students
7.   Expanding The Supply Of High-Quality Teachers

Chart 4.1

visit successful schools, something jumped off the page at me. It was the impact and the influence that great principals have. It really begins with the principal. You have to have a principal who embraces this kind of reform effort for it to succeed.

Great principals will inspire great teachers because their leadership is critical. If a principal does not buy into this, no reform effort will ever work in that kind of culture. High-quality instruction of low performing students is part of the BEST Plan, which is probably a little bit different than the TAP model; we insist on putting our best teachers in our lowest performing schools and our most difficult classrooms. We think that is critical to making this kind of an opportunity work. It's one thing to put the highest performing teachers in the most affluent communities, in the best, newest schools, and they would always have good results, but it's a different thing to be able to move, transfer, and shift them around to make sure that our best teachers are in our most difficult situations.

Expanding the supply of highly qualified teachers is the number-one challenge any state has. We all know that in the next decade we need 2 million teachers coming into this profession. Florida is a fast-growing state. On average, we would probably have 60,000 additional students come into our system every year. We need approximately 15,000 to 20,000 new teachers every year. Our colleges of education produced 4,000. That's the challenge. Florida's been blessed because we've had an ability to recruit across state lines, particularly in the Northeast. But when this becomes a national crisis, our ability to extract the best teachers from other states will end. Therefore, if we are not looking for and willing to embrace systemic changes in the ability to build, construct, recruit, and retain teachers, then we are going to have a devastating problem on our hands in less than a decade.

The pilot program began in January of 2004, and that's why they call it a pilot. Four districts were chosen, including Broward County School District. For those who are not based in Florida, I believe Broward County is the fifth largest school system in America. It is a very large school district with roughly 250,000 students. Pasco would be considered medium size. Hillsboro, which is Tampa, is another large district, and Sumter is a small, kind of rural county, and it's actually implementing the TAP plan as written. So four counties implemented BEST in January, and it is going very well. BEST has an evaluative process that goes with it, much like TAP, for schools that are not doing the exact TAP model.

In the Broward County model, teachers at the highest level—the mentor level—have an ability to earn $92,000 a year. I think that is exceptional. I know we have some Florida teachers here not from Broward County, and I hope they don't quickly put their resumes in to transfer to Broward County. But Broward is doing it in a way that creates the kind of reward system that we know will work. This is a pretty extensive program, and my good friends from the Milken Family Foundation ought to put this in their brochures because I think they can probably pretty much declare that the BEST plan is TAP or TAP junior, or TAP light, or TAP senior, or something. It is going into 519 schools and will affect more than 38,000 teachers and over half a million students. This will be the largest implementation of a performance pay plan for professional teaching anywhere in America. It will give us the ability to look at results.

Florida also, as you may know, has a high-stakes test called the FCAT. It is a test that is often considered controversial because it determines third grade promotions and graduation for 10th graders going through the 12th grade. The FCAT is a state test that is used for determining many things and, because we've constructed this test at every grade level, we actually have the ability to measure learning gains. We're one of only a few states that can actually look and determine how much learning is going on.

One of the great questions that our governor asks me routinely is that he wants to know if a student is getting a year's worth of learning in a year's worth of time. How can we know that? We have built a numerical scale score, so we can actually look at where a student starts and where a student ends to determine how much learning is going on.

I think that's important because, as we talk about performance pay, that sends shivers down educators' backs because they think back to the old days of different kinds of structures, merit pay structures. They think immediately of those good-old-boy systems where some old football coach who's now the principal is going to pick his favorites to determine who the best performing teachers are and who's going to get the bonus.

When I talk to teachers, I've never met a teacher who is afraid of accountability. I've never met a teacher who's afraid to be measured. But they want it objectively. They want a fair system. Florida has gone to great lengths to construct a system that we think is fair and equitable so that teachers who may be dealing with a harder-to-serve population and are starting much further behind, we're only going to measure the amount of learning that goes on, not just where a student ends up. That kind of system certainly wouldn't be fair to teachers who teach, for example, in the inner city. This is a system that looks at learning gains. In some respects, this system may attract more teachers to serve such environments, because they actually have honed in their skills and know that they have a lot of opportunity to bring a student from very low to very high. I think that will make the system fair and better.

Multiple career paths are important for teachers. Some teachers want to be classroom teachers. That's all they want to be. They don't want to aspire to be more. They don't want to assume additional responsibilities. They don't necessarily want to be in charge of curriculum or a department budget or practice development for teachers. They want to be classroom teachers. Multiple career paths—this creates opportunities for teachers to be where they want in the profession.

Market-driven compensation—you've already heard me talk a little bit about that in terms of the spread and the compensation. I think that's important. And I know teachers will tell me, "Hey, I'm not in this profession for the compensation." I would bet you that is probably true. But that's not the question we need to ask. The question is, who's *not* in this profession because of the compensation? That's the question that we need to ask. I think that as long as we have an archaic system that was invented well over 80 years ago that's based upon the amount of years in a classroom and the number of degrees that you could simply put on the wall, it's not going to get the job done. We've been on an industrial model, with the agriculture calendar, and now we're living in the digital age. We need to recognize that the artificial supply of talent coming into this profession is not going to continue.

The education profession has changed a lot. If you look back 150 years in the teaching profession, it was reserved for White, single women. In the

1850s, you had to get permission to date and it was only on Sundays. If you got married, you were kicked out of the profession. So we've made significant progress.

I think now it's time to take that next step and truly create a profession where you have multiple levels, you have different tiers, you have more opportunities, and the compensation is tied in part to performance. That doesn't mean that everything will be tied to a student's test scores, but it does mean that we cannot continue to rely on a salary schedule that is compressed, where the best are paid like those who are not the best. Veteran teachers are paid almost the same now as beginning teachers. We need to make sure there's an adequate spread. We need to create a structure that will attract the best and the brightest into this profession.

Performance-based accountability—of course, I think that's important. We have to be willing to look at accountability. We need to look at performance-based systems. Ongoing, applied professional growth and professional development are critical.

We have maybe 6,000 different programs in Florida for professional development. Teachers have told me that 80% of them were worthless, and they, the teachers, desire high quality professional development. It's sort of a field of dreams: build it, and they shall come. I think it's really up to us; with technology, we clearly have the ability to bring it to your desktop right now. I think it's critical that we continue to have professional development on a 24/7 basis, not 4 days in the summer. Internet-based training will not get the job done exclusively; it has to be a hybrid mix of teachers working together online and in various other settings. It has to be when you need it, when you want it, and tailored to your specific needs.

School leadership—you've heard me talk about that. It is often left out of this equation. Yet it may be the most critical part because none of these other pieces are going to work if that principal is not in tune with this. High-quality instruction of low performing students—you've already heard me talk a little bit about that and how we need to make sure that's in the equation. Expanding the supply of high-quality teachers is a big one for us in Florida, and we have enacted a class size amendment that will create an annual need for at least 7,000 more teachers than we would normally have in any given year. We also know that we're a fast-growing state, averaging 60,000 more students each year. We're also a state that has an aging teaching workforce, where the significant part of the workforce is going to retire in the next 2 or 3 years. That vast institutional knowledge needs to be there to help these younger teachers learn the trade. Clearly, we know that some of our veteran teachers are doing outstanding jobs, and we really can't afford for them to hang up their cleats now. So, that last piece is a big challenge for us. Just look at the sheer numbers; I would bet you in almost any state, you're facing the same kind of situation. Our colleges of education fund 5,600 slots a year. Roughly 4,000 of those will ultimately teach in a public school in Florida. In an average year, I need 15,000 new teachers, probably now in the neighborhood of 20,000 because of the class size amendment that we've passed.

We must face the reality of this profession and how we can better attract more talent into this profession. I will tell you there are many great reforms and Florida embraces most, if not all of them, including accountability. But the ultimate education reform will be the transformation of this profession. It will be an ability to attract the best and brightest, put them in the classroom and turn them into professionals. Give them some school-based authority, let the decisions be made by those closest to the students and watch the numbers fly. We're seeing a rise in the student achievement in Florida and we're proud of that. But we have to go the rest of the way.

BEST is just but one pilot program and I have to give you the bad news too. The bad news is that we actually had to delay BEST going statewide this coming school year because we didn't get funding to do so. I certainly hope that next year will be a better year in terms of some dollars for the program. I'm a firm believer in this model and that this model will revolutionize the teaching profession.

Things are good in Florida. We're proud of the results we're getting in Florida. And we're particularly proud of the great teachers that we have in Florida. You know, we probably are not the most highly compensated teachers in the nation; but I will tell you, even with all the odds and all the challenges they face, there are an incredible amount of good things going on in the state of Florida. We're working on this big project. It's my number-one priority on a personal level to see this through. Thank you very much.

Lisa Graham Keegan

Thank you so much for being here and most of all I want to congratulate you and say thank you for what you're doing. It's an honor to be here and it's been a great privilege in my life to work with outstanding teachers—both as a professional and as a mom, because my kids have certainly been blessed and had them.

I want to talk about this in the context of how teacher quality becomes greater in the nation through capitalizing on the capacity of great teachers out there, and the capacity of people who want to come to us and be great teachers. Secretary Paige talks all the time about the importance right now in this moment that Commissioner Horne has talked about, of needing so many new teachers, thousands of new colleagues for you all. How in the world are we going to we attract all these people into the profession? What Secretary Paige says is that we're in the business of raising standards and lowering barriers. I support initiatives that promote teacher quality and embrace high-quality, outstanding, and fabulous teachers, while lowering the barriers that prevent us from bringing them into the classroom. I believe that much like the paradox of student expectation—that higher expectation, higher challenge is not, as it turns out, a bigger barrier to learning. That it is actually a recipe for success in learning. The same is true with the teaching profession—higher standards, higher expectations for how we bring teachers into the profession is resulting in additions to the teaching core that are absolutely outstanding.

At the state level, the Education Leaders Council is involved in a partnership that created something called the American Board for Certification of Teacher Excellence which Cheryl touched on briefly. The idea behind the American Board is that the country was greatly in need of a way to certify those individuals who have proven content knowledge, knowledge of instruction and pedagogy, and have proven that they are prepared, through whatever life experience or educational experience, to become a beginning teacher.

I say to become a beginning teacher because I think all of us in the profession understand there is no such thing as a perfectly educated and ready-to-roll teacher. There is a perfectly educated and prepared, ready-to-roll beginning teacher who's going to need mentoring, experience, all of the nasty, in-your-face stuff that happens when the plan meets reality. My husband is a military guy and is fond of saying "no plan withstands contact with the enemy." Nothing could be truer than teaching second graders for example. You think you're ready and then you meet them. Nothing can prepare you other than at that point; for all of your content preparation and all of your knowledge, at that point you need an adult. You need an adult to say to you, "That was good, that was terrible, let's not do that anymore, this was great, you ought to expand here." That process of mentoring is integral to the teaching profession. All of us know it.

The American Board says we are going to figure out who has the academic preparation and the content knowledge necessary to teach effectively. American Board certification is a process where you sit for examinations that collectively take about 6 hours. They are in content and pedagogy. The content in those tests is spectacular. You sit down, watch streaming video of a child reading and then determine the best way to resolve his weaknesses. They ask: What are you hearing? What's next? What does this look like to you? How do you intervene? American Board certification uses technologies in ways that take us way down the line, while also creating an opportunity to bring new folks into the profession without going through traditional college prep pathways. You can also come through the traditional way, but this benefits the many thousands of people who would like to teach but are mid-career changers.

One of the best examples was just on *Fox News* in Idaho. Idaho has adopted the American Board as one route to certification besides the traditional route. This man was a West Point graduate and an engineer in the military for 20 some odd years. For those of you who have had military lives as my husband and I have, retirement comes around mid-40s. So, here's this engineer, a natural born dweeb who had taught for his entire career, yet he was not a certified teacher. He wanted to teach mathematics in high school; with the traditional path, he'd have to go back to school. Should we not create a system by which he can sit for an examination that says, "Oh, yeah, you're good, very good in mathematics, very good in understanding pedagogy and instruction, and you are ready to be a beginning teacher and to be mentored"?

That is what the American Board is bringing us. Its adoption is ongoing in a number of states, and I think it will add enormous capacity to the quality of the teaching profession. Who is opposing it? Obviously, it is being opposed by the traditional system and by those who are suspect. They say, "You can't just sit for a pen and paper test and instantly become a teacher." Neither, however, can you discount the availability of thousands of potential teachers around the country whose lives have prepared them to be excellent teachers somehow. We have to embrace them and call them colleagues. We need to mentor them as beginning teachers and get them up to speed to let them be part of the team.

I also think that the charter school movement which our organization promotes and which I have been a part of in Arizona, is a fabulous open door for the teaching profession. One of the things about teaching that I find so phenomenal (and it's actually Lowell who put it into words for me and I've been stealing his words shamelessly ever since) is that there are few professions, think about it, in which the people who know the profession best are not systematically free to bring their skills to the marketplace. For example, say you are a great doctor and have a great practice somewhere, and you have a particular technique that you like and works well. If you know your other colleagues who love that technique, you can go start your own practice. That's a normal situation in the medical profession. Same with being a CPA or an engineer; you take your skills and you say, "You know what? We do this just a little bit better and would like to do it ourselves in the marketplace."

Teachers who are exceptional do not have, or did not have, a regular route to bring their skills to the market to improve the education marketplace. How do we deal with special education kids? How do we deal with kids who are just gifted in mathematics but struggling in reading? We have hopes of attracting exceptional teachers, yet the only way to create a system or a school under this current system has been through the school board detecting growth in the attendance boundaries, and then building a school. Then we at the school board pick the teachers. That can be an OK system, but it doesn't allow for innovation among the excellent tier of teachers they want to add. It happens every now and then. Teachers get together and convince their leaders or their school boards that we ought to be able to start a little something special here or there, but it is not routine.

I believe that charter schools are only the beginning. I don't think we understand yet how powerful it can be to have two teachers at the head of where the next step in schooling goes. They ought to be driving that for us and I think the charter movement has been a great addition to teacher professionalism.

Cheryl said we weren't going to talk about TAP much, but I never pay attention to instructions. So I want to talk about what happened in Arizona. Arizona was the first state to adopt TAP. Commissioner Horne spoke briefly about Lowell's speech at the Milken meeting. I will tell you that Lowell gives many great speeches, but that speech was a V8 moment for so many of us and we still call it "Lowell's speech." For me, what was so critical—and I obviously remember it to this day and hopefully have acted on it since—was that in pursuing merit pay; in pursuing ways to reward excellent teaching, we were thinking about it in a way that was, excuse me, just so constipated. If you take the salary schedule and you do a better job we are going to compare you to the teacher in the next classroom, and then we are just going to pay you more. Lowell said that is not ever what happens in the real universe. In the real universe, when you excel, your supervisor, or whomever you are working for, or whoever is a leader, says to you, "Well, you are really outstanding. We will pay you more, but you will give us more." Your job changes, and within schools we don't have that regular possibility to excel where we say, "Oh my gosh, this young man has come in, and he is just fantastic. Not only is he teaching his kids, I can see his gain scores are fabulous."

Like Commissioner Horne, I believe value-added gains are what need to be used in rewarding successful teaching. I believe that the one-size-fits-all contract has to disappear. It is a huge barrier to innovation and fabulous addition to the teaching force. As a professional, I want to be able to say that I would be more than happy to give the month of June. Let me take a cadre of teachers in the summer and train them during the month of June, but certainly pay for that month. It would take two or three of us.

The whole notion of performance-based pay being differential pay for the same job I think is faulty. There is nothing wrong with bonuses for excellence, which I'm a big fan of, but I don't think that's how we want to be talking up bonuses as the best way to advance the teacher profession. It comes from getting more of your time into our classrooms. When we experienced this with TAP, it was so clear to me what was going on in TAP schools. Full-time mentors in those schools were feeding back into the younger teachers and had a regular system of professional development. It's not professional development in sort of the tired way that we've done it—take a class and then try to export that back into your life experience. Effective professional development is real time, real experience, and ongoing professional development, not classes. It is somebody feeding back to you immediately on whether that class was successful or not and why.

We run a program at ELC called Following the Leaders where we go out and we help schools take their curriculum, align it to state standards, make sure that they have ongoing feedback about how their schools are doing. This year we expanded that into a series of TAP schools in Arizona. We do training and expect to see usage figures. We're monitoring that all the time. In Arizona at a particular TAP school, we did not see those usage figures start to pop after the training. When that happens, you get a visit from Mom (a.k.a. Dr. Taylor) because she runs the program, not me. Dr. Taylor was going to go out and we were going to discuss why we don't see usage figures. I went too because I know these schools very well. What they said to us was so fantastic, and I continue to learn so much about the need to be humble, which for me doesn't come easy.

We sat with a group of educators and said, "You know what, we're not seeing usage yet on this new program. We're not seeing you guys online. You don't seem to be using this." Their answer was that since the inception of TAP in those schools, they are very careful about additional programs and any add-ons go through their own system of alignment. "We know alignment," they said to us, "We see these things and we like this product. But it has to work from the top, those of us in the leadership team down through every single classroom teacher. We will wait until everyone has agreed to what each is doing. Then we'll start using it, and we will let you know."

Wow. So as it turns out, their usage numbers were almost higher than anybody else's. Just a great lesson for those of us who are in charge of policies, our job is to make sure that we are facilitating the power of excellent teaching. All we can do is make sure that those doors are open and those people are able to do their job. We reward teachers for that. We provide pathways for greater excellence and then we just get out of the way. Thank you very much.

Ray Simon

I know this is, at least in recent history, a unique experience for the Milken Family Foundation to be in Washington, D.C. I too have only been here since January 6. It's a different experience than anything I've ever done in my life. I don't know how far from work I live. I don't have a car. I live in a one-bedroom apartment on the Metro system. I know that I go in a hole in the ground on one end and 15 minutes later I come out of a hole on the other end and I'm at work. I say that to tell you that if there's anything in this town you want to see, if it's not on the Metro line, it's not worth seeing. But I feel safe and secure to take the Metro and it'll get you anywhere you want to go.

I also learned that the Department of Education in Washington has a face. Many times the state departments of education that you have to deal with don't have a face. They seem to be very cold entities that only come around when something's wrong. We're trying to change that in Washington and I know that in working with your state chiefs they want to change that in terms of No Child Left Behind implementation. No Child Left Behind really has not had a face up to this point in time. It's mainly been a series of what I call form issues being debated. Starting points, end counts, AYP and highly qualified teachers is one of those "form issues." Those are important to discuss. You need form and structure with any law. In putting a face on No Child Left Behind, specifically putting a face on the Highly Qualified Teacher Provisions of the law, I think it's important to understand what it does and doesn't say and the difference between what it does and doesn't require.

Back in September the Department began to visit with individual states through Teacher Assistance Core. Forty-five teachers, researchers, and people who have active experience in the classroom went around and visited all 50 states. The meetings were conducted in an environment that we call "Conversations Without Consequences." That just means whatever is said in this room doesn't leave this room. Because of those meetings and a number of teacher roundtables that the Department conducted throughout the country in conjunction with regional meetings, we determined that there was much misunderstanding and misinformation about the highly qualified provision. There were teachers who were angry and teachers who were afraid of what this meant for them—and we're talking about our veteran teachers now—that they were going to have to go back to school. They were going to have to take additional classes, maybe even get other degrees. They might have to take tests to prove they were highly qualified. None of that is true. So our challenge was to work with states to first make sure they understood what the provisions in the law were. Then they had to communicate that to the teachers.

States have great latitude in how they define "highly qualified." Cheryl mentioned the three requirements and they're pretty broad. It's up to a state to set what those requirements are. There's no reason for a veteran teacher that has taught physics for 20 years to wake up one morning and be declared not highly qualified. That doesn't make any sense. If that's happening, then there's miscommunication somewhere. So we want to work with you. If you yourself are in a position where something unreasonable appears to be happening to you in terms of your designation, or if you have a colleague who you feel is concerned about where he or she will land in all these highly-qualified teacher discussions, give us a call. We have a Website, we have e-mail. There's a teacher toolkit that we've published that's available on our Website which answers a lot of practical questions we've heard from you about the Highly Qualified Teacher Provisions.

What we have to be sure of in Washington, and what your states certainly should be sure of, is that we respect the work you've done. You're veteran teachers. You're very special teachers. But we don't have Milken Educators in every classroom in our country. I just spent the weekend with my 2 year-old grandson. Alex always teaches me something before I leave, or he asks me questions that I try to remember. Two things stood out in this particular visit. First, he said, "Granddad, where's your hair?" I think he's known that for a while, but he just never asked. Then Monday, the day before I left, we were going somewhere together, and he said, "Granddad, you're my best friend." Man, it was tough to leave that little guy yesterday morning. But I use Alex in a number of my conversations with teachers. I say Alex is going to start school in a few years. Three more years and he'll be in kindergarten. I don't want it to be the luck of the draw that my best friend gets a good teacher in kindergarten. I don't want it to be the luck of the draw that my best friend gets a bad teacher in first grade. He shouldn't have to worry about that.

The Highly Qualified Teacher Provision is at least a first positive major step to help guarantee Alex always has a good teacher. It's not meant to punish any good teacher. It's meant to try to get teachers where kids need them and to make sure that our poorest children, our children of color, our children whose first language is not English, that those children don't have the luck of the draw, which many of them do now. It's luck of the draw whether they get a good teacher or not. That's just not right. We want to work with you to try to make sure this works.

This past April, we invited, through the Milken Family Foundation, some current and former Milken Award winners, principals, and teachers and spent a day with them. We learned a lot that day. They told us: our teachers are afraid because some of our teachers don't believe we can do the mission of NCLB, the mission of every child at grade level. We're afraid because we haven't been able to do that before as a group and we're worried we're not going to be able to do it now. Our principals are afraid because they're under a lot of pressure when state AYP lists are announced because for some reason being on school improvement has been equated with failure, which it was never meant to be. But our principals are afraid. So they're doing foolish things in response to that fear. They're doing things that we know as teachers don't make a lot of sense and that are not good for kids. We need help in being convinced that we can do this job. The educators in the room that day were convinced they could do it. But they're hearing from their colleagues that they don't think it can happen.

The United States Department of Education is going to try to alleviate those fears. We've taken some steps to do that. We've recently announced the sponsorship of seven workshops around the country this summer, starting in June. We sent out invitations; we're limited this first year to approximately 200 participants per session. If you haven't signed up, it's too late. We've had the enrollment out for just a couple of weeks and every session is now full. The session will simply be your fellow teachers from throughout the country whom someone has identified as being very special, and being identified as someone who has made a difference in the classroom, who has closed the achievement gap, who has gotten 100% of children proficient in his or her classroom. Those teachers are going to come share what they did to make that happen. When your colleagues can see success stories standing in front of them, then they know it can be done and the fear should be gone.

This summer we're also going to sponsor a research-to-practice summit in Washington. We will bring together individuals who have made this work in the classroom, with researchers, to talk about what works and what doesn't. Your colleagues who came to us in April also said one of the foolish things that's being done in their school districts is the elimination of professional development at a time when that is what we need the most for our teachers—when that's one thing that states can use to designate whether a teacher is highly qualified— is to provide them with quality professional development.

In the president's budget, there is over $5 billion set aside specifically for teacher quality issues. Over $3 billion of that can be used by the states. You can pay bonuses with that money. You can provide professional development. There are unprecedented levels of federal funding now given to states for the express purpose of working with teachers. Helping make sure little Alex and all his buddies have a good teacher every year. We look forward to continuing to work with you. We're going to invite other teachers back for visits. We want to continue dialog with you; you can write me at Ray.Simon@ed.gov. I'd like to hear your thoughts about teaching, No

Child Left Behind, and highly qualified teachers—particularly if you sense a problem or something that just seems to be totally out of place. We'd like to hear it. Thank you very much for what you do, and congratulations on your honor for being here today.

Janice Poda

Good afternoon. It's a real honor for me to be here. The whole time I've been sitting here, I've been trying to come up with a strategy that I can use to entice all of you to come back to South Carolina with me and be teachers there. I think I have two things that might interest you. This Friday night we're going to be announcing our state's Teacher of the Year, and we will be handing him or her a check for $25,000 and the keys to a Z4 BMW Roadster. That's the way that we acknowledge our state Teacher of the Year, and that's because of the role model that the Milken Family Foundation set by the honors they give to teachers. The other reason I'd love to take all of you home is because my own daughter will be a first-year teacher in the fall, and I'd like her to be surrounded by individuals who understand the need to help us mentor and induct our first-year teachers into the profession. I'm pleased that she's decided to follow my example and go into the teaching profession.

I usually would say to you that I bring greetings from South Carolina, the small, poor, rural state. But, the most recent flexibility provision from the U.S. Department of Education's definition of "rural school" indicates that South Carolina has no rural schools. So we no longer think of ourselves as a rural state, but we're not real sure what we are, so we're kind of having an identity crisis. Maybe I should say greetings from the metropolis of Columbia, South Carolina, or the urban center. I do want to share with you some of the things that we were doing in South Carolina before No Child Left Behind in the area of teacher quality. Then I want to talk about the risk of being the first state to have a compliance monitoring visit and some of the challenges that we're experiencing.

First of all, we've been requiring a content area exam for teacher certification since 1976. So for most of our teachers, the great majority of them will demonstrate that they have content knowledge through the test that they've taken. We've also developed a certification system for our middle-level teachers. We were in the process of phasing that in when No Child Left Behind was passed. I don't know if you've ever had the experience of standing up before 950 middle school teachers after they've taught all day and given statewide tests and to tell them that they may not be highly qualified. But that was one of the opportunities that I had just a few weeks ago. We also have a policy that requires that at least 90% of all teachers in each district, or in each school, are teaching in their field of preparation. We don't have any that even come close to nearing the 10% cap that we have on the number of out-of-field teachers. We were one of the first states to implement a comprehensive teacher evaluation system, a statewide system, where we have trained evaluators who look for the same criteria in each classroom. We have the third largest number of National Board Certified teachers in the nation. We pay each one of them an additional $7,500 per year for having achieved that accomplishment. We have five schools in our state that are participating in TAP and you've already heard a lot about TAP. This is our third year of the pilot and we've found great success from having that opportunity to be a pilot state.

Our teacher preparation programs are in the process of making significant changes to adapt to a standards-based kind of teaching environment. I would liken the responsibility of trying to implement the teacher quality aspects of No Child Left Behind to flying an airplane while you're building it, and you're still waiting for the parts to come in to finish building it. There are still a number of things that we have concerns about in our state, in terms of the implementation. I would like to just mention four of those.

I want to say upfront that one of the things No Child Left Behind has done for us, is that it has required us to go back and look at ourselves very closely, to do a very close examination of our policies, of the regulations that we had in place and the other requirements that we had in the area of teacher quality. It's given us the political will to do some things that we weren't able to do beforehand. For example, back in the early 1970s, our general assembly had passed a provision of a certificate called a "warrant," which meant that a person who had completed a teacher preparation program but never had passed any kind of exam for the teaching profession, could be allowed to teach. Every few years, they would put a cap on that amount of time and then they would raise the cap. So I was doing some research for some testimony that I gave in an equity lawsuit that was going on in our state a few months ago and found that there were teachers who had taken those kinds of exams as many as 29 times and never had been able to pass them. But because of the warrant certificate, they were still teaching in our state. No Child Left Behind will give us the opportunity to eliminate those kinds of certificates and to require teachers to demonstrate that they have the content knowledge that they need to continue.

It's also given us the opportunity to do a much better job of collecting and keeping data about teachers. I must say that this is one of the most underestimated challenges states face. I want you to envision for a minute people climbing around in a warehouse full of boxes, looking through old files for teacher test scores and doing that for 130,000 people, then entering them into a database. That is one of the challenges that we've been trying to do, as well as implement the other aspects of the law so that when we're finished, we will have a wonderful database with a lot of information. But getting there has certainly been a challenge.

One of my concerns, the first one that I'll mention, is that there are still some areas of certification where we have not given very clear direction on how a person can demonstrate that they're highly qualified. The first one has to do with special education, the other one is social studies. Those happen to be my two areas of certification, so perhaps that makes me a little more empathic with the fact that I'm the one who has to look at people sometimes and say, I don't think you're going to be highly qualified unless you do one of these things to demonstrate that you're highly qualified. That's hard to do, especially for the veteran who's been doing that job for 25 years. Then we have to say, perhaps you need to take some additional courses. I heard what Dr. Simon said and I'm going to make sure that I get some of my questions answered before we leave so I will have good answers to tell those teachers.

I think that once we do determine how special education teachers, especially high school special education teachers, can demonstrate that they in fact do have the knowledge of dealing with students with disabilities as well as the content knowledge they need in order to be highly qualified teachers, we'll have a better system for working with our students with disabilities. Then, hopefully all teachers will know more about how to work with children with disabilities and that'll be a good thing. If we don't do that in a way that will make it appropriate for those teachers, I think we'll be leaving many special education teachers behind. In terms of social studies, my fear is that if we require teachers to demonstrate content knowledge in every discrete area of social studies, like government, like geography, like political science, civics and history, that we'll actually in fact narrow our curriculum in what we teach in social studies, rather than giving students that broad view of the social sciences.

The second concern that I'll mention is that there is a tendency to compare one state with another, especially in the area of teacher quality. That's certainly something that happens in many areas, and I understand that watchdog groups like to do that. It's distressing to me to see those comparisons when, as you've heard, every state has the latitude to develop their own certification systems and the requirements for certification, their own latitude to develop their HOUSSE plans and also even defining a highly qualified teacher, as long as it's in the parameters of what the law states. So to make those comparisons from one state to another really isn't fair. Unfortunately, many of the watchdog groups are not nearly as patient as the states have been to receive all the information that we need in order to implement the law. So we're being evaluated at the same time that we're trying to implement this law.

The third thing that I'll mention is that we do need feedback. We need feedback from the U.S. Department of Education. We've been required to submit our plans on how we define highly qualified teachers and what our HOUSSE plan looks like. We really appreciate the fact that they've asked us for our input and our opinion; now we need to hear from them. Is our plan accurate? Does our plan meet the needs of the law and what the law states that it should be? Are we on the right track? I certainly would rather find that out before we have a compliance-monitoring visit, so I hope that would be forthcoming in the near future.

Finally, the issue I want to talk about is funding. While there's been a lot of discussion about funding, let me put it in a bit of perspective for you. Our state receives a total of $36 million for teacher quality. Twenty-six million dollars of that we received prior to No Child Left Behind for professional development and for class size reduction. So we have about $10 million new dollars that we're supposed to use for not only class size reduction and professional development, but also to ensure that every teacher is highly qualified and that every paraprofessional meets the qualifications of No Child Left Behind. There are about 18 different things that are outlined in the legislation that we can use that money for. Unfortunately, what we're finding as we go around—and we've done site visits to every district in the state, we've held several regional meetings with the districts in South Carolina—and what we're still finding is that the great majority of that money is being used for class size reduction and professional development. Very little of it is going into ensuring that the students who need the most highly qualified teachers are in fact receiving those. It's a real challenge that we still have as a state to find out ways that we can entice the districts to make those changes.

Funding is particularly insufficient in our small, poor ,and rural school districts. Those are the districts that usually have the limited staff to oversee the implementation of teacher quality efforts. They lack access to experts and they have an inherent lack of capacity to implement a broad and comprehensive strategy like teacher quality. They are especially challenged by the requirements of No Child Left Behind. The lawsuit that we have in our state is primarily focused on the teacher quality aspects. That's one of the most significant parts of the plaintiff school district's case about why we need more equitable funding in South Carolina.

I'll close by saying that I'm pleased, after a career of working with teachers, to help improve student achievement because teacher quality is on the radar screen of a lot of people, on the radar screen for Congress, for educational leaders, for parents, for teachers, for the average citizen. People are beginning to talk about teacher quality like they never have before. I think that the need that we have now, in the 2 years we have left to fully implement the teacher quality components, is we need to learn from the states, especially of the unintended consequences that are occurring as a result of implementation of the law— to get input from teachers, and I'm glad to hear that teachers are having a voice in the issues that we're facing, because otherwise none of us will move ahead. Thank you.

Cheryl Fagnano

As Lisa mentioned, the challenge that was placed before the school districts and the states for teacher quality was to raise standards while lowering barriers to entry into the profession, and I'm very interested in hearing specifically from both Commissioner Horne and Janice Poda. What are your states doing to raise standards for teachers while lowering barriers? What are the programs in place? Ray and Lisa, generally around the country, what do you see as the best things that are happening? What do you see not happening? Commissioner Horne?

Jim Horne

I think everybody recognizes that standards are critical. We must maintain high standards for our teachers and there's no real debate over that. However, when you step in the shoes of policymakers and then look at the challenges in terms of simply meeting the demands, the needs and a lack of supply, it becomes a perplexing problem. If we're just simply doing the math, you would make the argument that, OK, we need to create more paths and that sometimes is code word for *lowering of standards*, sort of a second-class or a different tier of teachers. I think that we've got to work very hard to make sure that doesn't happen. I think clearly, opening some paths to teaching that didn't exist before is going to be necessary.

Now, what I suggest— and this is just one person's opinion and we haven't been successful in moving very far to implement this model, and this works perfectly within the structure, like TAP or other models— is what we refer to as the West Point model. The military academies long ago recognized that they would not train all of the officers, but they would train the best. I think we need to go in the opposite direction of logic. Logic would say, lower the standards just to get all the bodies in here. I would suggest that we do the opposite— that is to raise the standards, particularly in the traditional teacher preparation programs. They would be our version of a military academy. They would produce the best. They would be given different privileges. When you create a professional pay plan or professional structure, or just simply create a profession, they may be given an opportunity to go into the profession at a higher level. Maybe the states could pay to provide them with a master's degree, for example.

Now for others, you would create opportunities for entry into the profession. Much like in the military, there are many officers who get what I'd call "battlefield commendations" and they rise up through the ranks. They just do an incredibly good job and are able to rise up to the highest levels of rank in the military. I think you would create those opportunities, but you would prove it out in the classroom. Of course, there has to be some minimal levels that we would just simply agree that you have to have because simply throwing in warm bodies who are unprepared to teach would be a disaster. But they would start at the lower level of the teaching profession, whereas, those who come out of traditional preparation programs come in as an officer, maybe at that next level, maybe even the third level. I think that would help us keep the standards high and would also open up and eliminate barriers to create the supply.

In Florida we have some big challenges such as teacher recruitment. We need 15,000 to 20,000 new teachers and our teacher prep programs are only producing 4,000 to 5,000. We recruit like crazy and California comes and recruits in Florida. I'll go northeast for the first snowfall, and we advertise, "Come to Florida." But that's not going to get the job done in the next 10 years. We are absolutely fooling ourselves if we just continue to work in this model. I would love to say, let's just raise the standards for everybody and keep them high, and keep no entry other than a traditional teacher prep program. But it will not work.

One thing I'm good at is math. I'm a CPA, I understand the numbers and I understand the bottom line—and that is not going to work. We have to create, and there's logic. You heard Lisa talk about situations with the engineer. There are many who want another career and they want to go in and teach. We need to make sure that we provide that opportunity for the right ones. I think that we can be adult enough that we can create a system that will keep out those who are not qualified, who don't need to be in the classroom.

In Florida, being the state chief, there are many different roles to play. We do programs to allow services for our teachers, but there's a regulatory part: I'm an edu-cop, too. Part of the time I have to go out and investigate 2,500 public school teachers every year, for a variety of things. For us to just simply pretend that if you come through a traditional prep program, that everything's going to be great, and that you're not going to allow a few bad apples into the profession—let's not kid ourselves. We get a few. You know, that's human nature. In a big system, you're going to get some of that; likewise, if you open up an unorthodox approach, you're probably going to get a little bit too. But I think that this model will work.

Janice Poda

First of all, I don't apologize for any of the standards we have for certification for teaching in South Carolina because I believe that not everybody can be a teacher, and that you have to have high standards to ensure you have the people you want in the classroom. We have tried to look at ways that we can eliminate barriers and we've done it through several ways. We have an alternative certification program that has been in place since 1984. It is now the largest producer of teachers in the state of South Carolina, producing about 400 teachers a year. Our next largest is Clemson University, which produces about 350.

The other thing we've done is tried to look at some of the bureaucratic things that cause problems for teachers. We have an online job application that every district in the state accepts. So you fill out one application and it can be disseminated to whichever districts you wanted to go to. Soon, that will also be the very same application you fill out for certification, so it'll be one-stop shopping for teachers. They can fill out one application, and the data will be used for both certification and for job searches.

We believe that's a way to eliminate some of the barriers that teachers experience. So I think that there are ways to streamline the process of becoming a teacher without lowering standards. I think we have to have standards to ensure that the people who are entering the classroom are capable of making the decisions and doing the work when children are involved.

Ray Simon

A number of school districts individually and states collectively are doing some good, very creative things. Denver: teachers' union there supported a pay system that links teacher pay to student outcomes. Chattanooga, Tennessee: working with value-added. North Carolina and New Mexico: have been putting many people through the alternative certification program, double the amount of teachers that they're producing. South Dakota, North Dakota, Arizona: are working closely with higher education institutions to increase content requirements for new teachers. Connecticut and Oregon: Those are just some that come to mind.

Lisa Graham Keegan

I think one of the best things that has happened to us, quite frankly, has been the presence of No Child Left Behind, because it has defined for us a natural aspiration. Also, in my vernacular, as the states have moved forward, the presence of No Child Left Behind is kind of a very gentle stakes up behind the car. You moved down the road and you don't go back now. Now we've said nobody gets to be invisible. Now we've said teaching has to be based on a demonstrated ability of standards that match student standards. It's a new ball game, and I think that is absolutely fabulous pressure.

One of the things that frustrates me, particularly in teacher certification as we move forward, is that in education we tend to be so ready to believe that if our own institutions created something, it was a great idea. If somebody else who doesn't look like our institution creates it, it's a bad idea. In education we don't always ask what the idea is first. We ask who thought of it. If the local college of education has a 3-week summer prep program for alternative certification, beautiful; if somebody who used to be a dean of a college of education starts a certification program with extremely high standards, but does not route you through a college of education, we are immediately suspect. I think we have to get over ourselves in that. I think this prevents us from seeing content rather than tradition and while there's a lot to be said for great traditions in our profession, I think we to have move on—because tradition will not get us where we need to go.

Audience Question

I am a professor at the University of Pennsylvania and I wanted to ask you a question about the discussion of barriers to the profession. I agree there is no question that the entry requirements for teaching have two problems. One, they keep out people who are good and should be teachers; and two, they do not keep out certain people who are bad and should not be teaching. In other words, you have some people who have trouble getting into the classroom because they have to go through all these requirements, and then you have other people who go through with straight As and really shouldn't be there in the first place. Of course, those two problems are true for all occupations and professions. We have people who would make great professors, but don't have a PhD; while on the other hand, we have people who got straight As at Harvard who really shouldn't be professors. What is puzzling to me about this whole discussion of barriers is what the yardstick is here.

Amongst those of us who study occupations and professions in general, the barriers to teaching are relatively low. This is one of the easiest occupations in the country to get into, far easier than the traditional professions. The requirements to get into teaching are much lower, the research shows us, than many other nations. So yes, sometimes these requirements are silly or irrelevant, but a deregulation argument always puzzles me because why pick on teaching? Would you also deregulate academia, accounting, or engineering? Commissioner Horne's instance of the person in the military who faced barriers to becoming a teacher, of course if they had wanted to do a quick mid-career switch to some profession, it would have been far more work to become an engineer, an accountant, a professor, a lawyer, or a doctor than to become a teacher. So my question is … I'm just puzzled by all this complaining about all these undue barriers to get into teaching when it's actually a relatively easy one to get into.

Lisa Graham Keegan

I'm not making the deregulation argument. I made the argument against barriers that don't add value. I don't think there's necessarily a value added to a person who's been teaching all his life, to go through a number of courses at a college of education to be told how to teach. I don't think that's a value-adding barrier. I absolutely agree with you; it's very easy in lots of ways, but I think that the access ought to be made easier for those folks who already have high quality. I think what we have is a *quality* problem. We have barriers to high-quality teaching.

Cheryl Fagnano

But would you raise the cut scores, for instance, on the certification exams or on the practice exams? When you look at them, very few states set cut scores that are higher than the national average.

Lisa Graham Keegan

We have to raise the test scores. You have to question some of the content. The tests that we use for most beginning teachers, in my opinion, do not reflect the high standards we demand of students. One of the best things No Child Left Behind does is enable us to take a little peek to see if those things match because that would be good if we are having teachers learn the same things we're expecting students to know. The praxis doesn't necessarily align well to the demanding content right now. Now, I think that's coming along and I think they'll come out with new examinations that are great and that will respond to that reality. But I would raise those requirements.

Audience Question

I am an elementary reading specialist in Harford County. This is my second Milken National Education Conference and I'm enjoying it very much. One of the things I think is missing here is that we're talking an awful lot about preservice preparation, testing, and not teacher quality in terms of pedagogy. I have to tell you that I am an alternative certification person. I started with a bachelor's degree from Dickinson College and Eugene Hickok was my advisor, and I spent 1 year at Towson University. However, when I got into the classroom I had no idea what I was doing. I had great content knowledge, passed every test. What are we going to do about making sure that the folks who are in there not only have content knowledge, which I agree is important ... but what about the pedagogy?

Janice Poda

I think that the pendulum has swung too far to the emphasis just on content knowledge at the risk of forgetting about the importance of pedagogy. I think that you have to have both. You must have content knowledge and pedagogy, and I wouldn't argue to diminish either one of them. To me the real problems in the schools of today are not content knowledge; they're the lack of teachers' ability to teach, to actually impart knowledge and to get the kids to be thinking on high levels. That's especially true with students in hard-to-staff schools where they are already behind; and as they go up through school, their achievement gets further and further behind. To me that's really where the challenge is. Finding ways to understand students, to meet their needs and finding strategies that help them learn are essential.

Audience Question

My name is Henry Johnson and I am state superintendent of education in Mississippi. I think the issue of content versus pedagogy is a false dichotomy. I think we need both. We need both very strongly, and I think that the traditional approach that we use tends not to get us there when we question first-year teachers, particularly, and ask, "What are your issues?" Most of them tell us, "I really wasn't prepared to do this well this first year." I'd like to see teaching look more like the medical model, where there is an extensive period of content development accompanied by an extensive period of on-the-job training, an internship and a residency to prepare for the "real thing." That would ensure that teachers have all the experience to go out and make a difference in learning outcomes for kids. But we don't seem to be willing to make that commitment as a nation.

Ray Simon

One thing Arkansas did a few years ago was to initiate a mentoring program for new teachers. Every new teacher was assigned a mentor who was an experienced teacher. The mentor was paid, the school district received a stipend to support the mentor, and the new teacher was given a temporary, initial license that was only good for up to 3 years—to make sure that the teacher did have an understanding of how to teach, and to have somebody there at his or her right arm all the time for issues that they weren't taught in school. We found that to be very beneficial, not only for the new teacher, because we kept a lot more teachers in the profession by having that supporting mentor there the first 3 years. We also heard from a mentor, "This has energized me. I was about ready to quit. I was about burned out. But when you gave me the chance in the state of Arkansas to be a mentor, it changed my career plans. I'm going to stay around awhile." They fed off each other. So that was a win-win. So I think you see many other states also adopting the mentor programs. Very good concept.

Jim Horne

I think we might see a new reality TV show about beginning teachers on an island. I agree with State Superintendent Johnson a 1,000% that we need an apprenticeship, and I think the TAP model and some of these other pay plans incorporate that important aspect, because that's a key piece. Where I come from in the business world, you will always have those pieces. You want to make sure there's a mentor, that there's an apprenticeship, because that is an important point and no pedagogical training prepares you for the pedagogy. There's nothing like the real-world experience when you step into that classroom for the first time because it's a very frightening, intimidating experience.

If I could change anything, I would change the teacher prep programs. I would take the traditional programs up a notch where, when you come out of the traditional prep programs, there's a higher rank for you. The problem with that is, it's always this sort of catch 22. You know the cart before the horse. We have to make this profession more attractive before anybody will go through a teacher prep program that has higher standards. If you're going to take up the teacher certification exam, you also have to make sure that there's an excellent opportunity for those who will do that. We're sometimes caught chasing our tail; sometimes we do catch up to the parked car, but we need to make sure that we don't zero in on one thing, one reform. It's a system of reforms to me, and if we don't change the profession and the pay plans, how can you have different career opportunities? I'm not sure the other pieces will have the impact that we want them to.

Cheryl Fagnano

I want to thank all of you for your questions and I particularly want to thank our very able panelists this afternoon. In summary, it seems to me from what I heard, that if we really want to reach the promise of highly qualified teachers in every classroom, there's a couple of things that we need to do as a society, as a country, as a government, as a school district. We need to make sure that there are opportunities for talented folks to enter the profession with high but not undue standards; and once there, we need to ensure that the best can advance professionally and that everyone has a chance for quality professional growth and development so that we can hold all of our educators responsible for their performance and their students' outcomes. Frankly, I would be very remiss in my responsibilities as the associate director of TAP not to urge you all to visit our Website at www.mff.org/tap, because it explains what our program really prescribes. Please take a look, and thank you for coming today.

NOTE

1. In fall 2004, the Foundation revised the description of TAP. The program was not changed, but rather the description was refined to better describe what is happening in practice. TAP is now based on four elements: multiple career paths, ongoing applied professional growth, instructionally focused accountability, and performance-based compensation. For more in-depth information on the TAP elements, please log on to www.mff.org/TAP.

PART IV

WHAT IT TAKES TO MAKE A
PERFORMANCE PAY PLAN WORK

CHAPTER 5

WHAT IT TAKES TO MAKE A PERFORMANCE PAY PLAN WORK

**Lewis C. Solmon, Frederick M. Hess,
Brad Jupp, Alan Krueger, and John Schacter**

Lewis Solmon

One of the good things about my job is that twice a year, at the Milken National Education Conference and at the Teacher Advancement Program Conference, I get the opportunity to invite some very smart people to sit down with me and just talk about issues that my colleagues and I at the Foundation are interested in. This morning we're going to do that with performance pay as the topic.

At the Foundation we've been interested in performance pay for quite awhile. Indeed, people have been talking about performance pay for a long time. Nearly 30 of the 50 states have passed legislation requiring some type of alternative compensation for their teachers. Most notably, Arizona, Florida, Kentucky, and Minnesota. Those are some of the places where performance pay has started and ended; more often than not, that is the pattern (Chart 5.1). There are a few places where performance pay plans have experienced continued success. A couple in Colorado and one

Improving Student Achievement: Reforms that Work, 109–156
Copyright © 2005 by Information Age Publishing
All rights of reproduction in any form reserved.

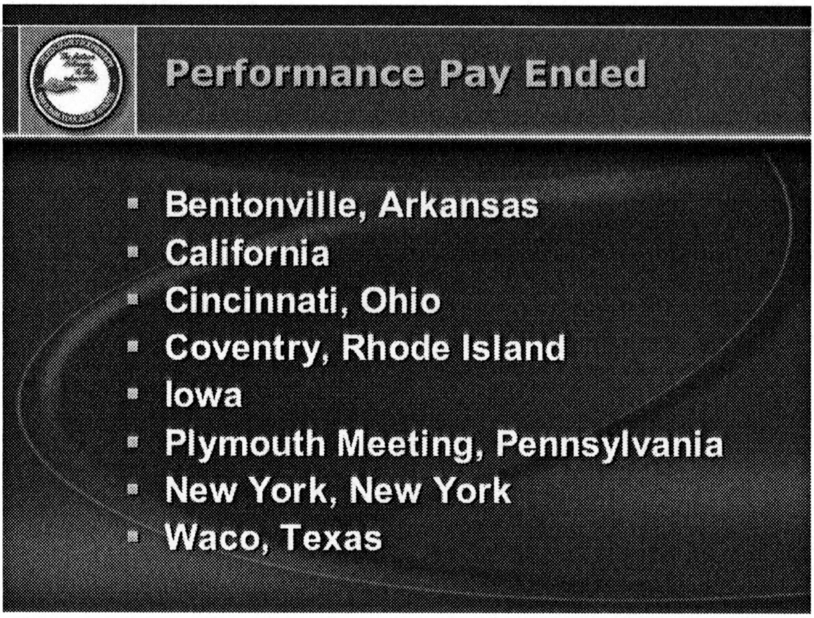

Performance Pay Ended

- Bentonville, Arkansas
- California
- Cincinnati, Ohio
- Coventry, Rhode Island
- Iowa
- Plymouth Meeting, Pennsylvania
- New York, New York
- Waco, Texas

Chart 5.1

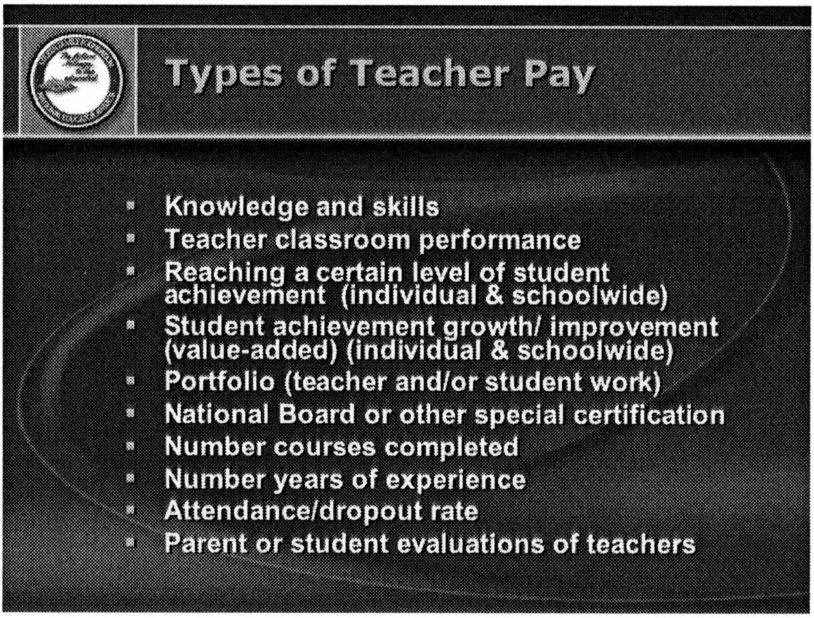

Types of Teacher Pay

- Knowledge and skills
- Teacher classroom performance
- Reaching a certain level of student achievement (individual & schoolwide)
- Student achievement growth/ improvement (value-added) (individual & schoolwide)
- Portfolio (teacher and/or student work)
- National Board or other special certification
- Number courses completed
- Number years of experience
- Attendance/dropout rate
- Parent or student evaluations of teachers

Chart 5.2

in Chattanooga, Tennessee, which has a very interesting program going on now.

One of the issues with performance pay is that there are a lot of different meanings of performance. This chart shows a list of them (Chart 5.2). Number of courses completed and number of years of experience are the traditional ways. Some people say that's performance. The longer you've been there, the more you have performed. The more courses you have completed, the more you performed. So we've actually even seen the situations where, when money is available for performance pay, some districts or states say, "Well, we're already doing performance pay." I don't believe that's what we really mean. There is knowledge- and skills-based pay and pay based on student achievement. Some even rely on evaluations by parents or students. So there are all these different kinds of performance pay plans.

I favor performance pay. I think it's a good idea, but maybe for a slightly different reason than the traditional one. Some say it provides incentives for teachers to make kids learn. What we have learned as we have traveled around the country and talked to many teachers is that all teachers want kids to learn. I don't think that you need performance pay to provide the incentives for teachers to want to make kids learn. It may play a role but I don't think that's the primary motivator. The problem is that often, due to their preparation, the lack of mentoring and things like that, teachers don't know how to make kids learn, particularly different types of kids. What teachers need and what we want to encourage them to do is have a lifelong learning mode and continue learning, continue acquiring the skills that are needed to help them make kids learn. That happens around the country in a variety of ways, but, it's a lot of work. What we've seen is that, oftentimes, teachers undertake major professional development efforts, or major self-improvement programs, but after some period of time, the enthusiasm wanes and the activity peters out.

What I've observed is that performance pay, among other things, is like a pot of gold at the end of the rainbow. It keeps teachers motivated to learn. That bonus when they succeed makes all the extra work worthwhile. Also, performance pay is professional. It rewards people for productivity. It's respectful and it's fair. We talk about fairness, and when I've talked to a number of people including some teacher association people, they've said, "We will accept performance pay as long as it's fair." I agree that it should be fair. But equal is not necessarily fair. If two teachers with different abilities, different energy, different amounts of work, putting in different amounts of time, different preparation and different student outcomes get paid the same, I don't think that's particularly fair. So, pay for performance seems, at least to me, a little fairer.

Over the years we have followed some of those pay experiments that we listed above. We looked at research and at newspaper reports, and even a few interviews with people on the scene. We compiled a list of actual and potential problems with performance pay plans. Some occurred. Some are just fears or potential problems. I believe that all of them can be addressed. Let us consider a list of some of the alleged problems. Here are some general teacher issues (Charts 5.3 and 5.4). If you have performance pay and you judge teachers based on student scores, you're just going to teach to the test. Well, that's a bad thing, except if you want them to know what's on the test.

The next one that I'd like to refer to is that teachers enter the profession because they love kids, not for the money. We don't want mercenaries in the classroom. We want people who love kids and want to make them learn. We want doctors who want to make people well or keep them from getting sick. We want lawyers who want to do justice. But that doesn't preclude them from being rewarded well, particularly if they're effective. Here are some of the union issues (Chart 5.5). No union will support a performance pay plan if everybody gets less than the current salary—that's logical. Why would anybody do that? That's one of the reasons why, in our own program (TAP), we've talked about bonuses adding on to the salary scale, rather than replacing the salary schedule. The number of programs that have resulted in teachers earning less have failed.

There are a lot of collegiality issues discussed in this context (Chart 5.6). One that I would highlight here is that if pay is based on performance, everybody's going to want to teach the kids most likely to learn. I think that our discussion is going to turn at least to some degree, to value-added. Obviously, if you look at improvement, maybe everybody's going to want to teach the lowest achieving kids because they've got more room to improve.

One of the problems is that plans may be implemented with too little teacher buy-in. I think that's very important. I think that we've had too much reform in education that is top-down, rather than bottom-up. The successful plans, which you'll hear about from some of our panelists, seem to me to be ones that will only proceed if the teachers are eager to have that happen.

The next set of issues are evaluation issues, and the issue underlying much of the problems people have with performance pay is that people have said, we don't really know what quality teaching is (Chart 5.7). Like pornography, we know it when we see it but we can't really define it. I'm not saying teaching is pornography but you get what I'm saying. Research is now starting to identify a series of behaviors, types of knowledge that are necessary and correlated with student achievement. I think the argument that we don't really know what quality teaching is, is starting to go away.

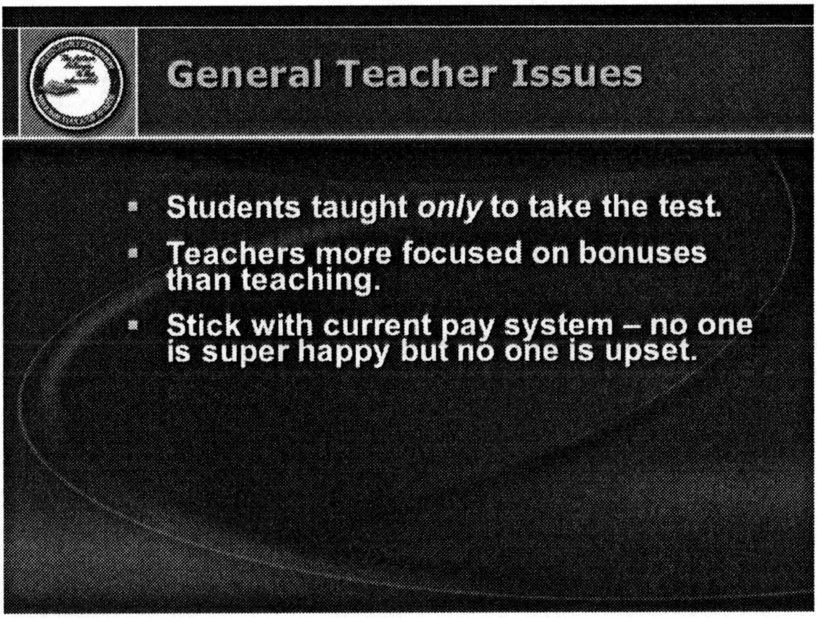

General Teacher Issues

- Students taught *only* to take the test.
- Teachers more focused on bonuses than teaching.
- Stick with current pay system – no one is super happy but no one is upset.

Chart 5.3

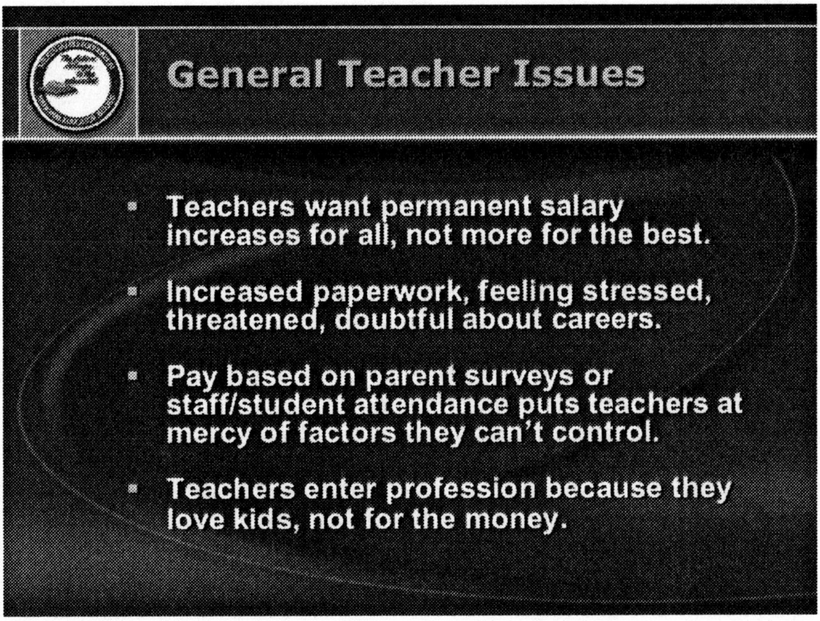

General Teacher Issues

- Teachers want permanent salary increases for all, not more for the best.
- Increased paperwork, feeling stressed, threatened, doubtful about careers.
- Pay based on parent surveys or staff/student attendance puts teachers at mercy of factors they can't control.
- Teachers enter profession because they love kids, not for the money.

Chart 5.4

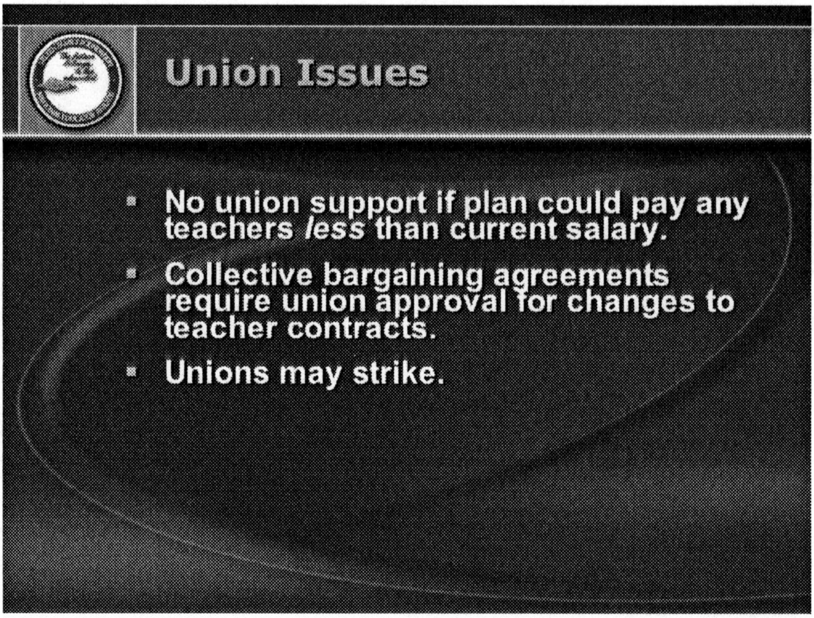

Union Issues

- No union support if plan could pay any teachers *less* than current salary.
- Collective bargaining agreements require union approval for changes to teacher contracts.
- Unions may strike.

Chart 5.5

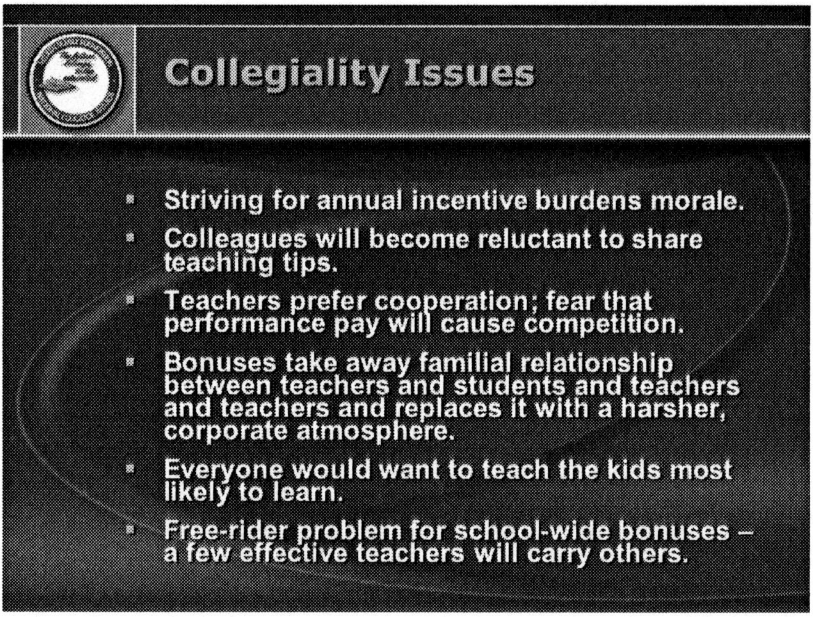

Collegiality Issues

- Striving for annual incentive burdens morale.
- Colleagues will become reluctant to share teaching tips.
- Teachers prefer cooperation; fear that performance pay will cause competition.
- Bonuses take away familial relationship between teachers and students and teachers and teachers and replaces it with a harsher, corporate atmosphere.
- Everyone would want to teach the kids most likely to learn.
- Free-rider problem for school-wide bonuses – a few effective teachers will carry others.

Chart 5.6

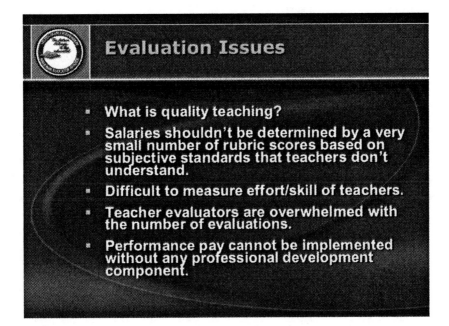

Evaluation Issues

- What is quality teaching?
- Salaries shouldn't be determined by a very small number of rubric scores based on subjective standards that teachers don't understand.
- Difficult to measure effort/skill of teachers.
- Teacher evaluators are overwhelmed with the number of evaluations.
- Performance pay cannot be implemented without any professional development component.

Chart 5.7

If we have performance standards and if teachers are not prepared for those new performance standards, there are going to be problems. That's why when you have performance pay, you need professional development to support it (Charts 5.8 and 5.9). And again, another evaluation issue is that test scores don't measure all of what kids learn. Well, that's true. But they do predict, pretty well, I believe. Some of our panelists may disagree, but it seems that test scores do predict pretty well what life chances are and how well people are going to do in life. They are not the only factor, but test scores are important.

One of the things that we've seen, and that could be a problem, is that some districts have said, yes, we want performance pay because we recognize that in today's environment, it's very hard to get significant across-the-board pay increases (Chart 5.10). We've seen in a number of places, where they've said, yes, we want performance pay but then they either define high performance as things that everybody does, like get extra courses, or they set the standards so low that everybody gets the maximum reward or they give every teacher the same evaluation so that everybody gets the same increase. If our goal is performance pay, we have to be careful not to use it as a back door into across-the-board salary increases.

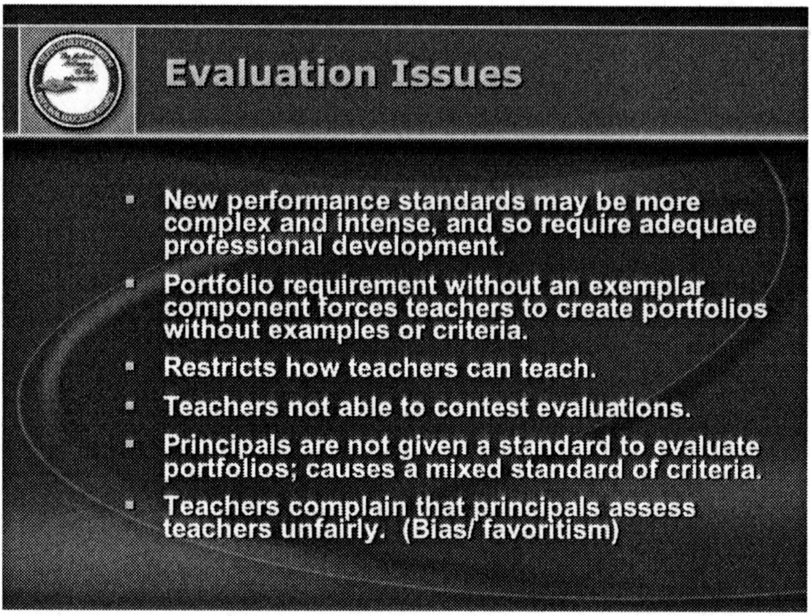

Evaluation Issues

- New performance standards may be more complex and intense, and so require adequate professional development.
- Portfolio requirement without an exemplar component forces teachers to create portfolios without examples or criteria.
- Restricts how teachers can teach.
- Teachers not able to contest evaluations.
- Principals are not given a standard to evaluate portfolios; causes a mixed standard of criteria.
- Teachers complain that principals assess teachers unfairly. (Bias/ favoritism)

Chart 5.8

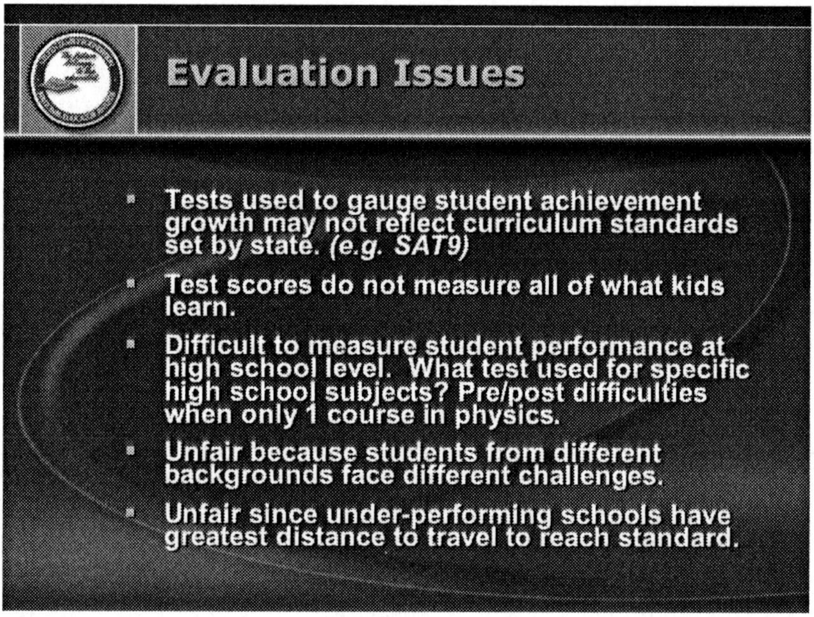

Evaluation Issues

- Tests used to gauge student achievement growth may not reflect curriculum standards set by state. *(e.g. SAT9)*
- Test scores do not measure all of what kids learn.
- Difficult to measure student performance at high school level. What test used for specific high school subjects? Pre/post difficulties when only 1 course in physics.
- Unfair because students from different backgrounds face different challenges.
- Unfair since under-performing schools have greatest distance to travel to reach standard.

Chart 5.9

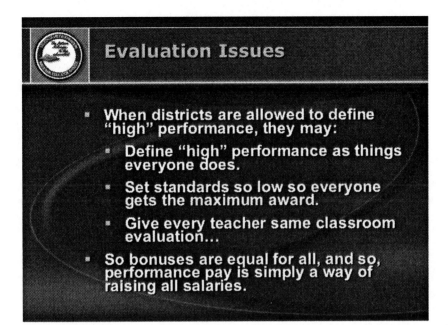

Chart 5.10

Then there are a set of outcome issues which are listed in here (Chart 5.11).

Let's turn to budget issues, where one of the big complaints is that we don't know, generally, how much plans will cost before the fact (Chart 5.12). Money is not sustainable, and that is a problem that we see. People get all enthusiastic about a performance pay plan and it's a good year, financially. There's money available and then, in the next year performance pay doesn't occur because money is not available. We've just got to be careful. Again, if this was a priority and people are willing to forego other kinds of spending, money can be found—and we've seen that a whole bunch of different ways, as money has been found for the Teacher Advancement Program and performance pay, in particular.

There is another set of issues that I call administrative issues (Chart 5.13). One of the saddest things is that we get an enthusiastic principal, district superintendent, state superintendent, but unfortunately sometimes the turnover is so great that the enthusiasm wanes again. That gets back to the fact that, if teachers are buying in, they're not going to let it die.

Let's go on to the parent issues (Chart 5.14). The issues here are that if parents know which teacher performs best, all parents will want their kids

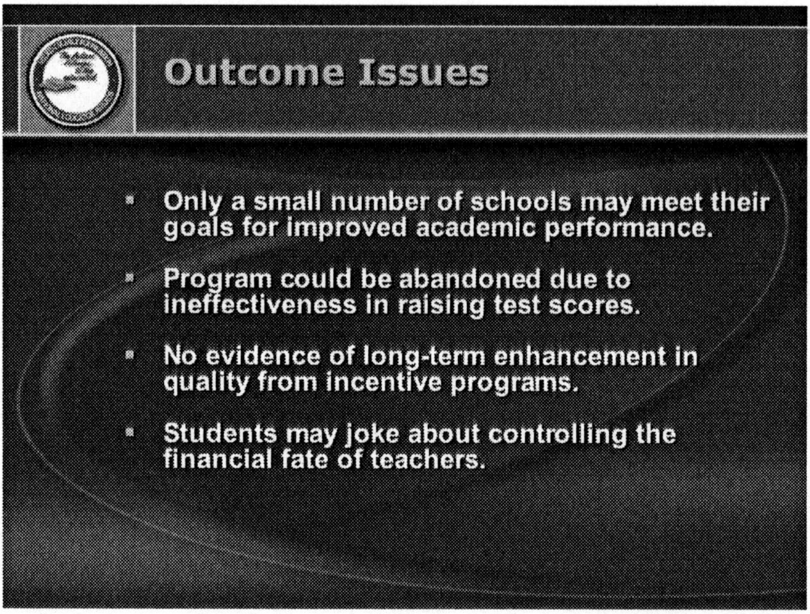

Outcome Issues

- Only a small number of schools may meet their goals for improved academic performance.
- Program could be abandoned due to ineffectiveness in raising test scores.
- No evidence of long-term enhancement in quality from incentive programs.
- Students may joke about controlling the financial fate of teachers.

Chart 5.11

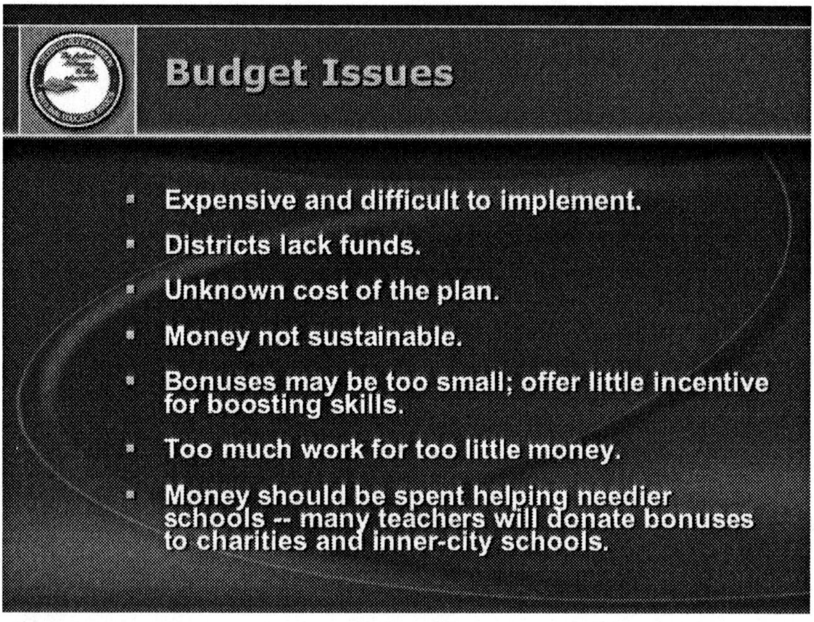

Budget Issues

- Expensive and difficult to implement.
- Districts lack funds.
- Unknown cost of the plan.
- Money not sustainable.
- Bonuses may be too small; offer little incentive for boosting skills.
- Too much work for too little money.
- Money should be spent helping needier schools -- many teachers will donate bonuses to charities and inner-city schools.

Chart 5.12

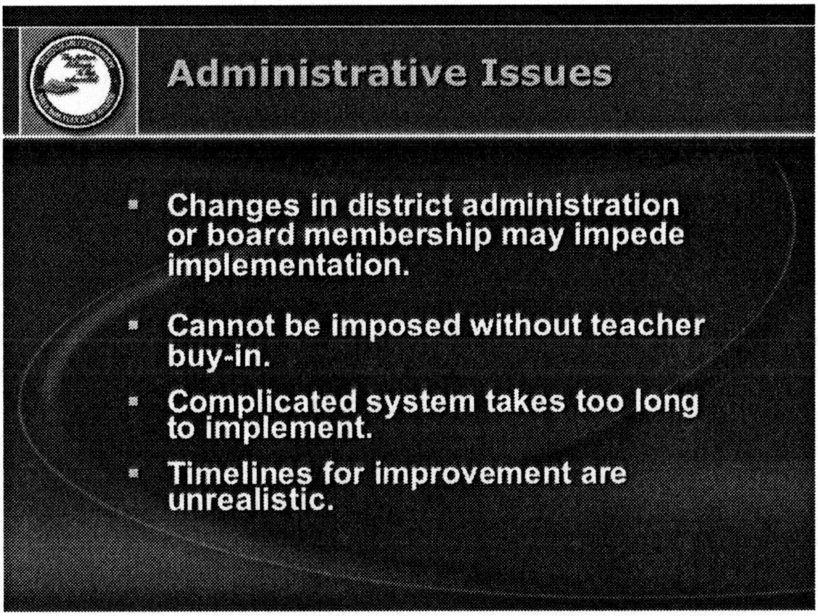

Administrative Issues

- Changes in district administration or board membership may impede implementation.
- Cannot be imposed without teacher buy-in.
- Complicated system takes too long to implement.
- Timelines for improvement are unrealistic.

Chart 5.13

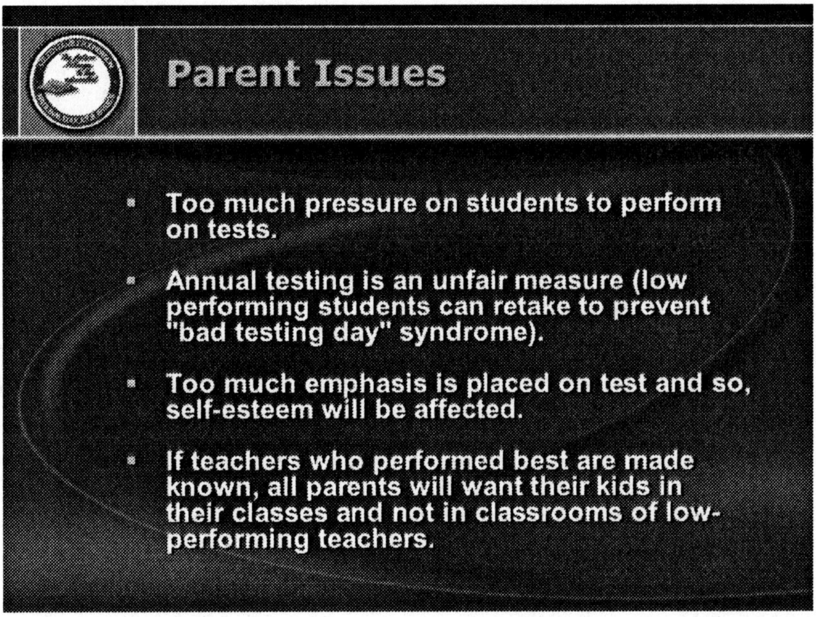

Parent Issues

- Too much pressure on students to perform on tests.
- Annual testing is an unfair measure (low performing students can retake to prevent "bad testing day" syndrome).
- Too much emphasis is placed on test and so, self-esteem will be affected.
- If teachers who performed best are made known, all parents will want their kids in their classes and not in classrooms of low-performing teachers.

Chart 5.14

in those classes and not in the classes of low-performing teachers. Why should some be stuck with low-performing teachers? Hopefully, some of the reforms that are going on now, including No Child Left Behind, will make sure that everyone has access to a quality teacher.

Those are some of the problems; others are listed here for completeness (Charts 4.15-4.16). The point that I want to make is that most of them can indeed be answered and be dealt with. I'd like to hear from a group of experts who have thought about the problem or have been right in the middle of the problem. Let me give a couple of sentences on each of our very prestigious and distinguished panelists. Frederick Hess is director of Education Policy Studies at the American Enterprise Institute and executive editor of *Education Next*, which is a really excellent education journal. He's written a number of books and I consider him to be one of the leading thinkers in education today.

Next is Alan Krueger, who is the Bendheim Professor of Economics and Public Affairs at Princeton University. Actually, his title is much longer than that and when we put together the program, I phoned him up and I said, "Alan, do we really have to say the four line title?" He was good enough to shorten it. He has double doors on his office because the plaque with his name on it is so long. Alan is the founding director of Princeton University's Survey Research Center and director of its Industrial Relations Section. He had a number of jobs in the Clinton Administration, has a column in the *New York Times* and really is regarded as one of the brightest economists today.

Next, we have Brad Jupp, who's a teacher in the Denver Public Schools, assigned to the Design Team of the Denver Public Schools, Denver Classroom Teachers Association pay-for-performance plan. Brad is one of the leaders in getting performance pay into Denver. Some of you may have been following that; it's been really a gargantuan task and just a beautiful example of success when it's done correctly. We are really interested in getting Brad's insights. Finally, John Schacter is president of SPP Enterprise Educational Consulting. He basically designed all the details of the performance plan in the Teacher Advancement Program. John worked for us for a number of years and moved to Northern California last year. We are glad to have him back.

Rick Hess

Good morning. It's a pleasure to be with all of you. I understand you all had a late evening last night, so I will try to be brief. Given that Alan, Brad, and John are going to talk a little bit about some of the specifics,

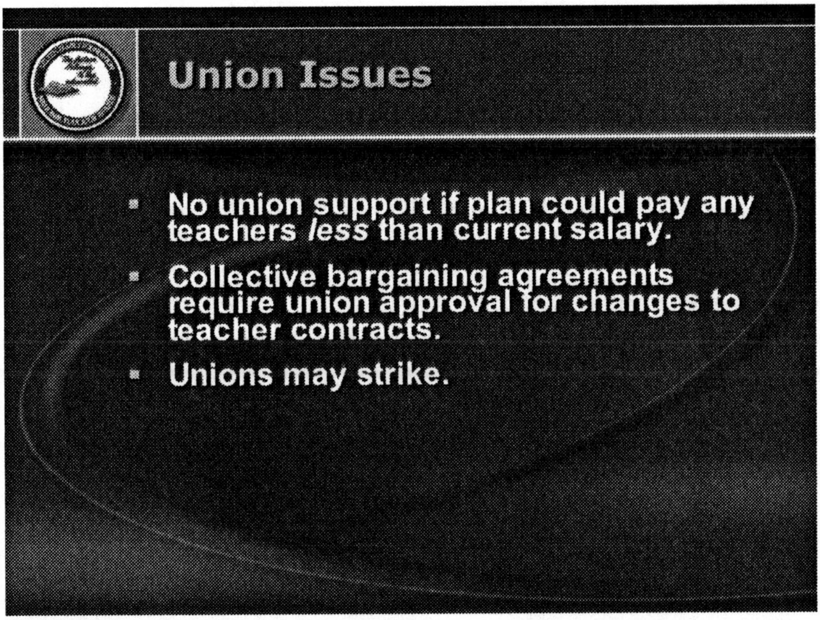

Union Issues

- No union support if plan could pay any teachers *less* than current salary.
- Collective bargaining agreements require union approval for changes to teacher contracts.
- Unions may strike.

Chart 5.15

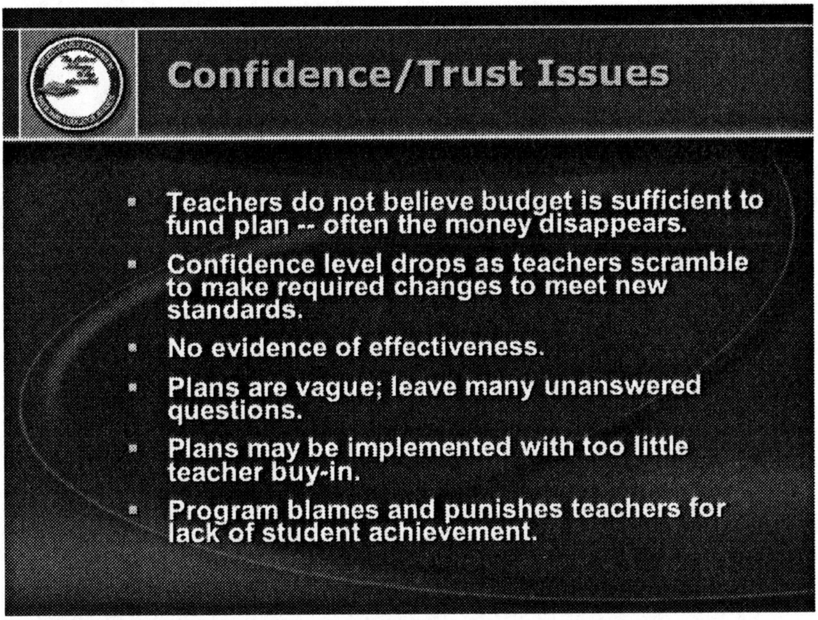

Confidence/Trust Issues

- Teachers do not believe budget is sufficient to fund plan -- often the money disappears.
- Confidence level drops as teachers scramble to make required changes to meet new standards.
- No evidence of effectiveness.
- Plans are vague; leave many unanswered questions.
- Plans may be implemented with too little teacher buy-in.
- Program blames and punishes teachers for lack of student achievement.

Chart 5.16

what I think I'll do is talk a bit about the context in which we talk about performance pay.

The first thing to keep in mind is that it's not helpful to think about performance pay, or whatever kind of label you want to hang on it, in isolation from broader questions of reforming and rethinking how we deliver education. One of the things that's always useful to remember is that the American system of schooling was never designed for the challenges that we face today, for the skills and knowledge our students need today, or to take advantage of the opportunities—technological and human—which we have at our disposal.

American education has its roots in the late 1700s, but it was radically expanded, particularly between 1830 and 1850, with the highlight being Massachusetts' reform effort. The whole notion of universal education for democracy was basically an accidental, helter-skelter kind of expansion, particularly driven in the early years of the twentieth century when there was a national, nearly religious faith in the power of the scientific method. The notion of scientific management was: To get the best out of people, you must lay out processes where you tell everybody what they are to do, down to the minutia of their jobs, and make sure they do it. Given in those days that all the difficult work was going to take place at higher levels, in terms of monitoring and measuring and making sure people did what they were told, it didn't make sense to differentiate in the way you paid people who were only filling the cogs.

In much of American society, nonprofits, for-profits, and government have been backing away from this notion of scientific management, which once made sense, but doesn't make sense given the resources, challenges, and opportunities in the world as it's played out in the last 50 years. In education, for a variety of reasons, we've never really unlearned those early experiences. We've never been able to radically reshape those institutional arrangements. What we need to think about is that performance pay is part of a larger effort, to rethink how we deliver schooling in a way that is accepting of excellence, insists on excellence, is intolerant of failure, and creates real room and opportunities for professionalism.

When we think about performance pay, we can't think about it in isolation from how we construct the work of educators, particularly how we handle benefits. Not just annual compensation but benefits, retirement plans, career opportunities, hiring and evaluation, and certainly the selection and incentives for managers. In particular, if we think about the way that we compensate educators today, the system was not built, but rather it emerged. It emerged from a system that largely took shape in a realm of a primogeniture. When first sons tended to inherit the family estate, we knew that most schoolteachers were either going to be second or third or fourth sons, or women in the premarriage years; this was the nineteenth century tradition. Teaching was an itinerant profession. And we began to reform teaching as we moved toward a notion of universal education.

We came up with a model that put men in charge as superintendents of systems or as principals. We hired largely men who typically had at least finished high school to become high school teachers. We hired women at the K-8 levels. We had an endless and phenomenal talent pool of women who would teach because there were really no other professional alternatives for educated women. There was nursing, but teaching was the more prestigious and rewarding of the two professions. We wound up with inequities between pay at the high school and the K-8 levels. You wound up with inequities based on race because the other talent pool was African American men and women, who had few other professional alternatives. So, they could teach in Black schools, and they were paid much less than their counterparts in the White schools.

When the unions and the teacher associations became active in the 1950s and when the UFT really became the modern AFT in the 1960s, the fights were about equity. The fights were about making sure we were paying men and women fairly. They were about getting the same pay for the same kind of work. They were about not discriminating by race, and they were about paying fairly, the same pay for the same work. And this was appropriate. It was necessary. It was the right thing to do at the time.

In the 1950s and 1960s, education was a lifelong profession. Women did it because this is what you did if you were a college educated, bright woman. We had a surplus of talent. People were going to do this stuff for 25 or 30 years because America was a much less transient society. We didn't have to worry about competing for talent against other white-collar professions because teaching was what you were going to do. We didn't have any data, no matter how sloppy, on student performance. We didn't have any agreement on exactly what schools were supposed to do. They were supposed to do a lot, but we couldn't really know how effectively they did any of it.

In a world like that, it made sense to pay all teachers the same because we didn't know who was doing well. We didn't have to worry about keeping the best people. What we had was an informal, eclectic culture built on the notion that we would always have enough talented people coming into the schools. In fact, we knew that these women were probably going to be in the communities after their husbands had passed away. Therefore, one of the keys was to make sure that the benefits and retirement plans were generous. Because we knew these women would stay in one place, we wanted them to stay in our schools for 25 years. After their husbands passed, we wanted to make sure they weren't an embarrassment to the local school district. So local superintendents and state boards pushed for increasingly generous retirement plans out of a sense of paternal obligation.

All of this has changed. We can no longer count on the fact that college-educated, talented women, and African Americans are going to choose teaching. We actually have data on how well educators are doing their jobs. True, it's often imperfect data, but nonetheless we actually have better data on how well educators of the group are faring than we have on attorneys or engineers or journalists or professors. In all of these fields, we feel okay about making distinctions based on the quality of work. Because we recognize, as we've said, that to not recognize differences in performance is to treat people unequally. Equal pay isn't fair if you're doing unequal work, if you're making unequal contributions.

There was nothing venal or wrong or inappropriate about the way that we traditionally compensated educators. It made sense. But, in a different era, with new challenges, with new opportunities, a different approach is now more appropriate to the task at hand. I'm going to briefly suggest three kinds of principles for thinking about how we compensate teachers.

One is the classroom contribution of educators. What are they doing with their kids? The problem with linking compensation to student-level of performance is that level of performance is a sum of three things: what you have done in your classroom, what everyone who's ever taught the kid has done in their classroom, and it's everything that happens outside of the school environment. That's not a real fair way to judge people. We don't tell doctors that we don't care if they work in Beverly Hills or Watts, we're going to judge them on the birth weight of babies. We ask doctors to do a reasonable job of improving the health of their patients. That's what we need to ask teachers to do.

Now, value-added measures are highly imperfect. In fact, I think Alan's got a little bit of data he'll share with you on this, and he's absolutely correct. Especially for small groups or for individual years, you want to put no faith in specific measures of value-added. These things tend to bounce. What we should do instead of coming up with algebraic systems of linking rewards to specific numbers—like the California kind of school reward system—is use the measures as a sensible guide. You can think of teachers in quintiles or quartiles or thirds over a few-year period say, "Are you generally doing as well as folks teaching similar students or are you not? Or are you doing better?" That's useful information, but we have to use it appropriately.

Second, we know that teachers do a lot more than just help their kids improve on the basic skills and content. Anybody who forgets that is making a huge mistake. Teachers mentor colleagues. Teachers help improve curriculum. Teachers teach particular skills that aren't assessed on exams, particularly if they're working with kids with special needs or if they're working with kids at an advanced level. There's a way to take this into account. It's called sensible judgment. Give principals the flexibility to make sensible decisions about who is contributing to the school environment, because principals are ultimately accountable for the performance of the school. Now, they shouldn't make this decision unilaterally. At elementary levels, teachers generally work in teams. Folks who work with teachers are in probably the best position to offer assessments. At the 9-12 level, teachers are generally arranged in departments. So, there are a lot of sources of information that principals can tap. There are reasons to distrust the principals on this front, and that's entirely fair. That's why we had to make sure that principals have both the skills and the incentives to make sensible judgments.

A third leg of any sensible plan to reward teachers for their contributions, which is really what pay-for-performance is about, is making sure we recognize teachers who take on more challenging assignments. If a value-added system means it's going to be easier to look good working with low performing kids, then we need to take into account teachers working with students who are higher performing. There are a lot of sensible ways to think about this, but it's a mistake to ignore either the school or classroom context in which teachers are working.

Finally, by way of closing, we make quality judgments about what people do every day. We do it in medicine and law and academia; we do it everywhere. It does not inevitably lead to cheating. It does not inevitably lead to favoritism. These are unusual occurrences. These are general signs of perversely designed systems or they're signs that we don't have competent, trained people making the decisions about quality and management. If that's a problem, and I've suggested for several years that it is, we need to really think about how we provide incentives and how we prepare and select principals. That absolutely needs to be part of this going forward.

Now, obviously, there are flaws. Obviously, there are going to be occasional mistakes. That's true, and anybody who denies that is blowing a lot of smoke at you. The fact is, given the changing economy, given the changing workforce, if we're going to compete for the talented, bright, hard workers, the kind of folks who are in this room, the old approach is going to prove less and less effective at getting and keeping the people we need to move forward. Thank you.

Alan Krueger

Let me begin by congratulating all of the teachers here. My wife is a high school math teacher, so I have a unique view into what teachers do after the 3 o'clock bell rings. I see how much time she puts into preparing homework, grading homework, writing tests, grading tests, preparing lesson plans—which translates to, "Alan, take care of the laundry. Alan, take out the garbage." So I want to congratulate the teachers for their hard work, and also their husbands and wives and partners, for their contribution as well.

Because my time is short, I want to be very clear about my main points. Lew asked me to examine the way we pay teachers. I'm going to offer some criticism about the way we reward teachers, and I'm going to point out some limitations about pay-for-performance. The current system for rewarding teachers does not work very well, and I'll show you some evidence on this. Alternatives can certainly be better and they can also be worse. This is a case where the devil lies in the details. I think greater reliance on performance-based pay makes a great deal of economic sense, if it's done well. This is an area where I'm going to paraphrase Voltaire: We shouldn't let perfect be the enemy of doing better because there is a lot of room for doing better. At the same time, we should try to avoid common pitfalls, many of which are predictable.

Brad asked me why an economist is talking about this subject. There's a long history of economists commenting on school rewards and teacher salaries. This is a quote from Adam Smith in the *Wealth of Nations* in 1776: "In modern times"—mind you, this is 230 years ago—"the diligence of public teachers is more or less corrupted by the circumstances which render them more or less independent of their success and reputation in their particular professions." Adam Smith was very disappointed in the system used to compensate teachers, particularly university professors back in 1776. He argued that it gave very little incentive for teachers to do a good job teaching. Many of the speakers yesterday referred to our education system as an industrial system. I was thinking that, in an industrial system, we usually use piece-rate to reward workers. This is very much a preindustrial system for rewarding teachers, and Adam Smith was writing in the preindustrial days.

Let me return to the current system. Chart 5.17 shows the relationship between teachers' education, whether they have a master's degree or not, and how well their students do. It also shows teacher experience and how well the students do. These graphs are based on the CTBS achievement test. This is from the Tennessee STAR Experiment where the teachers were randomly assigned. It wasn't the case that they were sorting and the teachers with the master's degree were assigned to the more challenging

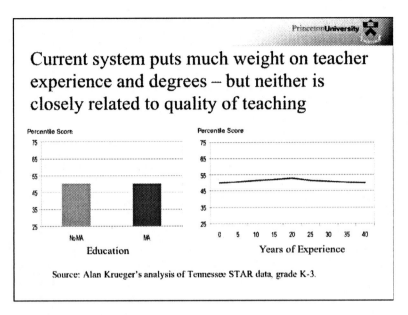

Chart 5.17

students. This is from the Tennessee STAR Experiment where the teachers were randomly assigned. You can see, there's no relationship between the teachers' level of education and how well their class does. There's a very weak relationship between teacher experience (measured by years of service) and how well their students do. It peaks after about 17 or 18 years, but it's a very gradual rise. The students are only doing about three percentile points better at the peak of the curve. That's just barely detectable statistically, yet these are the two main components that we use for setting teacher pay within schools. I would argue that they bear very little relationship with the type of job the teachers are doing. I think we should think of our current compensation system as, basically, rewarding teachers for being there.

That's why I say there's a lot of room for improvement. What would the requirements be for a pay-for-performance system? I think all pay-for-performance schemes must be viewed as fair, or else the teachers will find ways to rebel. The advice I have here is to first involve the teachers. This is often done, so it's not such great wisdom. But I can tell you a story: you may remember there were several problems with P235 tires from Firestone. It turns out that the problems can mainly be traced to very difficult labor relations that they had. Firestone insisted on a 30% wage cut. They wanted to change the piece-rate system in 1995, and that's when the problems began. Then, after the contract was settled, the problems went away. In my study, I could even look specifically at the plants where there was difficulty between management and labor, and other plants where there was smooth functioning. Most of the problems with the tires can be traced to the plants that were having faulty or difficult labor relations. This is a case where the lack of fairness, the lack of transparency, and the workers feeling that they weren't treated appropriately, caused major problems, not only for the workers, but also for the company.

Secondly, for incentives to matter in a positive way, they must be clearly defined and related to the outcomes that one ultimately cares about. A third requirement for pay-for-performance is that the teacher should have some impact over those outcomes that are being rewarded. You don't want to reward teachers based on things that they can't control or influence. If teacher effort is not related to the measures that you're looking at, then I think you have to think hard about whether those are the right measures on which to peg compensation.

Finally, I make a point which Rick also made, which is that the system must guard against manipulation of results. This happens in all fields. Those who are receiving incentives try to figure out ways of getting around the incentives or maximizing their returns under those incentives. This is just human nature.

Take a look at Chart 5.18. These are test scores of two classes in Chicago on the Iowa Skills Test. The top class was suspected of cheating. This is based on a paper by Steve Levitt at the University of Chicago and Brian Jacob at Harvard. In the black box, there's a very suspicious pattern. The numbers are incorrect answers and they refer to the letter that they filled in. The letters are correct answers. In the middle of the exam, there's this pattern: a number of students making the exact same mistake and the same students getting the correct answers, after having made several mistakes and having been weak students in the previous year, and then weak students, again, in the following year.

Levitt and Jacob went back to these classes and administered another test independently, and they found that in classes where they suspected there was cheating, the students actually did much worse when they were retested. They concluded that 4% to 5% of the classes had signs of cheating. They thought that was probably an underestimate. One thing that they pointed out, which is particularly worrisome for incentive schemes, is that the observed frequency of cheating appears to respond strongly to relatively minor changes in the incentives. What they proposed, which was

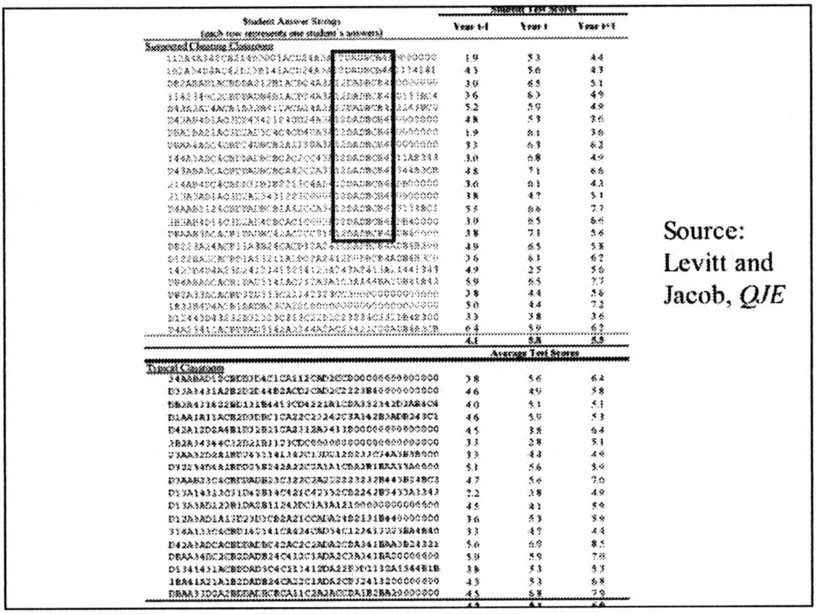

Chart 5.18

Source: Levitt and Jacob, *QJE*

quite sensible, is to have the teachers switch classes when they administer the exams. This is a very low cost way of guarding against cheating. Very little thought and resources go into avoiding manipulation of standardized tests. I suspect 4% to 5% of teachers cheating is on the high end, but nevertheless, that is a warning.

The main metric that's been used—well, not really the main one but certainly the current rage—is to look at "value-added." And I actually do think that value-added is related to real outcomes. If you look over time at workers' earnings and relate that to the gains on their test scores in high school, there actually is a positive relationship. It's not the strongest relationship in the world, but it's there. Even more importantly, the students' test scores and their gains in their scores are related to their ultimate educational attainment. That's probably why it affects their job success. I do think that there is signal in value-added.

Let me now turn to some limitations of using value-added. I don't mean to be the skunk at the garden party and, in fact, I think that value-added should get some weight. On the other hand, I also think it's important to be aware of the limitations. Once we're aware of them, we can try to think of ways of improving on them. The first limitation is one that Rick already mentioned, which is that, when we look at gains in test

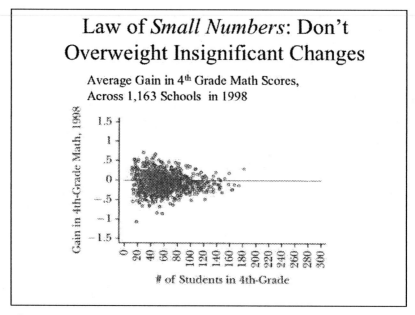

Chart 5.19

scores, they tend to be noisy, especially, if we look at a class, as opposed to a whole school. A study in Tennessee, by Michael Podgursky, found that only 20% of math teachers were statistically different than the average teacher. So, this is the opposite of Lake Wobegon where almost everybody was average, or at least you couldn't reject that they were average. The reason is that there's a great deal of noise when we look at the gains in test scores.

You can see that in Chart 5.19. This looks at changes in test scores across schools of fourth graders in North Carolina in 1998. Some of the schools were small, some were middle-sized, some were larger. The gains and losses are plotted against the number of students in the grade. What you see is kind of a sideways V on this graph. You get a lot more dispersion at the smaller schools. The reason is, you have a smaller sample. When you have a smaller sample, you get more variability. These are very big changes. These are measured in terms of standard deviations on the test score. You see no relationship between the size of a fourth grade cohort and how well the students are doing on the test, how much they're gaining. But you do see a big relationship in terms of the variability in the size of the gain. That suggests that, what we're largely picking up, particularly when we're looking at sizes of 20 or 30 students, is sampling variability.

One way to think about this is in terms of a baseball player. His batting average differs over the course of the season—he may have streaks and droughts—but with enough at-bats, you can get a meaningful batting average. Derek Jeter wouldn't want to be paid based on how he did in his last 30 at-bats. He finally did get a hit but it was kind of a rough spell. You need sufficient precision for a pay system to work—just like the batting crown requires a minimum number of at-bats. So you need large samples of students for value-added to have sufficient signal, and that's something to be concerned about—because often the number of students is small, and as a result, there is a lot of noise in their average performance. Now, because there's noise, it doesn't mean that there's no signal, but it means that there may be less than we think there is.

Another limitation I want to highlight is that the gain in test scores might be due to things that have nothing to do with schooling. I'll show you evidence on this in a moment. I'm sure that the gain is related to what goes on in the classroom, but I'm sure you all know there are many things that happen outside the classroom that also affect how well students do during the course of the year. Rick mentioned limitations of using the level of test scores. You don't want to grade the doctors by the birth weight of the babies they deliver. On the other hand, the behaviors are what led to the birth weights, and those behaviors are also going to affect the change in test scores or birth weights.

I have to say, I think the term *value-added* is a bit of a misnomer. I prefer to say "change or gain in test score" because the unique value added of the teacher is very hard to separate out from all of the other factors that contribute to student performance. You can see this by looking at what happens during the school year and during the summer. Let me show you quickly two slides on this. Chart 5.20 shows the over-the-school-year gain for first graders in Baltimore schools, starting in 1982 and then following the same students through 1986, broken down by socioeconomic status. These students were tested at the very beginning of the school year and then again in May at the end of the school year. You can see on the California Achievement Test (CAT), the children from the low-income families and the high-income families are making about the same gains each school year. Chart 5.21 shows you what happens over the summers. The children from lower socioeconomic status families are falling behind over the summertime. The children from the higher socioeconomic status families are gaining. This is looking at their math scores.

This pattern is not so surprising. A number of teachers have told me that they spend the first couple of months every year reviewing the material that the students learned in the previous year but forgot over the summer. I'm sure many of you have experienced that phenomenon. If you look at Chart 5.22 and look at the math scores over the school

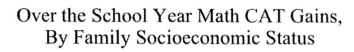

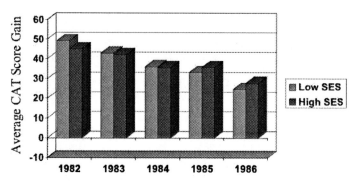

Source: Entwisle, Alexander, and Olson (1997), Table 3.1. Sample consists of 498 Baltimore public school students who entered first grade in 1982.

Chart 5.20

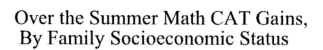

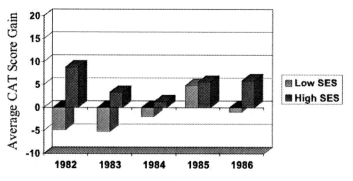

Source: Entwisle, Alexander, and Olson (1997), Table 3.1. Sample consists of 498 Baltimore public school students who entered first grade in 1982.

Chart 5.21

Cumulative CAT Gains By SES

SES	School Year	Summer
	Math	
Low	185.8	-8.0
High	186.3	24.9
	Reading	
Low	193.3	0.8
High	190.9	46.6

Source: Entwisle, Alexander, and Olson (1997), Table 3.1. Sample consists of 498 Baltimore public school students who entered first grade in 1982.

Chart 5.22

year, the students from the high and low income families made about the same gains. But the gap expanded between them over the summer months, having nothing to do with school, unless you think it's the school's responsibility, which, to some extent it may be, to give work for the students to do over the summer. But it's definitely hard to enforce that.

If you look at reading, the reading scores show the same pattern. When I talk about the reading scores, I call this the "Harry Potter divide." I actually examined data from a Gallup poll and found that children from low-income families are much less likely to read Harry Potter over the summer months than are children from high-income families. Clearly, low-socio-economic status households do not emphasize education to the same extent as high-socioeconomic status households. I think we need to be cautious about putting too much weight on a measure which is influenced by what's going on outside of school.

One thing to think about is that we probably penalize teachers who are teaching children from more disadvantaged backgrounds because the children are not getting the enrichment at home. One way around this is to test in the beginning of the school year, and you can reward for what happens during the course of the school year. Although, I think we also have to be somewhat concerned about spending all of our time testing, and having less time for instruction.

Another limitation of value-added is that it puts a great deal of weight and a great deal of reliance on the testing companies, on the way that they scaled these exams. Psychometrics is a relatively new science. As an economist, I prefer to look at real outcomes. The economists pride themselves at looking at tangible measures, like, is someone working and or in poverty? Are they on welfare, are they in prison? Did they vote? How much income do they make? And so on. It's going to take a long time to evaluate the third grade teacher on those kinds of outcomes for her students. So we need to look at intermediate outcomes. I think that's just the nature of life here. But do we trust the measures enough to say that a gain in the test score, from 20 to 25, is just as easy or just as difficult as a gain from going from 80 to 85? Are the scales validated in such a way that we would want to put so much weight on them?

I think that there is some signal, as I said earlier. On the other hand, I think this is where we do need to have more research, and I'll just give a plug: I've been working on a method with colleagues to try to evaluate teachers based on how well their students do compared to other teachers with students who start in a similar place. Specifically, we look at the change each student who starts at percentile X moves to percentile Y (e.g., X and Y can represent 5 percentile point gains). In this way, we can see if a given teacher's students do better than the average student does with the same starting place. This is one way of trying to get around the problem of scaling of tests.

When you get into more sophisticated statistical schemes, however, you begin to face the problem of not being very transparent. I would also be concerned that maybe the teachers won't trust this type of benchmarking; although, I wonder that if they knew what was coming out of the testing companies, they might not trust the way that the scores are already being assigned. Let me say clearly that if done right, performance pay has great potential to improve incentives for teachers.

Another aspect of performance pay is that it can likely help to improve the recruitment and retention of high-quality teachers. It's not just incentives we're giving to a group of teachers, to point them in the right direction and to make sure they are assigning the right amount of homework and grading it, giving challenging classes, and so on. But it's also trying to bring the right people into the profession and to make sure that they stay in the profession.

My review of the limitations of the value-added method leads me to think that one would want to use a small number of performance indicators. Maybe four or five. No single one is perfect—here's where I think that getting the buy-in from the teachers in recognizing we're going to do the best we can under the circumstance and realizing that there are limits is crucial. Putting weight on the performance, the gains for the classroom, does make some sense, bearing in mind that we have all of these limitations. I think you might want to put more weight on it for a larger class, or maybe you would want to look over a few years where you could pool some more test scores together. I think putting weight on the school-level gain is also sensible. That would have more signal in it and also give classroom teachers and other staff an incentive for cooperation. Absenteeism is another measure I think one might consider, supervisor's evaluations, and so on.

One thing I haven't mentioned is class size. Having smaller classes, I think, does help teachers to be more effective, but it's also very expensive. If you had two teachers who could do the same job, one has 30 students and the other one has 20 students, and they're teaching the students equally well, I think the teacher with 30 students ought to be rewarded more generously. I could tell you, from my wife's experience, there's a lot more homework and tests to grade in a larger class. So, rewarding teachers more for taking on a heavier load also seems to me to make economic sense.

Last, because no single indicator is perfect or exhaustive, I think trying to use a well-rounded set of measures makes more sense than using any single measure. I also think that rewarding multiple indicators will help reduce the inclination for manipulation of the incentives. If no single measure is getting all of the weight, then there is less incentive to subvert any single measure. This would be one way to mitigate the kinds of problems that were documented in Chicago. Thank you.

Lewis Solmon

Before Brad speaks, I want to just make a couple of comments. Number one is, I think both of the insights that we've received were very helpful, and it's encouraging to see that in our Teacher Advancement Program (and we'll discuss more of this later), we've covered a lot of the problems that were mentioned.

Second, when I was in graduate school a hundred years ago, Adam Smith was one of the bibles. Our microeconomics book had a footnote on one page that said, students should read the whole of Adam Smith except page 482. So, all students ran to Adam Smith to read page 482. What it said on that page was that college professors should get paid according to the number of students they had in their class, which is consistent with both what you said at the end, and it's performance pay. If you weren't good enough to attract a lot of students, you wouldn't get paid as much. So our professor said, or the author of the book said, don't read that page. Brad.

Brad Jupp

It is an honor to stand before this many excellent teachers, recognized for their performance by the Milken Family Foundation. It is also an honor to speak at an event convened by the Milken Family Foundation. From my perspective, as a teachers' union leader, the work of the Foundation in honoring excellence in teaching needs to be recognized too. As an audience, you've already done a remarkable job. You have listened to three economists in a row. I hope to give you a break from that.

Let me tell you a little about myself. I am a teacher in Denver Public Schools. I have been appointed to the Design Team of the Denver Public Schools/Denver Classroom Teachers Association Design Team, which is the collaborative body of two teachers and two administrators working to build a compensation system that pays teachers, at least in part, based on the academic growth of the students they teach. I am also a leader in the Denver Classroom Teachers Association (DCTA). My local president appointed me to this position. Furthermore, I have helped negotiate the labor agreement between the union and the district since spring 1988.

On March 19, 2004, we got 59% of the union membership of the DCTA to vote in favor of a collective bargaining agreement that replaces the single salary schedule with a pay system that recognizes teachers for their professional accomplishments. We call the system the Professional Compensation System for Teachers, or ProComp. It is not a perfect replacement for the single salary schedule. What we did in Denver is to take a huge step forward in the right direction, or, to choose another metaphor, an open door through which many other school districts and teachers unions will pass in the next few years.

In the short time I have today I am going to provide you with a brief description of it. Then I will talk to you about what we've learned about the perceptions of teachers from the campaign to get ProComp passed. Finally, I will close with a challenge.

ProComp is an attempt to take the district's single largest expenditure, teacher compensation, and link it more closely to the district's three goals: to hold high expectations for all, to improve the performance of all students, and to close the gap between poorer and better performing students. At the same time, we have introduced a system where an individual teacher builds a professional pay package by drawing from a menu of different compensation elements.

As a compensation system, ProComp moves away from the set of professional pigeonholes we call the single salary schedule. The single salary schedule is little more than an array of boxes with numbers in them, an artifact of an era of ink and ledger paper. In Denver, the salary schedule has 13 steps for experience and seven education lanes. It starts at about

$33,000 and allows teachers with 13 years of experience and a PhD to earn a little more than $65,000. It is composed of 91 pigeonholes, into which we situate all 4,250 teachers in Denver. Needless to say, it is an awkward fit for some.

ProComp replaces the single salary schedule with a fully funded, uncapped system, one where each teacher becomes her own compensation reference point. Teachers enter at the same level, about $33,000, but they can earn more and continue earning through their entire career—no more maximum at the end of 13 years. Teachers compose their own professional compensation package from a menu of ten different elements. As a system, it cannot be worked out on ledger paper. Rather, it is a fully hypertextual system that relies on many spreadsheets layered on top of each other.

Under ProComp teachers will be recognized for their professional accomplishments in four core areas:

1. acquisition and demonstration of new knowledge and skills in the classroom
2. demonstrated performance in the classroom observed by a principal or peers
3. commitment to hard-to-staff schools and hard-to-staff assignments
4. meeting and exceeding measurable high expectations for student learning

Teachers who acquire and demonstrate new skills and knowledge are no longer limited by the cynical game of paying for graduate credit to advance their salary. Instead, they are allowed to earn salary increases for spending time learning new skills and then demonstrating in the classroom what they have learned.

Under ProComp, the system for observing teacher performance will focus much more closely on what teachers do in the classroom. Non-instructional behaviors—whether a teacher comes to work on time, whether a teacher wears shorts, or whether a teacher volunteers for committees after school—do not have as direct an impact on student learning as those behaviors that are directly related to instruction. Furthermore, teacher misbehavior should be addressed through some system more quick and direct than a teacher evaluation system linked to compensation. If you want a teacher to stop wearing shorts in class or if, for that matter, you want a gym teacher to start wearing shorts in class, you cannot wait for the full year of a professional evaluation cycle to turn before you correct that behavior.

ProComp introduces some simple market incentives. We learned that in Denver teachers move away from the toughest schools and assignments. Positions like the center placement classroom for emotionally disturbed students is a revolving door assignment—a first- or second-year practitioner lasts about 6 months before trying to find another place to work.

Finally, ProComp introduces ways for teachers to earn salary increases and bonuses for student learning. We realized that, even measuring student learning is not completely developed, we could not wait until it is to reform our compensation system. Therefore, we introduced into our compensation system some pragmatic and low-stakes elements that take into account the impact teachers have on the learning lives of the students they teach.

The greatest surprise about ProComp is that we got 59% of the union's membership to vote for it. To do so, we had to realize that the perceptions of teachers about the way they were paid might be different than we presumed for many years. As a profession we have done far less investigation into teacher perceptions about the way they are paid than we should. We are most familiar with results from the surveys conducted by teacher unions. Since the audience is largely teachers, I can rest assured that most of you are familiar with these kinds of surveys. They ask multiple-choice questions like this:

What kind of cost of living adjustment do you think you deserve?
  1. 0%
  2. 3%
  3. 6%
  4. 9%
  5. 12%

The outcomes of these investigations to teacher perceptions were pretty much predetermined. As someone who's composed surveys like this, I have always wondered who was stupid enough to select choice 4 or 5?

Beginning in 1994, the DCTA began asking some very different questions of our members. As we did, we began to get some very different information back from them. We began to realize that teacher perceptions about the way they are paid are like figure over ground problems—you know that exercise where you can look at a picture of an old haggard lady and if you adjust the way you see it, a pretty lady with an umbrella emerges from the same drawing? Well, we gradually discovered that we might be looking only at the picture of the old hag and missing the picture of the pretty lady.

In 1996, prompted by *What Matters Most*, the report of the National Commission for Teaching and America's Future, the DCTA asked teachers questions about their interest in incentives for working in hard-to-serve schools and hard-to-staff assignments. At that time I was a pretty traditional union negotiator, and I thought the teacher responses would be largely negative. To my surprise, nearly 50% of the teachers said they thought this was a good idea. We've asked the question on many surveys since 1996. Each time we have, the number of teachers saying they support this idea has grown. Now, nearly 70% of our members say they believe that teachers who work in schools with predominantly poor students should receive bonuses, and over 60% say that teachers who work in assignments where the supply of licensed professionals is low—like special education centers, middle school mathematics, or speech pathology—should receive a similar bonus. For me, this became the first hint that we may be looking at the wrong image. Instead of looking at the image of collective gain in a simple sense of an equal raise for all, perhaps we should be looking at enriching the earnings opportunities for the profession.

In 1998, we began asking a more challenging question on our surveys. It asked:

What portion of your salary, if any, should be based on accurately measured student growth?
1. 0%
2. 1% to 10%
3. 11% to 25%
4. 26% to 50%
5. 51% or more

The initial response affirmed to traditionalists like me that teachers did not want their pay based on measurable student growth. About 68% selected choice 1, saying, "No, none of my pay should be based on student results." What we failed to realize then was that in fact 32% selected a choice other than the first. In other words, a sizable portion of the teachers represented by DCTA—by inference about 1,360 of a workforce of 4,250—expressed something very different than the obvious majority: "We are confident that some portion of our pay should be based on the results we get with the students we teach." We have continued to ask this question. By spring 2004, the number selecting something other than choice 1 exceeded 50%.

As we got closer to the ratification of the ProComp Agreement, the surprises kept on coming. We did very close surveying of member perceptions during this period. We learned a great deal about how our members felt about ProComp as a system, too much to summarize in a talk like this. One stands out above all, though, and should be noticed before I conclude. We asked our members if they were likely to vote in favor of this new collective bargaining agreement, one that replaced the single salary schedule with an uncapped system in which a teacher's earnings were based in part on student learning. The group most likely to support it was male teachers in secondary schools with more than 13 years of service in Denver Public Schools. We could speculate on the many reasons why this was true, but we must recognize that these are the teachers who are most likely to be stereotyped as resistant to radical changes.

By way of conclusion, let me offer you all a challenge. Please realize that what we've done in Denver is open a door, not create some final solution to the problem of finding a better way to pay teachers. There was a whole lot of hoopla in Denver on March 19, 2004. That hoopla was generated because we opened a door. Our challenge now is to follow through and implement the system our members have approved. On March 20, we woke up and realized that now the teachers have said, "Go ahead," and we now have to deliver.

My challenge to you is to look through the door we've opened and honestly assess what we have accomplished in Denver and, more important, what you might be able to do in your district. Look through and discover that you and your colleagues may want more from their compensation system than they are currently getting. They may want to leave an ink and ledger paper compensation system behind and replace it with a different set of opportunities, opportunities that allow people like you to get the recognition you deserve without having to get on a plane and fly to Washington.

Thank you very much.

John Schacter

First, let me say, it's an honor and a pleasure to speak to such a distinguished group. You see, I taught at the elementary level. At the end of each year, I asked my students to evaluate my teaching. Here's what one student wrote: "If I had 20 minutes left to live, I'd want to spend them in Mr. Schacter's classroom, because every minute with Mr. Schacter feels like an hour!" There's an old saying that teachers are the bones on which children sharpen their teeth, and I can tell you, I know that saying firsthand. Now, Lew said that I have about 10 minutes to share with you my opinions about performance pay. We've heard from historians, economists, and a union president. What I'd like to share is an educational psychologist's perspective of performance pay.

There are two reasons why I think we should try performance pay. The first is incompetent people don't realize that they are incompetent. Let me share with you a true story. In 1995, McArthur Wheeler walked into a Pittsburgh bank in broad daylight wearing absolutely no disguise, and he robbed the bank. He was arrested later that night, after the videotape from the bank surveillance camera was broadcast on the evening news. When police showed Mr. Wheeler the videotape, he incredulously mumbled, "But I wore the juice, man. I wore the juice." McArthur Wheeler thought rubbing his face with lemon juice rendered it invisible to videotape.

Believe it or not, Mr. Wheeler's behavior is not that unusual. You see, two Cornell psychologists recently published an article in the *Journal of Personality and Social Psychology* that found that people who are highly unskilled and highly unknowledgeable don't realize it. Here's what they did: They gave these participants tests of humor, grammar, logic and problem-solving. The people who scored in the bottom 12th percentile thought that they performed near the top. So, that's my first reason for why we should try performance pay.

The second reason is, there's nothing less motivating than seeing a person receive the same pay and benefits for doing a task worse and for putting forth much less effort. Professor Krueger can probably tell us the name of the economist who won the Nobel Prize for discovering this. I found a recent study in the journal, *Nature*, that tells us this also is present in animal behavior. In their study, researchers Sarah Brosnan and Frans de Waal analyzed capuchin monkey work-and-reward behaviors by dividing a group of female monkeys into pairs and rewarding them with a cucumber slice every time they gave the researcher a piece of granite. After 2 years of training 95% of the time, the monkeys exchanged the granite for the piece of cucumber. Then, the scientists began paying one monkey partner with a succulent grape, while the other continued to receive the cucumber. What happened was that the monkeys paid in cucumbers, which had been handing over the granite 95% of the time, now decided to do so only 60% of the time.

Next Brosnan and de Waal tweaked the experiment a bit more by giving grapes to monkeys in the pairs that did absolutely nothing. Seeing this, the outraged working monkeys exchanged the granite for the cucumber only 20% of the time. So, that gets me to my point: the researchers in this *Nature* article said they think that this concept of fairness has been embedded into the human psyche over eons and eons. And that by encouraging incompetence we discourage high quality work.

Thus, the inability of incompetent people to know that they're incompetent, along with the highly unmotivational factor of seeing incompetent

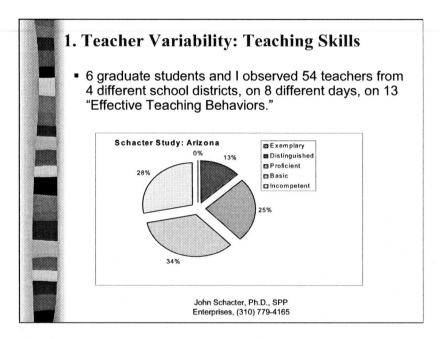

Chart 5.23

people get equally rewarded, are two reasons for trying performance pay in education. There are other compelling explanations as well.

As in almost any job, employees vary in terms of their skills, knowledge and performance. For teachers, researchers have measured this variability in basically two ways. One, they've looked at how well they teach. The other way is in terms of how much their students actually learn. Chart 5.23 is a study that I conducted with six graduate students, where we observed 54 teachers from four different school districts on 8 different days over 432 hours of instruction on 13 effective teaching behaviors. We scored the teachers' performance on a scale from 1 to 5, with 5 being best. After each observation, we then summed and averaged our ratings to come up with a final score. You can see that the results definitely show a tremendous amount of variability in teaching performance.

Not only do teachers vary in terms of how well they teach, but they also vary in how much their students learn. In another study of 384 second- to sixth-grade Arizona teachers' classroom achievement gains, Professor Thum and I found that about 30% of teachers' student achievement declines, that about 30% remains the same, and about 40% actually gain (Chart 5.24). We weren't alone in this discovery of how much teachers vary in terms of how much their students achieve. Over 30 years, William Sanders found a 54% difference (Chart 5.25).

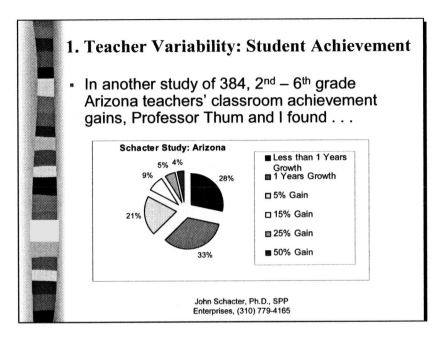

Chart 5.24

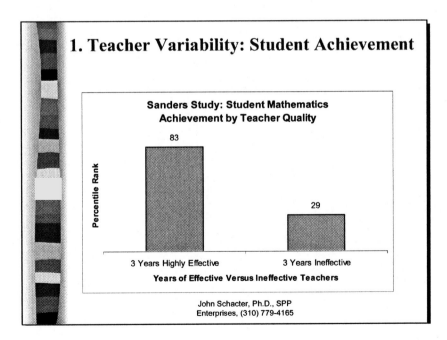

Chart 5.25

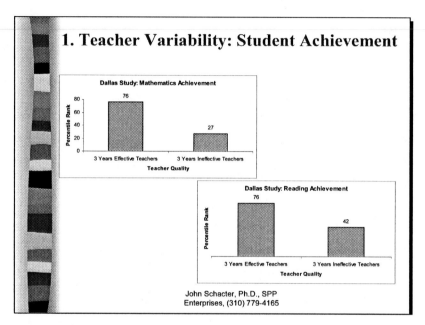

Chart 5.26

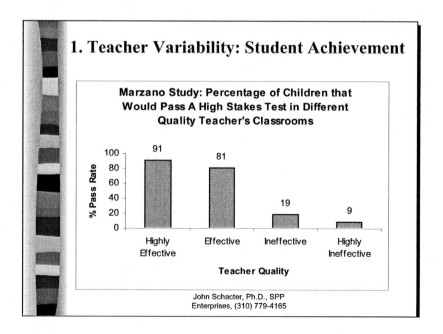

Chart 5.27

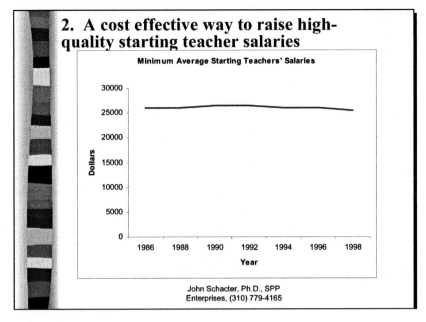

2. A cost effective way to raise high-quality starting teacher salaries

Chart 5.28

The Dallas Independent School Researchers, Mendro and colleagues found similar variability in student achievement gains both in math and in reading. (Chart 5.26) Finally, Dr. Robert Marzano, using a statistical technique developed by a Harvard statistician named Donald Rubin, came to these conclusions. So, as you can see, there's a lot of variability in both how well teachers teach and how much their kids learn (Chart 5.27).

Another reason that I thought some of the panel members were going to talk today, but didn't, is to try to raise the salaries of the most effective teachers, especially early in their careers. Chart 5.28 from Dan Goldhaber's research shows that teachers' starting salaries in current dollars basically haven't changed over time. These low starting salaries compared to other professions may be one reason why highly capable people don't choose teaching as a career. Think about it. If you can earn $10,000 more a year in a sales job, and $15,000 to $20,000 more a year in an engineering or computer science job, becoming a math or science teacher really doesn't factor in to your decision (Chart 5.29).

The final reason we should consider trying performance pay is: Better teaching leads to better learning. Now, every teacher in this audience, along with my wife, always says to me, no duh. The problem is that researchers have had a very hard time actually defining what better teaching is. And so far, this seemingly obvious link hasn't been empirically validated.

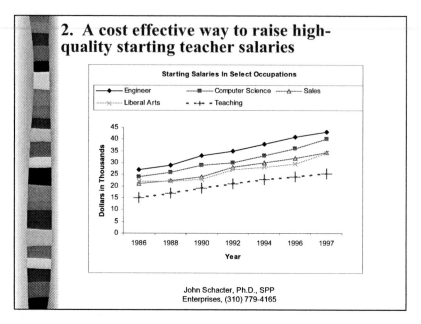

Chart 5.29

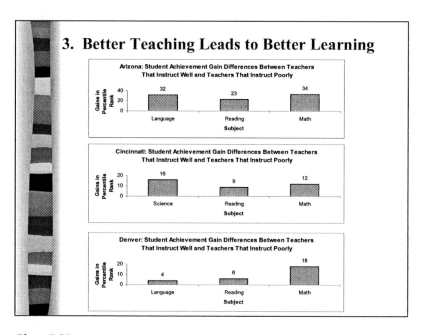

Chart 5.30

In the study I conducted, better teaching, which is defined by our 13 effective teaching behaviors, resulted in 20 to 30 percentile point gains in reading, language, and math. In a study conducted in Cincinnati, better teaching, defined by 21 teaching behaviors, resulted in 9% to 16% differences in reading, math, and science. In a study conducted in Denver, better teaching, as defined by crafting high-quality, measurable learning objectives related to student achievement, resulted in 4 to 18 percentile point differences in reading, math, and writing (Chart 5.30). These are some reasons why I think it's worthwhile to at least consider reforming the way we pay teachers and, most importantly, the way that we evaluate teachers.

The million-dollar question that we really haven't had answered here today is: Does performance pay work? What I did was, I looked at answering this question in three ways. Does performance pay improve teacher attitudes? And you heard a little bit about this from Brad. Does it change teacher instruction? Because, this is part of why we have these incentive systems. And does it lead to better student achievement?

So, does performance pay improve teacher attitudes? In the United Kingdom—which actually has a nationwide performance pay system, and in Cincinnati, where the teachers recently voted down their performance pay system—there is just tremendous resistance to performance pay. The teachers report it causes jealousy and discourages teamwork. But if we look at the TAP reform, we see that the teachers are much more supportive. Only 30% seem to be against performance pay (Chart 5.31). A universal conclusion from the research in education and business about attitudes regarding performance pay is this: Employees rate working with high quality colleagues, having good leadership, working in an institution recognized for innovation and excellence, and having access to continuous learning, all as more important than earning a raise or a bonus for your performance.

Second question: Does performance pay produce changes in teacher instruction? Again, we see that the results of these other, strictly "performance pay initiatives," are not too positive. In the United Kingom, 91% of administrators say instruction hasn't changed at all. In Denver, 80% of the teachers reported that they're teaching basically exactly the same as before the performance pay initiative came in. In TAP, we see that we have close to 70% of our teachers saying they're teaching differently (Chart 5.32).

Finally, let's look at the third question: Are there changes in student achievement? In the United Kingdom they haven't done studies on changes in student achievement due to performance pay, so I wanted to look at two of the biggest studies: the Denver study and the TAP study of performance pay. The Denver middle schools, over the course of 4 years,

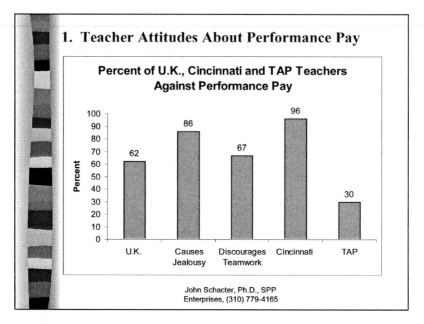

Chart 5.31

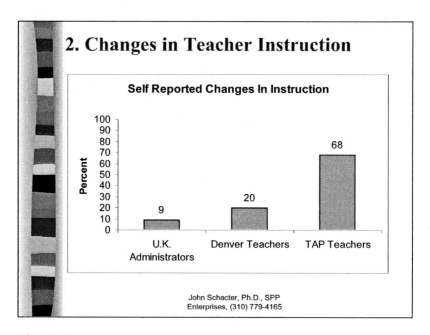

Chart 5.32

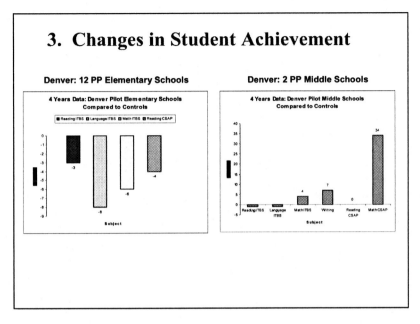

3. Changes in Student Achievement

Denver: 12 PP Elementary Schools

Denver: 2 PP Middle Schools

Chart 5.33

appeared to do better in math, and the same in reading. But in the elementary schools, the students in performance pay pilot schools ended up actually doing worse, in all subjects. Some of them aren't statistically different, but some are. For the Milken reform, a different story emerges (Chart 5.33).

In TAP schools, roughly 65% of these schools are doing better than controls, in reading, language, and math, on standardized tests and on state standard assessments. The results seem to hold for both Arizona and South Carolina. Next year we'll actually have a study out of five states. In several instances, the magnitude of the differences between TAP schools and control schools is quite large. Arizona school 3 gained 113% more than its controls over 3 years. Arizona school 2 gained 51% more. Arizona school 5, in just 2 years, is already out gaining its control by 50%. In South Carolina, after just 1 year, we see the high performing TAP schools are out-performing their controls by 14% to 24% in math, and 6% to 26% in reading (Chart 5.34).

So what does all this mean for performance pay? Well, performance pay, when you implement it as an isolated system (Rick Hess said it and so did Alan Krueger), is not going to work. It's not going to work because it's unsystematic; if they force a performance pay system on a school without other reform elements to help teachers improve, the teachers are not

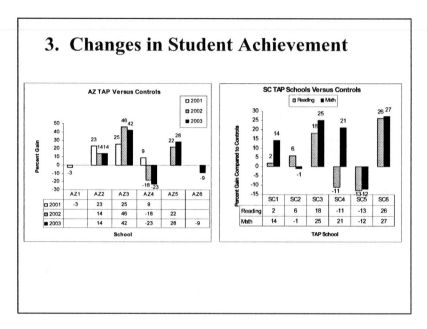

3. Changes in Student Achievement

Chart 5.34

going to get better. If I say to you, I'm paying you based on your performance, and you don't know what good performance is, and you don't know how to perform well, and you're marginal, and nobody's going to help you get better, why do you think all of a sudden you're going to start performing better? You're not.

In lots of performance pay systems in education, the criteria for pay are problematic. A lot of the criteria are ambiguous, one dimensional, and have no research base. Performance ratings have also been deemed unreliable. Support is lacking in performance pay systems that don't work. They don't have professional development, they don't have distributed and quality leadership. They don't have a sense of collegiality. And most systems lack rigor. In the United Kingdom, 97% of teachers earned a performance award. In Denver, I think it was close to 93%. So, the systems don't seem to differentiate or pay the better teachers for better performance.

To conclude, in TAP, performance pay appears to be working. Why? Because there are four elements of the TAP reform, and performance pay constitutes only one. Not only is TAP measuring and paying people for better performance, but TAP is teaching teachers how to teach better. TAP is teaching them how to conduct data analysis. TAP is distributing the leadership throughout the school, so there's support and mentoring and help and continuous guidance. TAP is expanding the pool of quality people to hire from. So, in my opinion, when you put performance pay into a larger system, into a larger context, where you actually reform other elements of the system, I think that there's great promise for the idea of performance pay. Thank you very much.

Lewis Solmon

I think it's important for you all to get a chance to ask some questions, so why don't we go straight to questions from the audience.

Audience Question

I'm from a large urban district in California. I have two questions. The main concerns that I hear in my district, regarding performance pay is that if we're going to adopt a business model, the problem that a lot of the teachers that I talk to see is that they can't fire their employees when they don't perform. So they have to show up to work the next day and some-how inspire and motivate and still produce, with students who—and in our district it's a reality—that it's not just one or two kids in our class, but a good 70% or 80% of our class—have two or three jobs, their parents are working jobs, the students are raising their brothers and sisters. And, in the hour and a half that I have with them every other day, I try to inspire and perspire and do all the right things; but when they go home, I'm not guaranteed that the skills I give them are being reinforced, kind of like the summer model that we saw. So, I want to know: How would we address that in a large urban district if I want to take this back and be an advocate and be an ambassador?

The second question is: If we're considering class size as part of the performance pay, what do we say to the elective teachers? I know at our school, senior year, students can choose from a litany of English electives. I know that my elective will not be filled as quickly as film analysis, which counts as English. I know that teacher is going to be making a million and two dollars, and I'll be making five. So how do I address those concerns when I go back?

John Schacter

Everybody on this panel has talked about having multiple parts to a performance pay system. In TAP, 50% of the bonus is based on teaching,

30% on classroom achievement gains, and 20% on school-wide achievement gains. So actually, TAP is getting a large picture of how well you're performing. We don't have any components in there about class size.

Lewis Solmon

Do you want to answer the class size part?

Alan Krueger

Well, I was going to answer the first part about firing; we had this issue at the universities. I don't know if you realize that academic pay is largely pay-for-performance. It is mostly based on publications, not performance in the classroom. We also have tenure, like many teachers have. So, we don't fire the low performers. On the other hand, the pay does turn out to be a motivator, and there are ways around different assignments and so on. People do often get signals to leave, rather than get to a point where they would be fired when they couldn't be fired in the first place. So, that doesn't seem to me to be insurmountable. Especially if it's layered on top of a system where there already is tenure.

Lewis Solmon

I would like to address the more general point where you say you've got students that are in very desperate situations and they can't go up. One of the points of our next panel, dealing with No Child Left Behind, is the underlying assumption that all students can learn. When we look at improvement, even those kids who have such deprived situations that they are at a very low level, one has to hope, and there's evidence—whether you look at the KIPP Academies, or whether you look at some very successful schools in inner cities. There is evidence, not just hope. There is evidence that low SES kids with a lot of ostensible problems can learn in the right environment, so we don't want to say, "Well, we can't do performance pay because you have kids who can't learn. I'd like to go around a school and have you and others pick out the kids in the first grade who can't learn." We believe all kids can learn. We look at how much they improve, not where they end up.

Audience Question

My question is for the gentleman from Colorado. You said that the teachers basically put together their own plan. Could you elaborate just a little bit on what you meant there?

Brad Jupp

I'm not sure I said the teachers put together their own plan.

Audience Question Continued

You said they layered it.

Brad Jupp

Here's what it boils down to: Teachers are going to be given a menu of compensation choices. Three of the choices are going to be ones that they draw upon routinely to get salary increases, but the other seven are going to be ones that are more difficult to attain, and you may have to do special things in order to get them. You may have to perform extraordinarily well to get them. In the end, what teachers will do, instead of just getting a pay increase for working another year or getting a pay increase for getting 30 hours of graduate credit, is that they'll have to pick and choose from these compensation elements to make their pay. It becomes much more like a professional pay package that way.

Lewis Solmon

Brad, does it mean that if they pick some of the more difficult things, they have the potential of getting even more income?

Brad Jupp

Exceptionally more, yes.

Audience Question

Did you ever consider involving parents? Teacher contribution is limited to 10%.

Brad Jupp

The best way to think about this is that you have to accurately measure the impact they have in the 10% of time they've got, because that's the time that matters. We more or less have seen a change in not just our union leadership, but our union membership that says we can't blame the parents anymore. We can't say that a poor child performs poorly in school just because his parents were poor. We have to begin to say that it's our duty to take the children of the poor and advance them as far as we can. Now all of these people around me can tell you that there are some tough measurement issues that you have to unpack in order to get that right. One of the things that we're doing in Denver is working hard to get that right, not only at a psychometric level, but also at a pragmatic level, so that teachers can understand it. Ultimately I think it is educational malpractice to say that we can't teach kids because their parents are poor.

Lewis Solmon

As a matter of fact, the evidence definitely shows that teacher quality has a significant impact. We are beyond the Coleman days, when he said everything depends on the family.

Audience Question

I'm from Boston, and we have a wonderful union that I work with. What you've done is extraordinary. What I want to know, is your phone ringing off the hook now that you've stepped in? What's happening nationally with other unions? Are you getting the kind of calls, and are you on the road trying to elicit the kind of support, that are needed to move education in the right direction?

Brad Jupp

Yeah, the phone's pretty busy. Obviously, I'm here. Normally I don't get invited to these kinds of things.

Lewis Solmon

For the record, Brad, this is the second time.

Brad Jupp

True enough. I think that my local union is in for a fun ride at this year's NEA convention, and I'm sure that there are going to be some people from New Jersey and California who give us a whooping, or think they're giving us a whooping. Our best resource in the past 5 years has been the teacher union reform network, which includes Boston, Los Angeles, New York, Cincinnati, and others. They've helped us think outside the box. The NEA and the AFT as organizations have been, by and large, somewhere between inquisitive and supportive. They haven't been trying to hold us back.

Alan Krueger

It doesn't seem to me that a unionized setting is antithetical to having pay-for-performance. It has some advantages. Take for example, grievance procedures; if teachers are worried about fairness, there is the union and the grievance procedures for enforcing fairness concerns. In addition, if you're going to involve teachers in forming the system, having a union there is a natural way to do it. On the other hand, I think it probably takes a great deal of effort. I told Brad before when he said we only had a 59-41 vote Washington an 18-point victory is a landslide. It takes quite a bit of work to bring the unions on board. In the long run, I don't see it necessarily as an impediment.

Lowell Milken

First I want to apologize for Lew's analogy when he spoke about the difficulty of quality teaching relating it to pornography. Second of all, I want you to know that when John Schacter used to work at the Foundation, we didn't have monkeys running around the office. I have two quick questions; Alan, you showed a slide, and if I read it correctly, it was about K-3 and teacher experience and degrees? Do you have similar work for high school science and math, as to what effect the degree has in student learning? I'd be curious, if you've looked at that. Brad, in the case of your Denver initiative, could you just speak for a moment more about your funding source? What kind of tax increase? You mentioned $25 million. The question is what was the nature of that?

Alan Krueger

I haven't personally looked beyond K-3 in education and the performance of classes. I can tell you the literature generally finds very little connection when looking at general master's degrees. If you look more closely at whether a teacher has postcollege education in the field in which they're teaching, then there is more of a connection. There is more of a connection between having a graduate math degree, even an undergraduate math degree, and how well the teacher does in teaching math based on the performance of their students. Also, if you look at standardized tests of teachers in the fields in which they teach, a reading teacher who scores better on reading tends to be a more effective teacher—which is not necessarily degrees, but it does say that teacher competence in the field, not very surprisingly, is related to their performance.

Brad Jupp

We are going to go to the voters of Denver in November of 2005 and ask for a $25 million property tax override. What that will do is to create a continuous revenue source to pay for the alternative compensation system that we call ProComp, on an ongoing basis. One of the things that was talked about before I presented, it was one of Dr. Solmon's remarks, was that we rarely look at how we're going to fund compensation systems for teachers over time in a different way. When we were doing our planning in Denver, we hired an independent financial analyst and examined teacher pay systems using an actuarial model. We determined that the system we were inventing would use the $25 million over a 50-year period in an economically stable way. We wouldn't drain the revenue source too quickly or drain it too slowly. It's actually one of the longer and more interesting things that we did. The safe thing to say is that we knew we needed continuing revenue if we're going to make a lasting impact on teacher pay.

Lewis Solmon

Why don't we end here and thank our panel for a very informative discussion.

PANEL CONTRIBUTIONS

CHAPTER 6

RECOGNIZING DIFFERENCES

Lewis C. Solmon

For more than a century, public education has worked under a single salary schedule that compensates teachers for college credits, education degrees, and years of experience, but not for their effectiveness in the classroom (see Figure 6.1).

In fact, research shows that the degrees, courses, and experience that teachers have, beyond the first few years of teaching, are unrelated to how much their students achieve. Furthermore, the current salary schedule does not normally take into account the fact that teachers work in schools offering different levels of nonmonetary benefits, such as a safe, pleasing environment. Nor does it recognize that students come to class with different levels of preparation and home support.

Paying all teachers with the same experience and credits the same salary also ignores the fact that graduates of different fields have vastly different alternative career options; think of a physicist compared with someone having a bachelor's degree in elementary education. School administrators report that it is very difficult or impossible to fill elemen-

Improving Student Achievement: Reforms that Work, 159–167
Copyright © 2005 by Information Age Publishing
All rights of reproduction in any form reserved.

Reprinted with permission from *Education Next,* a publication of the Hoover Institute, Stanford University. *Education Next* Vol. 5, No.1 (Winter 2005), 16-20.

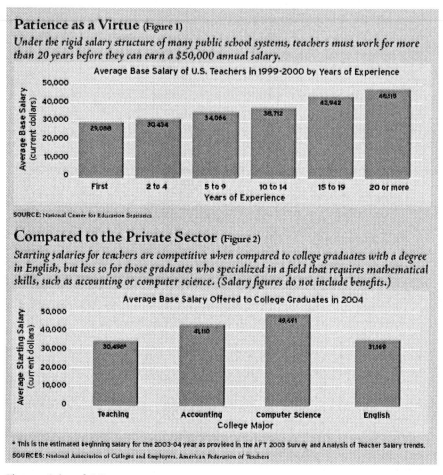

Patience as a Virtue (Figure 1)

Under the rigid salary structure of many public school systems, teachers must work for more than 20 years before they can earn a $50,000 annual salary.

Average Base Salary of U.S. Teachers in 1999-2000 by Years of Experience

SOURCE: National Center for Education Statistics

Compared to the Private Sector (Figure 2)

Starting salaries for teachers are competitive when compared to college graduates with a degree in English, but less so for those graduates who specialized in a field that requires mathematical skills, such as accounting or computer science. (Salary figures do not include benefits.)

Average Base Salary Offered to College Graduates in 2004

* This is the estimated beginning salary for the 2003-04 year as provided in the AFT 2003 Survey and Analysis of Teacher Salary trends.

SOURCES: National Association of Colleges and Employers, American Federation of Teachers

Figures 6.1 and 6.2

tary teaching positions about 6% of the time, while positions in math, physical sciences, and special education are difficult or impossible to fill more than 30% of the time. According to the American Federation of Teachers, the estimated starting salary for teachers with a BA, in 2003–04, regardless of discipline, was $30,496. The National Association of Colleges and Employers tells us that the average starting salary for accountants that year was $41,110, and for graduates in computer science, $49,691 (see Figure 6.2) Starting salaries for mathematicians with a BA, the year before, averaged $40,512; for physicists with a BA in 2002, according to the American Institute of Physics, $78,000. Is it any wonder that it is so difficult to hire and retain math and science teachers?

Extra pay for those in hard-to-staff fields would acknowledge the laws of supply and demand—greater opportunities for math or science majors bid up their earnings in other careers, so getting them into teaching requires competitive salaries. It would not mean that physics teachers are more important than elementary teachers.

In the current system, an increase for one teacher requires increases for all. If, for instance, we decided that our teachers are underpaid, as state officials from all parts of the country tell me, current practice would make a meaningful pay increase prohibitive. Just to bring the salaries in the below-average states to the national average would cost $8.5 billion—an amount that is fiscally irrational. It may seem like a meaningless argument, except that such an amount is dictated by the current uniform salary schedule, which requires those below-average states to raise each teacher's salary. It would be much cheaper—not to mention more educationally effective—to raise the salaries of just the most-effective teachers, those deserving of the increase, rather than all teachers. Then there would be money available to give larger raises to the very best teachers.

It would be similarly impossible to bring all teachers' salaries up to the average level of other professions. Why would we want to pay more to the least-effective teachers anyway? What we end up with, then, are paltry average annual increases (as teachers gain experience and course credits), ranging from the high of a $1,498 average increase in California to a meager $503 at the low end in South Dakota.

In the Madison School District in Arizona, the lowest salary for a new teacher with only a bachelor's degree is $31,304 and the highest salary after many years and 72 postbaccalaureate credits is $57,251, an 82% increase over a career! Compare that with the legal profession, where the lowest-paid 10% earn less than $44,490 and the highest 10% earned more than $145,600—a 227% difference! The flat salary schedule for teachers is a good reason for those in Madison to welcome the stipends of $6,250 that the district offers to its "master" teachers, who take a leadership role among the faculty, and the bonuses averaging $3,400 to teachers who exhibit outstanding classroom performance and student achievement.

The traditional K–12 compensation system is obsolete in that it is no longer useful, but, sadly, it is not obsolete, because it is still in use.

THE TEACHER ADVANCEMENT PROGRAM

For the past 4 years, the Milken Family Foundation, founded in 1982 and based in Santa Monica, California, has been working through its Teacher Advancement Program (TAP) in Madison and in more than 60 other schools—mostly elementary and middle schools and a few high schools—

around the nation to change the way teachers are evaluated, helped to grow professionally, and compensated.

The TAP is a systemic reform of public schools intended to attract, motivate, develop, and retain high-quality talent in the teaching profession. It has four key elements:

- Multiple career paths allow teachers to pursue a variety of positions throughout their careers—career, mentor, and master teacher—depending on their interests, abilities, and accomplishments. As they move up the ranks, their qualifications, roles, and responsibilities increase—and so does their compensation. When teachers take on more responsibilities, they should receive more pay. The old career ladder programs failed because the best teachers were honored with new titles and more work, but with meager, if any, extra pay.

- Performance-based accountability evaluates teachers' effectiveness through a comprehensive, research-based system that combines such criteria as position responsibilities, classroom observations, and students' gains in test scores.

- Ongoing applied professional growth requires a change in the school schedule that allows time during the regular school day for teachers to learn, plan, mentor, and share with other teachers so they can constantly improve the quality of their instruction.

- Market-driven compensation allows schools to compensate teachers on the basis of their performance and the performance of their students.

ATTRACTING—AND KEEPING—EFFECTIVE TEACHERS

One of the things we all seem to know is that there are few careers, except teaching, in which professionals are not held accountable for their failures and rewarded for their accomplishments. So why, political constraints aside, do we insist on giving raises to reward a teacher's longevity instead of his or her job performance?

For the past 17 years the Milken Foundation has worked with state superintendents to recognize and reward K–12 educators with a $25,000 gift—no strings attached—for outstanding and effective performance. Of the 1,977 recipients of the Milken award, we know that 1,653 of them are still working. Of these, 281, or 17%, have left their school buildings to take jobs at a district office (154), a nonprofit organization (47), a university (41), a federal or state government office (24), or a private company (15).

Unfortunately, we do not know whether this 17% turnover among Milken award recipients is better or worse than among those equally experienced and outstanding teachers who do not receive the awards. But we do know that 46% of all teachers leave the profession in the first 5 years and that, anecdotally, the Milken awards have created an aura of excellence about the profession that enhances the environment that our TAP research shows is so important to teacher retention. The very fact that these teachers have opportunities beyond the classroom increases the attractiveness of the profession as a whole.

However, when no compensating salary is awarded for teaching in difficult or undesirable schools, it is easy to understand why the best teachers may choose to teach in the most rewarding and pleasant environment available, moving from low to high socioeconomic status schools when the opportunity arises. Extra compensation is thus needed for those teaching in hard-to-staff schools where conditions are difficult, dangerous, or unpleasant. Defying that pattern, however, some very talented teachers in Arizona are moving from socioeconomically advantaged schools that are not using the TAP to schools of low socioeconomic status that are. Over the past 3 years, 61 teachers have started working at the two schools of lowest socioeconomic status in the Madison school district, both of which are using the TAP. Of these teachers, 13 (21%) have come from schools in high socioeconomic areas in Madison or nearby districts, and they are among the best teachers from the area. They are attracted by the more interesting professional development, the enhanced collegiality, and the opportunity to earn more by being effective.

We want teachers who love kids and want to help them learn, but that does not mean they cannot be interested in compensation as well. Physicians seek to prevent or cure diseases, and some lawyers seek to dispense justice, but that does not bar the best of them—but not all of them—from earning large incomes as well.

STUDENT OUTCOMES COUNT

Teachers should be rewarded for producing useful student outcomes, most notably, student learning gains, measured by value-added standards (i.e., improvement) rather than by levels of achievement at the end of a course. This method takes into account differences in where students start as well as differences in out-of-school factors that teachers cannot control. Looking at gains rather than levels of achievement also adjusts for the fear that performance pay will make all teachers want to teach the highest-achieving kids. When student improvement is rewarded, there may be financial benefits to teaching students who have the longest way to go—it may be easier to get a 25 percentile gain from someone starting at the 30th percentile than a 15 percentile gain at the 80th percentile. Providing incentives for teachers to make their students learn more may encourage teachers to do so, but, perhaps more importantly, it will compensate them for the extra effort required to improve the skills that will help their students achieve.

Another issue involves incorporating a school's nonacademic goals into a merit pay system. As we know, schools are expected to develop students' social behavior, career preparation, and positive attitudes. The most hackneyed of these has been enhanced student self-esteem, which sometimes is used as a reason for not failing students who deserve to fail. Let it simply be said that a great way to enhance a student's self-esteem is to have her achieve something academically. Holding teachers accountable for students' academic achievement gains is not inconsistent with students' accomplishing other things in school.

STANDARDS WITHOUT A STRAITJACKET

Despite the need to keep the focus on academic achievement, the Teacher Advancement Program acknowledges that research has identified pedagogical methods that help students learn, so it includes evaluation of classroom skills as part of its teacher compensation system. This allows teachers to be rewarded if they do everything right, even if their students' scores do not increase.

A key to this part of the performance evaluation, of course, is developing clear criteria for measuring those classroom skills. Multiple evaluations are conducted by certified evaluators. This helps overcome teachers' fears of bias and nepotism in their evaluations. Moreover, by including principals in the school-wide performance bonus system, they too will have an incentive to ensure that the most-effective teachers are rewarded.

Will such rubrics reduce teachers' opportunities to be creative in their teaching, to try new approaches, to teach as they like? Probably not, because the other test of teacher competence is better student outcomes. Thus the rubric gives credit for the skillful exercise of proven teaching methods, regardless of student outcomes, as well as rewards for student success, regardless of teaching method.

FIX THE WHOLE SYSTEM

The initial success of these performance- and responsibility-based compensation systems suggests that there are alternatives to the traditional "step-and-column" pay in which no one will earn less than in the traditional system. All teachers who reach certain goals get a bonus; but 50% of that bonus is awarded for teaching skills (a classroom-based evaluation) that are not tied to student outcomes and 50% for student achievement gains that are not part of the teaching skills evaluation. Furthermore, half of the student outcome bonus is based on school-wide gains and half on gains by an individual teacher's students.

In the 3 years that we have been using the TAP system, we have found that the school-wide rewards part of the bonus encourages teachers to work together to make everyone more effective. There is the possibility of the "free rider," of course: ineffective teachers reaping benefits from the achievements of their more-effective colleagues. Thus we expect part of the bonus to be based on individual teacher results. All bonuses must be significant or the extra work involved in implementing such a system will not be deemed worthwhile. That means, for instance, that a master teacher in Madison, Arizona, could get a bonus worth as much as 17% of his or her salary compared with the 2–3% bonus that current salary structures usually set as a cap for such expert teachers.

We have learned that performance pay alone is not enough. It must be supported by a strong, transparent, and fair evaluation system, and by a professional development plan that helps teachers to deal with revealed deficiencies and to improve. Teachers may resist evaluation not because they are unwilling to be held accountable, but instead because they fear they do not know what to do to improve student achievement. If professional growth opportunities are available to help teachers improve, the resistance to being evaluated fades.

A professional development program should use student data to identify areas where teachers need help. It should then have teachers help other teachers improve their teaching and student learning. This fosters collaboration and reduces the competitive attitudes that some fear are engendered by performance pay. Indeed, as long as my receiving a bonus does not preclude anyone else's getting one also, fears of competition and failing to collaborate go away. At schools using the TAP, striving for the annual performance awards improves teaching and enhances collegiality and morale.

One cautionary note: Most school districts are constantly trying to get more money for their teachers. So some will agree to a performance pay plan, but then transform it into an across-the-board salary hike: defining high performance as things everyone does (taking classes toward an advanced degree), setting standards so low that everyone gets the maximum award, or giving all teachers the same evaluation. Districts must guard against such behaviors.

CAN IT LAST?

Merit pay plans are expensive, especially if the performance awards are added to the salary schedule, so there are questions about whether the extra funds will continue to be available during the next economic downturn. What if the superintendent or school board turns over? Will results be demanded too quickly, and will the program be discontinued if test scores do not rise in a year or so?

Establishment of a dedicated funding source, such as an increase in the property tax levy or sales tax, could ensure sustainability. The former has been accomplished in Eagle County, Colorado, and the latter has the potential to support performance pay in the state of Arizona, where voters passed a law in 2000 to raise the sales tax by $0.006 and dedicated 40% of the proceeds to performance pay. In fact, most districts in Arizona ended up defining performance pay in ways that gave all teachers the same increases (for example, by allowing more course credits to fill the requirements for meritorious work). The district using the TAP was one of the few that actually used the money for real performance pay. The bottom line, though, is that support and advocacy by teachers is key to sustainability.

Although many teachers initially view performance pay and accountability as contentious issues in reform, absolute levels of acceptance for all the principles embodied in the TAP are high. Since the inception of the TAP, surveys of teachers' attitudes toward the elements of the program show that collegiality and teachers' satisfaction have remained strong in the schools using the TAP. This finding refutes many who argue that pay for performance leads to increased competition and divisiveness. These attitudinal results reflect the holistic approach of the TAP, which combines an accountability system having clear rewards and a professional development system to support all teachers (veteran and novice) in improving their classroom instruction.

Another important way to ensure sustainability is to show that the program is working. There is always the fear that results will be demanded too soon, and then the program will be discontinued if test scores do not rise in a year or so. We now have 3 years of results from TAP schools in Arizona and 2 years from TAP schools in South Carolina. We compared 25 year-to-year changes in student achievement in TAP schools to control schools. In 17 of these cases, or 68% of the time, the TAP schools outperformed their controls. This compares favorably with the results of a RAND evaluation of schools that have initiated other comprehensive school reform programs. RAND concluded that 50% of the schools with these reforms outperformed the control schools in math and 47% outperformed the control in reading, although these schools had been operating for a substantially longer period of time than the schools using the TAP. One important anecdotal explanation for the success of the TAP is that teachers in schools using the program improve significantly because their performance evaluations are related directly to TAP teaching rubrics.

Any pay-for-performance plan in K–12 education will succeed only if teachers buy into it from the start, if it is fair, and if it is embedded in a systemic reform that supports all aspects of performance reward, especially those that encourage teachers to become better at their craft. Such a pay plan will be revolutionary, but will not become obsolete in any sense of the word.

CHAPTER 7

THE UNIFORM SALARY SCHEDULE

Brad Jupp

For at least 2 and a half decades, political leaders and opinion makers have been telling teachers and union leaders like me that it is high time to move away from the single salary schedule. For a long time it was easy for us to dismiss those calls for change. This was partly because as a profession we are more remote from the policy debate than we should be, but it is also because we believed that many of those engaging in the debate were ax grinders, more interested in dismantling public education as an enterprise than improving it.

Recently, though, with more voices joining the choir calling for change, it has become difficult to write off the differentiated pay advocates. The 1996 report of the National Commission on Teaching and America's Future, "What Matters Most," was a wake-up call. Here was a report that placed the highest value on the teacher, even as it recommended "develop[ing] a career continuum and compensation systems that reward

Improving Student Achievement: Reforms that Work, 169–174
Copyright © 2005 by Information Age Publishing
All rights of reproduction in any form reserved.

Reprinted with permission from *Education Next,* a publication of the Hoover Institute, Stanford University. *Education Next* Vol. 5, No.1 (Winter 2005), 10-12.

knowledge and skill." Since then, other important pro-teacher groups, like the Progressive Policy Institute, Public Agenda, and the Teaching Commission, have taken even stronger positions. In his paper "Better Pay for Better Teaching," Bryan Hassel, who is a researcher for the Progressive Policy Institute, raises the stakes by saying, "In addition to better pay, we must move toward a better pay system. We should reward teachers not just for experience, but for their skills, knowledge and, ultimately, the performance they bring into their classrooms."

Less obvious was the pressure from within the ranks of our profession. With the exception of Public Agenda's report, "Stand by Me," I have found little research on teachers' perceptions of alternative compensation. In Denver, however, my union, the Denver Classroom Teachers Association, which represents approximately 4,500 teachers, and independent researchers commissioned jointly by the union and the Denver Public Schools, developed an extensive body of perceptual data that showed teachers as open-minded to changes in the ways they are paid.

SURPRISING DATA FROM TEACHERS

Though Denver had a typical salary schedule (see Figure 7.1) our data overthrew many of the preconceived notions held by teacher unions, school administrators, policy leaders, and opinion makers about how teachers perceive compensation systems. Since 1998 our union has asked its members what they thought about incentives for "teaching at schools with the highest percentage of high-need students." By 2003, when the last available survey was conducted, the number of people favoring these incentives had reached 89%. The percentage of teachers who favor incentives for "teaching in content areas of short supply" is only slightly less, at 82%.

The union has also asked its members, "What percentage of your pay should be based on accurately measured student growth data?" Respondents were given multiple-choice options of none, 1 to 5%, 5 to 10%, 10 to 25%, and 25 to 50%. In 2002 and 2003 no single choice received more than half of the responses, but the fact that fewer than half of the teachers surveyed selected the first choice, none, is remarkable; it means that for 2 years' running more than half of the union members surveyed believe that some portion of their pay should be based on accurately measured student growth.

In fact, Denver teachers have shown surprising open-mindedness about merit pay programs. The Denver Public Schools, with the collaboration of the teacher union, launched a Pay for Performance pilot program in 1999 and, when it ended in 2003, started a more comprehensive

Denver's Salary Schedule (Figure 1)

With relatively low starting salaries and guaranteed raises over time, the current Denver Public Schools salary schedule is typical of compensation schemes for teachers. Each step represents a year of teaching.

	B.A.	M.A.	DOCTORATE
New Hire	$31,320	$31,779	
Step 1	$32,971	$33,454	$39,169
Step 2	$33,073	$33,697	$40,903
Step 3	$33,225	$35,101	$42,642
Step 4	$33,480	$36,503	$44,377
Step 5	$33,785	$38,053	$46,251
Step 6	$33,988	$39,671	$48,219
Step 7	$35,421	$41,337	$50,290
Step 8	$36,912	$43,087	$52,449
Step 9	$38,456	$44,924	$54,702
Step 10	$40,092	$46,860	$57,057
Step 11	$41,784	$48,843	$59,521
Step 12	$43,566	$50,944	$62,082
Step 13	$45,546	$53,401	$64,919

SOURCE: Denver Public Schools

Figure 7.1

Professional Compensation System for Teachers (ProComp). Our independent researchers discovered a surprising amount of support for merit pay by teachers in both programs.

The hallmark of the Pay for Performance pilot was paying teachers $1,500 bonuses for meeting measurable objectives set collaboratively with their principals and based on the academic growth of the students they taught. When asked in the spring of 2003, just as the pilot program was ending, to rate whether setting measurable objectives for bonuses of up to $1,500 had an impact on "cooperation among teachers," 53.2% of the participating teachers said the impact was positive; only 2% said the impact was negative. While this positive response is certainly dependent on the special nature of the objective-setting process in Denver—a process in which teachers collaborated directly with their principals to set goals based on individually measured baselines for the students they taught, in the subject matter they taught—this response still flies in the face of preconceptions that teachers fear pay for performance based on student growth because it will harm collegial relations.

Even more surprising were the results that came from phone polls conducted in January and March of 2003 asking teachers their opinions on ProComp just before the vote to adopt the new program. When we ran demographic cross-tabulations of the results, we found that the teachers most likely to ratify ProComp were male secondary teachers with 13 or more years of service in Denver Public Schools. Though perhaps influenced by the special circumstances ProComp created—it lifted a cap on annual salary increases that, due to our single salary schedule, became effective following the 13th year of service—the results refuted the stereotype of the change-averse senior teacher.

PUTTERING TOWARD REFORM

The common perception that current salary scales are set in stone also overstates the case—at least with respect to the Denver metro area. The salary scales in each of the nearby districts we examined displayed evidence of gradual tinkering in response to political pressure. I have not found rigorous national research on this subject, but comparisons of metro Denver salary schedules conducted during the development of ProComp found, according to independent researcher Douglas Rose, that all the public school districts routinely "showed strong hints of incremental decision making." When experienced teachers, for instance, want additional salary increases, steps are added at the top. And boards of education want to compete in the marketplace for entry-level teachers, so early sections of the salary schedule are artificially inflated. Lower rates of pay are also established for probationary teachers or teachers with emergency licenses. Some districts in our area have even made nominal efforts at reform. Denver has market incentives for teachers of English Language Acquisition. Another district, Jefferson County, experimented for a couple of years with a program granting rewards to teachers for completing approved projects.

For all of the changes that have been slapped onto the existing schedules, however, it is safe to say they amount to nothing more than accommodations to internal and external pressures, small alterations that accomplish little or nothing in the work lives of teachers or the learning of students. These are not the radical new systems called for by the

National Commission for Teaching, the Teaching Commission, Public Agenda, or the Progressive Policy Institute.

WHAT THE MILE-HIGH CITY DID

In Denver, we developed ProComp to take our teachers further down the road toward a new form of thinking about compensation (see Figure 7.2). Compared to the system that it replaces, ProComp is a comprehensive approach to merit pay:

- It ties teachers' pay directly to professional accomplishments, including demonstrated knowledge and skills, as well as to student academic growth;

Merit and Battle Pay in Denver (Figure 2)

Denver teachers hired before 2006 have a choice between the traditional salary schedule and this four-dimensional merit pay system. Teachers hired after January 1, 2006, will automatically enter the new system.

Learning Gains
- Teachers who exceed expectations for student growth as measured by a statewide Colorado test will receive a sustainable 3% raise.
- All teachers will set two student growth objectives with the help of their supervisors. Teachers who meet both objectives will receive a 1% raise; those who meet one objective receive a 1% bonus.
- Teachers at schools identified as distinguished will receive a 2% bonus.

Evaluation
- Teachers found to be unsatisfactory will have their salary increase delayed for a minimum of one year.
- Probationary teachers will be evaluated every year in their first three years of service and will receive a 1% raise if they are judged to be satisfactory.
- Non-probationary teachers will be evaluated every three years, and will receive a raise of 3% if they are deemed satisfactory.

Battle Pay
- Teachers working in assignments identified as hard-to-staff and in schools termed hard-to-serve will receive a 3% bonus.

Credentials
- Teachers with active licenses from the National Board for Professional Teaching Standards (NBPTS) will be awarded a salary increase of 9%.
- Teachers who complete one Professional Development Unit (PDU) in their concentration will receive a 2% raise.
- Teachers who complete an advanced degree relevant to their assignment will receive a 9% raise.

SOURCES: Denver Public Schools and Denver Classroom Teachers Association

Figure 7.2

- Salary incentives are also provided for work in hard-to-staff assignments and hard-to-serve schools;
- A "menu" of extra earning opportunities, available to the entire work force, is spelled out, as are bonuses available to specific job categories;
- Teachers are eligible for every incentive earned—there is no cap on such earnings. A special-education teacher, for instance, teaching in an English Language Acquisition assignment and working in a school with the highest level of students receiving free and reduced-price lunch, would receive three bonuses, one for each of three eligible areas.

We also designed the system so it could be sustained across education careers. Using a financial analyst, we developed a 50-year model so that teachers could count on career earning expectations and not just pick up an extra bonus or two now and then. At the same time we built a system around a commitment to change. ProComp is grounded in a 9-year collective bargaining agreement, instead of the normal 1- to 3-year cycle. This should ensure that it is not a policy du jour, but lasts long enough to establish and prove itself. And we tied the system to larger district goals in order to provide clear educational incentives while keeping pressure on the bureaucracy to both perform and improve.

ProComp has its limits—it is rooted in compromise; the timeline for implementation is slowed by the need to build district financial and instructional capacity; it does not raise entry pay and provides relatively slow growth in annual earnings; many incentives are too small to really meet demands of the market—but I believe it points in some important new directions.

For people impatient to see the single salary schedule get out of the way, ProComp is not ambitious enough. In the final analysis, I think they are correct. ProComp is not an educational "silver bullet" or even a comprehensive solution to the unsolved problem of how to build a new form of teachers' pay.

We recognize, however, that we are in an exceptional moment, one where the single salary schedule can no longer support the pressures placed on it by the expectations of a twenty-first-century public education system. Fortunately, Denver teachers recognized those new realities. On March 19, 2004, the proposal was ratified by a decisive margin (59% to 41%) of union members, with 2,700 of the union's 3,200 voters—well over half of the district's 4,500 teachers—casting votes.

We look forward now to testing what we have developed. We want to use the momentum for change to improve both the teaching profession and the schools where our teachers work.

CHAPTER 8

TEACHER QUALITY, TEACHER PAY

Frederick M. Hess

A rare point of agreement in the debates about how to improve American schooling is that we need better teachers. Simply put, today's teaching force is not equal to the challenge of the new century. The way in which we compensate and manage this force, the legacy of a time when talented women lacked other options and would teach in one school for decades, serves to dissuade talented candidates while rewarding and insulating ineffective teachers. It is time for straight talk on teacher compensation and sensible steps to reform the way teachers are paid and managed.

Even veteran teachers and teacher educators have concluded, as Vivian Troen and Katherine C. Boles write in *Who's Teaching Your Children?* (2003), "The number of good classroom teachers, and therefore the quality of teaching itself, is in perilous decline and will continue to worsen." Academically stronger students tend to shun the teaching profession. Undergraduate education majors typically have lower sat and act scores

Improving Student Achievement: Reforms that Work, 175–189
Copyright © 2005 by Information Age Publishing
All rights of reproduction in any form reserved.

Reprinted with permission from *Policy Review,* a publication of the Hoover Institute, Stanford University.

than other students, and those teachers who have the lowest scores are the most likely to remain in the profession. The lower the quality of the undergraduate institution a person attends, the more likely he or she is to wind up in the teaching profession. From 1982 to 2000, the percentage of teachers who had earned a master's degree in their subject area fell from 17% to 5%. Professional licensing exams are so simple and the standards for passage so low that even the left-leaning Education Trust concluded they exclude only the "weakest of the weak" from classrooms. While none of these data points alone is damning, together they paint a troubling picture.

Left and right have heralded the need to resolve the teacher quality challenge and meet the federal mandate, legislated in No Child Left Behind, that every child have a "highly qualified" teacher by 2006. Reformers of all stripes recognize that teacher compensation is a crucial element in hiring the teachers we need and steering them into the schools where they are needed most.

It is in deciding how to tackle the challenge that reformers split. Superintendents, education school professors, teachers unions, and professional associations are united in the conviction that the crucial step is the need to pay teachers more. Today, almost everyone "knows," in the words of *Washington Post* national columnist Richard Cohen, that "Teachers make lousy money." There's one problem with this analysis: It just isn't true.

TEACHERS AREN'T UNDERPAID

The case that teachers are underpaid is a weak one. Teacher pay is actually quite reasonable when considered in context. The average teacher salary in 2001 was $43,300, compared to the average full-time worker salary of $40,100 (see Nelson, Drown, & Gould, 2002). While a starting salary of $30,000 may seem shockingly low to some, it's actually higher than what many Ivy League graduates earn when starting in the policy world, advertising, or similar nontechnical jobs. According to the *Chronicle of Higher Education*, for example, those 2002 graduates of journalism and mass-communication programs who were able to land positions earned a median salary of $26,000 if they had a bachelor's degree and $32,000 if they had a master's.

Economist Richard Vedder has observed that the Bureau of Labor Statistics National Compensation Survey shows that teachers earn "more per hour than architects, civil engineers, mechanical engineers, statisticians, biological and life scientists, atmospheric and space scientists, registered nurses, physical therapists, university-level foreign-language teachers,

[and] librarians." In fact, the Bureau of Labor Statistics reported that the average pay per hour for all workers in the "professional specialty" category in 2001 was $27.49, while public secondary school teachers earned $30.48 and elementary teachers $30.52—or about 10% *more* than the typical professional.

How can this be? Don't we *know* that teachers are woefully underpaid? Let's consider the facts. Most Americans work about 47 weeks a year (with about 3 weeks of vacation and 2 weeks of assorted holidays). Teachers, on the other hand, work about 38 weeks a year (teaching for 180 days and working additional professional days). In other words, after accounting for vacation, most Americans work about 25% more than the typical teacher. This doesn't even factor in the fact that, according to the U.S. Department of Education, during 1999-2000 (the most recent year for which data are available) about 5.2% of teachers were absent on a given day—a rate much higher than the 1.7% absentee rate reported by the Bureau of Labor Statistics for all forms of managerial and professional employment, as economist Michael Podgursky has recently observed. The availability of substitute teachers makes teaching very different from professions like medicine, sales, law, or journalism where there is often no one to stand in for a worker in the event of an unscheduled absence. That translates into the average teacher missing an additional 9 days during each 180-day school year. So, technically, the truth is that the typical teacher works 36, not 38, weeks a year. While some teachers might prefer more money and less time off, this is a lifestyle choice that teachers make when choosing a career. Teaching, for instance, with its summer breaks, regular schedule, and lack of travel, is particularly family-friendly.

Public educators also receive generous benefits, including "defined-benefit" pensions that do not require any contribution from the teacher. A career teacher, without ever having to contribute a nickel, can normally retire at age 55 and receive close to 70% of his or her salary for life. There are hundreds of thousands of retired teachers drawing annual pensions of $40,000 or more—many young enough to begin second careers. About half of teachers also pay nothing for single medical coverage, compared to just one quarter of private-sector professional and technical workers. Public school teachers receive benefit packages worth about 26% of their salaries whereas the typical private-sector workers' package is worth 17% of theirs.

Teacher advocates protest that none of these considerations factor in the long hours that teachers put in at home. After all, according to the National Center for Education Statistics, teachers claim to work slightly more than 49 hours a week during the school year, including 38 hours in school, 3 hours with students, and almost 9 hours at home. There are a couple of problems with claiming that this represents an extraordinary workload. First, when people are asked how hard they work, they tend to overestimate the actual figure, so that 49-hour figure is really more of an upper limit than an unbiased estimate. Second, the typical workday for nonprofessional workers often stretches from 8:30 to 5:30, or 45 hours a week, and is even longer for many professionals. It is not unusual for journalists, accountants, engineers, technology workers, or other college-educated professionals to routinely work 50 hours or more each week and to take work home at night or engage in professional travel. Of course, these work days often include a lunch break, and a worker who is at the office for 9 hours with an hour-long lunch is said to work a 40-hour week, not a 45-hour week.

On the other hand, it is apparent that teachers are counting every minute they are at school in reporting their workweek. Since teachers report working 38 hours a week at school during the school day and most district contracts specify that teachers' entire school day runs about 7 and a half hours—or about 37 to 38 hours a week—it is clear that the reported working day includes lunch breaks and preparation periods. If teachers use much of their lunch break and preparation period to relax, eat lunch, and socialize—which is the norm in my experience as it is in almost any line of work—they are actually teaching, planning, and grading about 6 and a half hours a day in school, or about 33 hours a week. Accepting at face value teachers' self-reports about their workload at home and with students after school, the typical teacher is working about 45 hours a week, all told. This is perfectly respectable but hardly unusual.

While, on the whole, teachers are not underpaid, good teachers, those working in tough circumstances, and those with critical skills are often wildly underpaid. The flip side is that mediocre teachers are overpaid, sometimes substantially. In the past few years, the notion of the "$100,000 teacher" has come into vogue. In books like *The Two-Percent Solution* and *The $100,000 Teacher*, authors such as Matthew Miller and Brian Crosby have called for paying good teachers $100,000 or more. Miller and Crosby are right. If we are serious about attracting and retaining the energetic and talented practitioners we want, we need to pay our best, hardest-working teachers that kind of money. Overlooked in these discussions, however, is that a number of teachers already earn that kind of money. The most recent systematic data, collected 5 years ago by the U.S. Department of Education's 1999-2000 Schools and Staffing Survey, estimated that over 5,500 teachers were earning more than $100,000 a year. Between 1999 and 2004, teacher salaries have steadily increased to the point that one can reasonably estimate that today at least 15,000 to 20,000 teachers earn more than $100,000 a year for their teaching duties. In 2000-2001, for instance, the median teacher salary was above $70,000 in more than one third of New York school districts. This means that half of the teachers in those districts earned at least that much. In Scarsdale, New York, half of all teachers earned more than $91,000 during 2000–2001 (see Podgursky, 2004).

The problem is not the total amount paid to teachers but the fact that basing teacher pay on experience and credentials rather than performance means that pay isn't necessarily going to those teachers who deserve it. Highly paid teachers earn their salaries not because they are exceptional educators or have tackled tough assignments but because they have accumulated seniority in wealthy school systems where pay is based on longevity. Providing raises in such a system is enormously expensive because so much of the spending is soaked up by the undeserving.

Some experts urge us to pay teachers more but simultaneously argue that money doesn't really motivate teachers. Scholars like Harvard University professor Susan Moore Johnson point out that private school teachers earn less than public school teachers but are generally happier because staff morale is high at their school, they feel valued, and they enjoy parental support. Of course, this is true. It should not, however, distract us from the need to fix a broken compensation system (see Kelley, Odden, Milanowski, & Heneman, 2000). While money may not be the only way to attract the teachers we need, it is a useful tool and one we can readily wield.

WHEN EQUAL ISN'T FAIR

Rafe Esquith, 49, is a bearded 20-year veteran who teaches fifth grade at Hobart Boulevard Elementary, a school in the Los Angeles Public School system. He teaches his class of 32 from 6:30 a.m. until 5:00 p.m. and skips his 9-week vacation in order to meet with students. Esquith is able to offer the extended school day and school year because families choose to enroll in his class. Esquith teaches his charges algebra, gives a daily grammar test, has students reading adult novels by authors like Steinbeck and Dickens, and has the class perform Shakespeare regularly. In 2002, his students read at the 88th percentile while the school's fifth-graders overall scored at the 42nd percentile (Mathews, 2003.) The suggestion that Esquith ought to earn the same salary as any other 20-year veteran is a farce. He works longer, harder, and more effectively than most of his colleagues. Simple fairness demands that he be paid more, far more, than the typical fifth-grade Los Angeles teacher.

Equal pay and equal treatment are fair only if individuals are equal in their effort and their contribution. If they are not working equally hard or confronting similar challenges, then treating them equally is manifestly *unfair*—and that's what we do today. The status quo response is offered by union officials such as Paul J. Phillips, president of the Quincy Education Association in Massachusetts. "Teachers almost never treat salary as a competitive concept," Phillips recently argued in *Education Week*, and they are not bothered "when an ineffectual teacher earns the same salary as ... high-quality teachers." Our existing compensation system encourages career-squatting by veteran teachers tired of their labors, discourages talented young college graduates from entering the profession, frustrates those educators who pour their weekends and summers into their work, and attracts candidates who are often less motivated than those who got away.

Union officials claim that it is nearly impossible to gauge teacher quality and that, even if the occasional principal can do so, principals in general cannot be trusted to treat teachers fairly. As an editorial in the National Education Association's *NEA Today* proclaimed, "Basing teacher pay on student performance is no answer—it's a thinly disguised assault on us. Every day, we educators do the best we can, often under horrific conditions, with the best of intentions. No single determining factor— least of all student achievement—should dictate who among us will be paid more than others." Howard Nelson, a senior researcher at the American Federation of Teachers, the nation's second-largest teachers union, has declared that allowing principals to evaluate teachers "is one of the most irritating, unfair, inaccurate things that could happen."

A very different line, however, was adopted by the man who founded the AFT, Al Shanker. "I'm worried about how to prevent the pay-for-performance issue from becoming dysfunctional, dog-eat-dog," Shanker once said. "But I'm sure that we can develop such a system and that it would be pretty good. Its flaws would be very small compared to what we have now or compared to what you would have without such a system" (as quoted in Haycock, 2003). Classroom teachers generally agree. A 2003 Public Agenda survey found that 78% of teachers agreed that "in [my] building, it is easy to spot who the truly great teachers are," and 72% agreed that "most teachers in [my] building could pretty much agree on who the truly great teachers are." Even in the world of higher education, where "hard" evidence on performance is less prevalent than in K-12 schooling, faculty raises are based in large part on how much faculty members are seen to contribute as scholars, teachers, and community members.

Sensible reform requires, of course, that district and school leaders be held accountable for performance so that they will have self-interested reasons to identify and protect good teachers. Meanwhile, the research suggests that principals who do not have to abide by certification requirements are especially likely to hire and reward teachers who attended high-quality colleges, who possess strong math or science training, or who put in more instructional hours (see Hoxby, 2001). For all its imperfections, performance-based accountability gives principals a better gauge of employee performance than is available in professions like architecture, law, accounting, or engineering, where evaluations are rendered on an annual basis.

It would be a mistake, however, to rely simply on assessments of student performance to gauge teacher quality. There's more to schooling than standardized test results. Tests are imperfect and incomplete measures of learning, and it's crucial to remember that a teacher can contribute to student learning in a slew of ways that may not show up on a given assessment. A teacher may mentor other teachers or help to improve the effectiveness of colleagues in other ways. She may counsel troubled students, help maintain school discipline, remediate students on material that will not be tested, and so on. We should not reduce the definition of teaching excellence in this way, yet that's a mistake that some reformers risk in their eager rush to embrace performance-based compensation.

It is unfortunately true that apologists have used the imperfections of test-based accountability to excuse ineffectiveness and deny that teachers ought to be held accountable. However, there's nothing to be gained—and much to be lost—by going overboard in response. Rather than trying to judge teachers with mechanical precision, we ought to develop sensible instruments for evaluation and permit managers to make reasoned decisions. This is an area where public- and private-sector firms have made enormous progress in the past 15 years and where a wealth of experience is readily available from fields like journalism, consulting, and civil service reform.

Beyond teacher effectiveness, however it is measured, there are several other considerations that districts should acknowledge and compensate: the relative challenges an educator faces, the desirability of the work environment, and the relative scarcity of the teacher's skills. Educators who take on low-achieving or unpopular schools may find it exceptionally difficult to produce performance gains or to attract students. Compensation and evaluations should reflect such disparities as well as the fact that it's often harder and simply less enjoyable to teach low achievers in a gritty, crowded school than to instruct more advanced students in a well-lit, spacious, comfortable school. For instance, researchers have estimated that Texas school districts could retain teachers with 3 to 5 years' teaching experience in low-achieving, high-minority schools at the same rate as in suburban schools if pay were boosted by about 26% (Hanushek, Kain, & Rivkin, 2004). Differential pay need not rely on guesswork but can be based on this kind of deliberate analysis.

Similarly, it is time to end the fiction that schools should pay English, social studies, and physical education teachers the same amount that they pay science or math teachers. After all, there are many more competent candidates for English and social studies jobs than for math or science positions. School administrators report that it was "very difficult" to fill elementary teaching positions less than 6% of the time but "very difficult" to fill secondary math or physical science positions more than 30% of the time (Podgursky, 2002).

SALARIES

Today, just 5.5% of traditional public school districts report using pay incentives such as cash bonuses, salary increases, or additional salary steps to reward excellent teaching. Only five states offer retention bonuses to keep teachers in high-need schools. Meanwhile, the majority of teachers back differential pay. The 2003 Public Agenda Survey of teachers found that 70% supported giving extra pay to teachers in "tough neighborhoods with low performing schools," 67% supported it for "teachers who consistently work harder ... than other teachers," and 62% supported it for teachers "who consistently receive outstanding evaluations from their principals." School districts frequently provide piecemeal stipends for coaching or teaching English as a second language, yet they don't reward those teachers who mentor colleagues, critique lesson plans, or otherwise work to make the school successful.

Few things are more frustrating for high performers than to be treated exactly like their less committed peers. Today, the profession repels too many energetic practitioners by expecting teachers to willingly sacrifice professional growth, advancement, and reward.

The steps that need to be taken are straightforward. Teachers' compensation should be based on performance rather than simply on experience and credentials. Districts determine salaries using a negotiated "grid" in which pay is strictly a function of the years a teacher has taught in the district and the number of degrees or credits the teacher has accumulated. A school district will pay all teachers who have a bachelor's degree and 5 years' local teaching experience one amount and all who have a master's degree and 12 years local experience another amount — regardless of the quality of their work (see Hassel, 2002).

Paying for performance and for critical skills does more than deliver rewards to the most deserving. When done sensibly, it sends a vital message about the organization's priorities and values. Russell Miller, a principal with Mercer Human Resource Consulting, has bluntly observed that for organizations that fail to reward excellence, "The biggest risk is mediocrity. Your stars are going to look elsewhere, and your average and below-average employees will say 'I'm going to stick around.'" Managers require the leeway to pay employees in accord with the difficulty of their jobs, the scarcity of their skills, and their performance.

Just as traditional companies structure compensation to keep the pay of those doing similar work within a general range, a sensible system would utilize broad "pay bands" of the kind long utilized in the private sector and favored in civil service reform. These proposals are hardly radical. In the past couple years, the federal Department of Homeland Security and the 750,000 civilians working for the Defense Department have been shifted to a pay system that uses five career groups and four pay levels—rather than the bureaucratic 15-grade general schedule long used by most of the federal government. Dozens of studies of test projects involving more than 30,000 Defense Department employees have found that the system improved performance and morale while retaining essential safeguards.

In the case of the Defense Department, the safeguards have included the creation of an independent Merit Systems Protection Board through which employees can seek a review of decisions. Systematic performance data and sophisticated information technology can prove invaluable in equipping managers to make good decisions and in flagging problematic management decisions. For instance, enterprise compensation management software produced by companies such as Kadiri Inc., Workscape Inc., and Advanced Information Management Inc. uses "disparate impact analysis" to determine whether any minority groups are being treated unfairly or whether the compensation for any individual is out of line. These kinds of checks and balances can help protect educators from managerial malfeasance.

Such a system in a district might specify that teachers with 7 to 10 years of experience would earn between $40,000 and $80,000, depending on the difficulty of their assignments, the demand for their skills, and their performance. If districts were paying $80,000 to 33-year-old math teachers who were doing an effective job in troubled schools, and recapturing the cost by paying $40,000 to history or English teachers in comfortable schools, we would find it miraculously easier to find and keep the teachers we need.

Districts like Charlotte, Denver, Cincinnati, Dallas, and states like Kentucky, North Carolina, and Arizona are gingerly experimenting with "school-based performance awards" and more flexible pay systems that reward individual teachers for excellence on a number of measures. These efforts to modify teacher compensation have typically been tepid, tacking small bonuses onto the existing salary system. For instance, states and districts devise plans to provide a bonus of $1,000 or $2,000 to teachers who are already making $35,000 or $50,000 a year. Bonuses that are one-time awards of 3% or 4% of annual salary are unlikely to have much impact (see Hanushek, 1994).[1] The president of the Wilson Group consultants, a firm specializing in performance-based reward systems, has derided merit increases of 4% as "a joke.... The after-tax difference [in pay] is a Starbucks coffee." Robert Heneman, a professor of business management and human resources at Ohio State University, has observed that the "research shows that you need [a] seven percent or eight percent [compensation increase] just to catch anybody's attention."

Proposals to reform teacher pay routinely suffer from several flaws, all readily remediable. First, the dollar amounts usually add up to a small percentage of teacher pay and are not linked to broader professional incentives. Second, these rewards are often structured in ways that limit the ability of individuals to influence their chances of winning. Many of the rewards are granted on a school-wide basis, which, though a nice sentiment, means that even a massive effort on the part of an individual teacher has only a tiny impact on whether she will win the bonus. Such systems encourage everyone to work more or less as they always have while hoping the others will shoulder the burden. Group bonuses are a healthy way to build cohesion when mounted atop systems that already recognize and reward individual effort, but are not by themselves effective at motivating individuals. Third, rewards are frequently given for acquiring certificates, like the one issued by the National Board for Professional Teaching Standards, rather than one's classroom performance. Finally, especially when rewards amount to $10,000 or more, they are often one-shot deals that feel like a lucky lottery ticket and which teachers expect to pocket about as frequently. It is far better to provide more moderate incentives that committed employees can realistically expect to claim year after year.

PENSIONS

Public school "defined benefit" retirement plans were designed for industrial-era jobs in which employees did not move or change careers. They reflect a mindset that assumes personnel should be strapped into a district for 20 or more years. These plans provide a formula-driven retirement benefit that disproportionately rewards educators who stay in place for 15 or 20 years at the expense of those who depart sooner. Most states mandate that educators stay in the retirement plan for 6 to 10 years before they become "vested" and can collect even a portion of their benefits. Matthew Lathrop of the American Legislative Exchange Council has noted, "The guaranteed benefit is only good for those who spend a substantial part of their career with one employer. That's an enormous drawback in today's economy, when even public employees are less likely to stick with a single employer."

This strategy made a certain sense when teaching was a profession for married women without other career choices, but it's a handicap in today's world where workers routinely switch jobs every few years. Dramatic rewards are provided for those who hang on for 25 years at the expense of those who don't stick around that long. As of 1998, for example, 35% of major teacher retirement systems required that teachers remain for at least 10 years before collecting any benefits at all. In other states, teachers are typically required to remain in place for 5 or 6 years before becoming eligible for any benefits.

With its emphasis on time served, the defined benefit model is hostile to entrepreneurs, discourages risk-taking, and is a better fit for a factory than for a knowledge-based profession. Existing pension policies reduce worker flexibility and leave teachers hesitant to consider positions in other districts, charter schools, or new start-ups. The result fosters excessive caution and helps stifle creative thinking. A commonsense approach would provide benefits in a more flexible fashion and one less conditioned on long service. The most important step to take is shifting schools from traditional pensions to "defined-contribution" arrangements, such as 401(k) or 403(b) plans. Such a step would reduce the number of veteran teachers who feel compelled to put in their time in order to collect a full pension, ease exit from and reentry into the profession, give teachers more geographic flexibility, and make teaching more attractive both for talented 20-somethings and for mid-career job-changers. Reducing the obligation to fund pensions would permit districts to pay employees higher salaries in the here and now. Alternatively, districts could provide a generous contribution on behalf of each employee, perhaps 5% or 10% of salary, to an account that is readily portable if the worker takes a new job.

Such a shift in retirement benefits would reflect broader changes in American life. In 1980, according to Labor Department statistics, just 20% of employers offered the more flexible defined-contribution plans; by 1998, more than 40% did. Meanwhile, the percentage offering defined-benefit plans declined during that same period from 39% to 22%. In other words, most employers are responding to a new and more mobile world by making it easier for workers to enter or exit their work forces without having to put retirement benefits at risk.

TENURE AND ACCOUNTABILITY

Currently, it is virtually impossible to fire poor teachers, especially after they serve 2 to 3 probationary years and become tenured. In 2002, the Los Angeles Board of Education encountered fierce resistance when it tried to remove about 400 of the 35,000 teachers in a chronically low-achieving district. In the end, the board was able to remove only three, and two of the three removals were overturned on appeal. New York City's troubled school system, with over 72,000 teachers, sought to dismiss only three over a 2-year period. In a survey, more than 80% of superintendents and principals reported that the local union fights to "protect teachers who really should be out of the classroom."

Nationally, public school districts report dismissing about one teacher a year for low performance. This amounts to a rate of well under 1%, compared to a rate of 4.9% in charter schools. Public school teachers have been caught sticking a child's head in a toilet, reading the newspaper while children gambled in the back of the room, and missing weeks or months of school at a stretch and yet kept their jobs (see Hess, 2002).

The notion of "tenure" originated in higher education, where it was intended primarily to secure scholarly inquiry by protecting scholars who pursued unpopular lines of research. Tenure has always been less obviously applicable to K-12 schools in which teachers are hired to provide instruction rather than to create new knowledge. Aside from that larger issue, however, higher education itself has spent the past 30 years struggling to reduce the percentage of tenured faculty. The percentage of full-time professors with tenure or on the "tenure track" fell by more than 30% from 1975 to 1995, according to the *Chronicle of Higher Education*, while the percentage working on short-term contracts increased by 50% during that period. From 1970 to 1998, part-time faculty grew from 22% to 42% of all instructors nationwide. Colleges and universities have taken these steps due to concerns about staffing inflexibility, lost efficiencies, and employee motivation.

Unable to remove inept or lethargic faculty, principals and superintendents learn simply to work around them. In one troubled district after another, poor teachers receive good evaluations from principals eager to pass them along. Teachers themselves recognize how hard it is to purge their ineffective peers, with 36% reporting that "between tenure and the documentation requirements, it's too hard for administrators to remove any but the very worst teachers" and just 14% reporting that inability to remove bad teachers is not a problem.

Reluctance to terminate weak educators is embedded in collective bargaining agreements and accepted by many administrators as a normal part of doing business. One high-ranking Texas district official wryly explained what it takes to fire a teacher in that nonunion state: "Firing incompetent teachers for poor performance or for engaging in misconduct is as time consuming and demanding as trying to convict someone of a crime.... Are we saying it can't be done? Of course not. What we are saying is that it requires almost 100% of a principal's time to *hope* to win a case to fire one bad teacher."

Even teachers agree that tenure protects teachers who should not be in the schools. Seventy-eight percent of teachers report that there are at least a few teachers in their school who "fail to do a good job and are simply going through the motions," while 58% say that tenure doesn't necessarily mean that teachers have worked hard or proven their ability. One New Jersey union representative confessed to the *Chronicle of Higher Education*, "I've gone in and defended teachers who shouldn't even be pumping gas." A Los Angeles union representative said, "If I'm representing them, it's impossible to get them out. It's impossible. Unless they commit a lewd act."

Especially telling is that apologist organizations like the National Commission on Teaching and America's Future can issue extensive reports on improving teacher quality, such as last year's *No Dream Denied: A Pledge to America's Children*, without ever addressing the need to remove ineffective practitioners. Private-sector managers regard purging low performers as a routine part of the job. In fact, widely admired firms such as General Electric make it a point to eliminate the least productive 10% of their work force every year. As former General Electric CEO Jack Welch has explained, "This is how great organizations are built. Year after year, differentiation raises the bar higher and higher and increases the overall caliber of the organization."

Accountability provides new safeguards for flexible firing. Measuring a teacher's value added helps flag ineffective teachers and protects good teachers from unfair treatment. Districts can use these measures as a way to monitor school management and detect individual principals who may behave irresponsibly. In an era when 78% of superintendents evaluate principals on their ability to judge and improve teacher quality, the case that teachers need to be insulated from cavalier management is an increasingly difficult one to make. Across America, employment is normally "at will," with workers free to quit any time and employers equally free to fire workers. That sensible standard should be the model for schooling.

COMMONSENSE REFORM

In an era marked by the No Child Left Behind "highly qualified teacher" mandate and the more prosaic challenge of finding the teachers we need on a day-to-day basis, simple truths have sometimes been drowned out by calls for more spending or fanciful new academic strategies. The critical first point is that, on average, teachers today are not underpaid. The problem is that good teachers and those tackling the important challenges are underpaid—and we need to find ways to compensate them appropriately. Amidst heated concerns that No Child Left Behind is underfunded and that schools lack the resources they need, the simple truth is that fixing the way we pay and retain teachers is the crucial first step in making schools work.

Moving to a more flexible system of rewarding and managing teachers is part and parcel of the larger national effort to move toward schools guided by accountability and competition. In accountable schools, leaders need the flexibility to monitor and reward personnel in sensible ways and to identify and assist or remove ineffective teachers.

It is in the most troubled systems that commonsense work force reforms will have dramatic effects. In these schools, administrators have tremendous difficulty finding qualified teachers. It is in these districts—with their large numbers of long-term substitutes, burned-out veterans, and unqualified teachers—that new applicants will be welcome, that offering generous compensation for effective teachers or those with critical skills will have the largest impact, and that explicit pressure and individual-level incentives will make a huge difference.

Reforming the teaching force in this way will foster a more flexible, welcoming, rewarding, exciting, and performance-focused profession. A culture of competence will beckon and energize the kinds of adults we want in classrooms: impassioned, hard-working, effective teachers and communicators who know the content they are teaching.

NOTE

1. For instance, Palm Beach County offered $10,000 to veteran teachers who would transfer to low-performing schools, and fewer than 10 of the 90 targeted teachers moved. To be effective, inducements intended to get teachers to leave familiar, comfortable environments for low-performing schools need to be large, sustained, part of a coherent package, and augmented by reforms designed to replicate the focus and collegial culture of high-performing schools.

REFERENCES

Hanushek, E. A., Kain, J. F., & Rivkin, S. G. (2004, Winter). The revolving door. *Education Next, 1,* 77-28.

Hanushek, E., with Benson, C. S., Freeman, R. B., Jamison, D. T., Levin, H. M., Maynard, R. A., Murnane, R. J., Rivkin, S. G., Sabot, R. H., Solmon, L. C., Summers, A. A., Welch, F., & Wolfe, B. L. (1994). *Making schools work: Improv-*

ing performance and controlling costs. (Washington, DC: Brookings Institution Press.

Hassel, B. (2002). *Better pay for better teaching.* Washington, DC: Progressive Policy Institute.

Haycock, K. (2003, May). *The elephant in the living room.* Paper prepared for Brookings Papers on Education Conference, "The Teachers We Need," Washington, D.C.

Hess, F. M. (2002). *Revolution at the margins.* Washington, DC: Brookings Institution Press.

Hoxby, C. (2001, Spring). Changing the profession. *Education Matters,* pp. 57-63.

Kelley, C., Odden, A., Milanowski, A., & Heneman, H., III, (2000). The motivation effects of school-based performance awards. Philadelphia: Consortium for Policy Research in Education.

Mathews, J. (2003, October 14). Pursuing happiness, through hard work. *Washington Post,* p. A13.

Nelson, F. H., Drown, R., & Gould, J. C. (2002). *Survey & analysis of teacher salary trends 2001.* Washington, DC: American Federation of Teachers.

Podgursky, M. (2004). Improving academic performance in U.S. public schools: Why teacher licensing is (almost) irrelevant. In F. M. Hess, A. J. Rotherham, & C. B. Walsh (Eds.), *A qualified teacher in every classroom?* Cambridge, MA: Harvard Education Press.

Podgursky, M. (2002). *The single salary schedule for teachers in K–12 public schools.* Houston, TX: Center for Reform of School Systems.

Troen, V., & Boles, K. C. (2003). *Who's teaching your children?* New Haven, CT: Yale University Press.

PART V

NO CHILD LEFT BEHIND

CHAPTER 9

NO CHILD LEFT BEHIND

**Lewis C. Solmon, Richard Ingersoll, Ken James, Jay Mathews,
Nina S. Rees, and Susan Tave Zelman**

Lewis Solmon

A lot of the discussion in the last couple of days, whether it was Lowell
Milken's panel talking about school reform or the Teacher Quality Panel,
inevitably turned to No Child Left Behind. Quite frankly, even though I
hear so much discussion of this law, I think we need even more discussion
of some of the claims and counterclaims, charges and responses to the
charges. That being said, we are very privileged to have this group of people to discuss this very important law.

I would like to start off by throwing up very quickly a number of charts
to make a point. You saw a couple of them yesterday. We're teaching and
graduating more kids today than ever before, and some people are very
proud of that. Perhaps we should be proud, but if we're graduating kids
who can't read or do math, I think we have a little less to be proud of.

What I'm going to be talking about are achievement gaps. These are
really what No Child Left Behind wants to close. Sixty-nine percent of
fourth graders are not proficient in reading, and the figure for eighth
graders is 68% (Chart 9.1). That leads to the international gap, where we
rank average or lower than other industrialized countries on literacy. Let's
go to the math right now (Chart 9.2). You can see that we've got very high

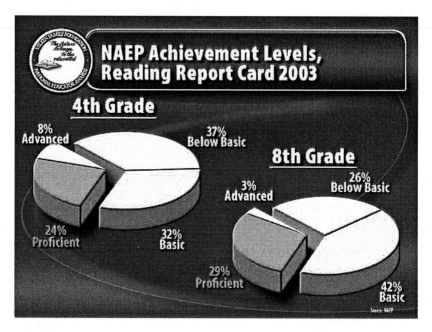

Chart 9.1

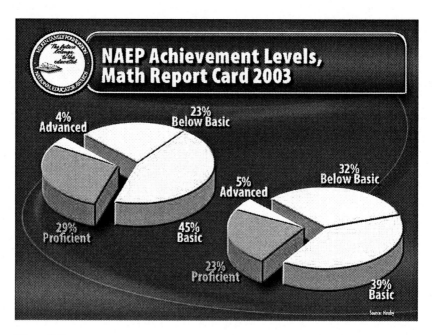

Chart 9.2

percentages at basic or below, as opposed to proficient or advanced. "Basic" means you can barely read, and "below basic" is really not acceptable at all.

Here is some evidence on the gap between ethnic groups (Chart 9.3). I would point out that we should not be too proud of even our White achievement. This is the percentage by race of kids below basic: 25% of Whites and 60% of Blacks in the fourth grade are below basic on the NAEP Reading Test. That's really horrible. The next chart shows that over the last 20 or 30 years, the gap between various ethnic groups has not narrowed substantially (Chart 9.4).

Let's go to the poverty gap or income gap. Looking at Chart 9.5. you can see that of those eligible for free and reduced lunch, the percent proficient in reading in the year 2000 was only 14%, as opposed to 41% of those not eligible for free and reduced lunch. The 45% in 2003 is nothing to write home about, either.

Progress is elusive among high-poverty students, as you can see (Chart 9.6). Fifty-two percent of high poverty eighth graders are below basic in math, while 43% percent are below basic in reading. There has been a slight improvement in math, but eighth graders are also showing a slight decline in reading. Then there's the urban gap (Chart 9.7). The national percentage of of fourth graders who are below basic is 38%, and there is a large increase in that number as you look at the District of Columbia which is at 69% or Los Angeles which is at 65%. One might say that by moving our conference from Los Angeles to Washington, D.C., we left the frying pan to get into the fire—as the top two cities, in terms of percentage of students below basic are Los Angeles and Washington, D.C. The gap in major cities is just startling. The percentage below basic is just startling in places like Los Angeles and the District of Columbia, and the same trend exists among eighth graders in reading (Chart 9.8).

The next chart shows the college readiness gap (Chart 9.9). The lighter bar is the graduation rate; the darker bar is the college-ready rate. "College readiness" means a student has to take a certain number of courses in high school, which colleges require for the acquisition of necessary skills, and has to be able to demonstrate basic literacy skills. That brings us back to the original point: If we are graduating people, they should be qualified to go on. However, they don't even have basic literacy skills, and that's pretty scary.

If we look at different randomly selected states, we can see the per-pupil expenditure differences (Chart 9.10). You can see expenditures in New Jersey and Connecticut are vastly different than in New Mexico and Mississippi. Also, the percent of Whites enrolled in these states, as shown in (Chart 9.11), again demonstrates significant differences.

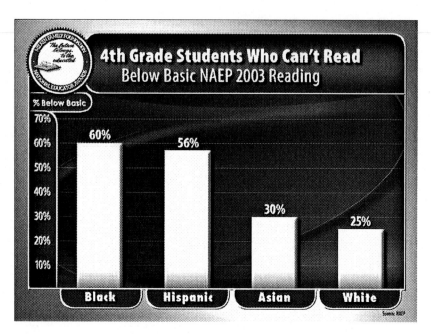

Chart 9.3

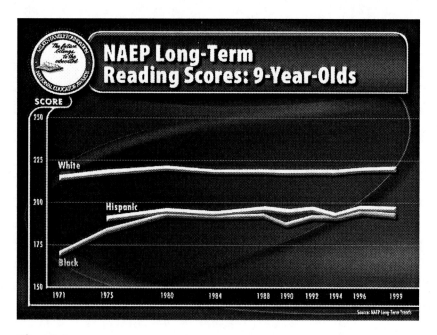

Chart 9.4

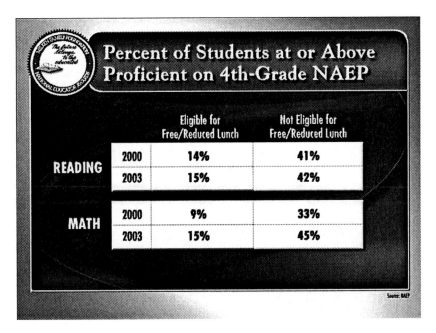

Chart 9.5

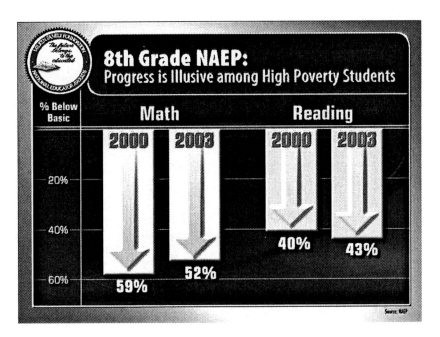

Chart 9.6

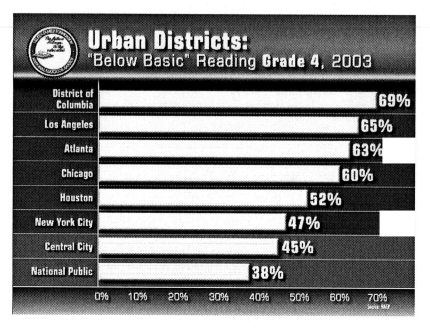

Chart 9.7

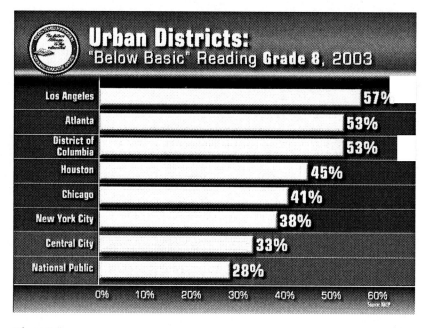

Chart 9.8

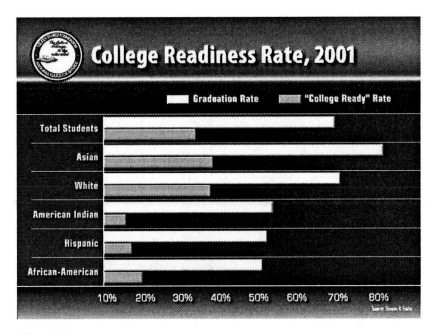

Chart 9.9

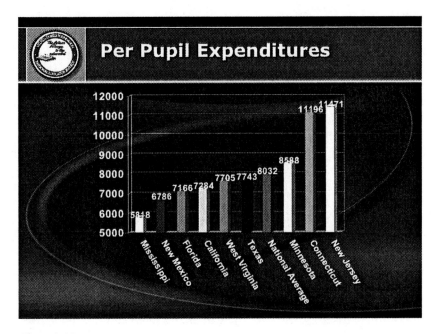

Chart 9.10

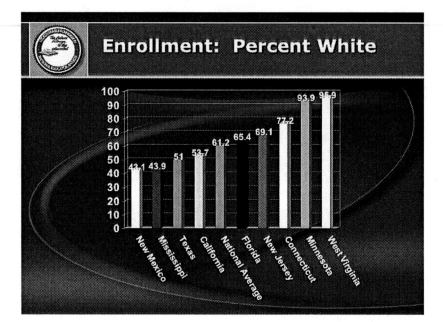

Chart 9.11

We looked at this group of states to see their fourth grade students' reading scores in 2003 (Chart 9.12). To give some perspective, every 10-point increase is roughly equivalent to one grade-level increase. For example, fourth graders in New Mexico are reading at 2.5 grade levels below fourth graders in Connecticut.

White eighth graders in West Virginia are reading at 1.7 grade levels below white eighth graders in New Jersey (see Charts 9.13, 9.14, 9.15, 9.16, 9.17, 9.18, 9.19, & 9.20). These slides show some significant differences by states in NAEP scores in math and reading, and by race. This makes me think of the fact that people are asking why the federal government has to get involved in worrying about student achievement and achievement gaps. Since we have left it to the states, there are dramatic differences in what has been achieved in reading and math. That may be an argument for looking at some national policy.

There are many ways to develop education policy. The simplest, albeit most ineffective way, is to give more education money to states and districts and let them do what's always been done, which is to make it as easy and enjoyable for members of the profession as you can. This approach will minimize protests, but nothing will change. No Child Left Behind, in my view, has taken the opposite approach by focusing on student achieve-

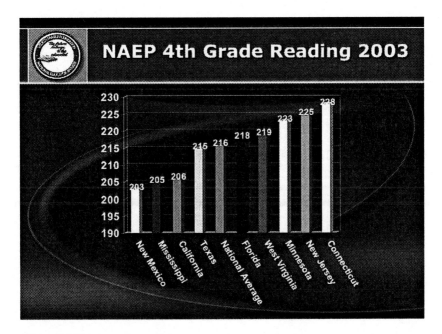

Chart 9.12

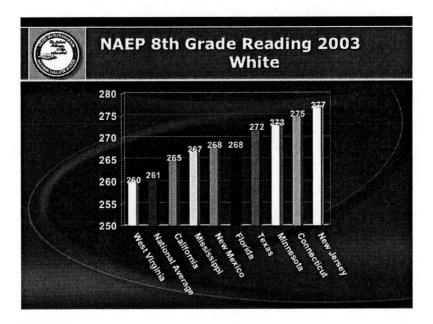

Chart 9.13

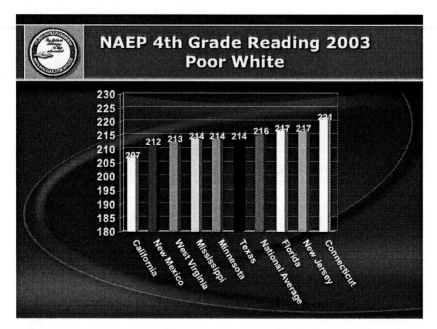

Chart 9.14

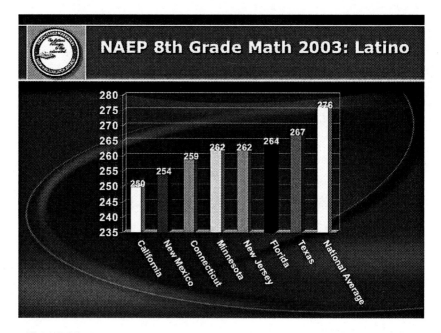

Chart 9.15

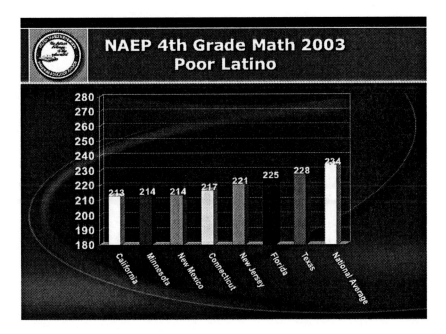

Chart 9.16

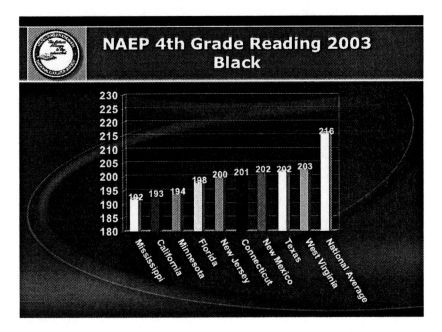

Chart 9.17

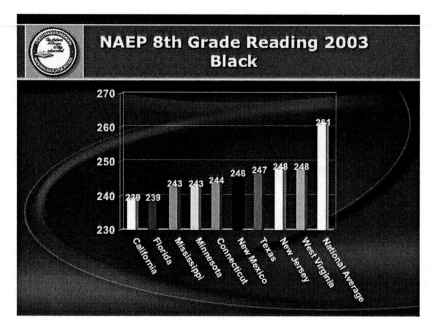

Chart 9.18

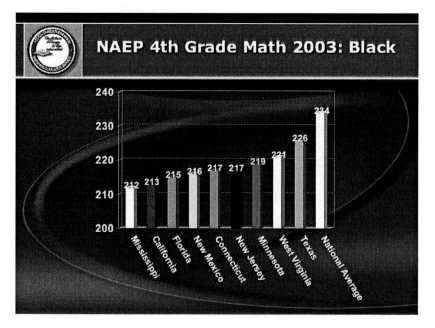

Chart 9.19

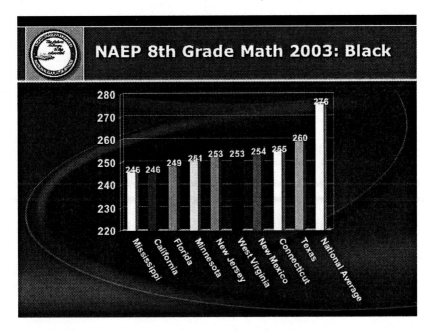

Chart 9.20

ment, insisting on standards, holding states, districts and schools account-able for teachers and students meeting these standards, providing resources to help meet the standards, and then having consequences for those who do not meet them (Chart 9.21).

Now, many teachers and teacher associations support the big ideas of No Child Left Behind, even if they quibble with some of the details. Inevitably, there will be protests from those who prefer the status quo. That might be a political liability, but it will also lead to student growth. By shifting the focus of reform from discourse to accountability with consequences and by insisting that subgroups (by ethnic group, poverty, special needs, etc.) all achieve and reach certain achievement levels, No Child Left Behind has incensed some observers of the education scene. When we add to that the impact of an election year, to the discomfort of educators being held accountable, there should be no surprise that criticism of No Child Left Behind has snowballed. This has become political. We heard Congressman Boehner say that he is walking arm-in-arm with members of the Democratic Party, and that's very encouraging. Although, when one reads the newspaper reports, it doesn't sound like that.

Today, we will hear from some practitioners, people who have been trying to apply No Child Left Behind in their districts or states; from some

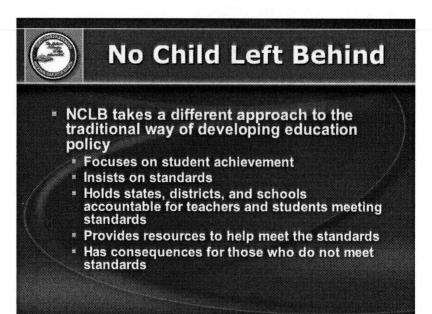

Chart 9.21

observers and researchers of the program or issues related to the program; and a representative of the Department of Education whose job is partially to make sure that No Child Left Behind gets implemented and implemented well. Our first speaker will be Susan Zelman, who is the superintendent of public instruction at the Ohio Department of Education. She has a very impressive resume, having been in Missouri and Massachusetts, having been a professor and done many interesting things. Next is Kenneth James, who has just recently assumed the position of director of education for the state of Arkansas. Several years ago, he was superintendent in Little Rock. He then moved to Lexington, Kentucky, and now is back as the director for the state of Arkansas.

Third, we will have Jay Mathews; many of you will know him from his columns in the *Washington Post*, where he's written for 33 years. He has a lot of accomplishments and awards, and is one of, if not the, preeminent education writers in America today. He will be followed by Richard Ingersoll, who has done some of the fundamental work underlying the ideas dealt with in No Child Left Behind and some of the ideas that stimulate our thinking in the Teacher Advancement Program. He will discuss some of what he has recently been studying. Finally, Nina Rees, who is deputy undersecretary for Innovation and Improvement in the U.S. Department of Education, will talk about her views on the progress of No Child Left Behind.

Susan Zelman

Thank you very much, Lew. First of all, I want to congratulate all the educators here because, clearly, these are the teachers that are leaving no child behind. So, thank you very much.

Second, I want to give you a little bit of a picture about Ohio. I also want to convey to you how the No Child Left Behind Act has really helped us in our educational agenda. The Milken motto is The Future Belongs to the Educated. We understand this motto only too well in Ohio. Ohio is the microcosm of the United States. One third of Ohio is in Appalachia, and we have eight large cities. We have both poor, rural areas and rich, rural areas. We have inner cities and suburbs. I personally always thought the song was wrong; if you can make it in Ohio, you can make it anywhere. Ohio is 40th in the nation in the percent of our population holding college degrees. We also understand that we have to reinvent our economy in Ohio. We call it the "third frontier," where education is integral to our new economic vision.

What we're hoping for in Ohio is that we'll have such great educational policy that we will create the global entrepreneurs of the future; that our students will be so smart they will be able to create jobs for the future in Ohio; that business will come here because we have the best, well-qualified workforce. Now, our theory of change is that we first should set high expectations for what we want our students to know and be able to do. I will tell you in terms of educational policy, when I came in 5 years ago, the first thing I did was try to listen and learn from our teachers. We had focus groups around the state with the governor. One of the things that our teachers told us was that they were teaching to the test, but they didn't know what was on the test.

One of the early things we did was to get a commission together, with a lot of educators on it. With the help of our teachers, we developed academic content standards, which spelled out what we wanted our students to know and be able to do, grade-by-grade. Then in the process of redesigning our assessment system, we created tests for accountability purposes, but also useful diagnostic tests. These will help teachers really figure out how to individualize instruction and make sure that nobody's surprised when a child gets to third grade and can't read or do mathematics.

We're putting that system in place. We also are working with teachers to develop model curriculum, which is juried and written by teachers. It's on what we call our Instruction Management System. We have revised our accountability system to deal with the whole issue of multiple measures. We felt we were very well positioned when No Child Left Behind came into being. The reality is we loved No Child Left Behind because in Ohio we never really disaggregated our data. We knew we had a problem with achievement gaps, but we didn't really talk about it. Now, with No Child Left Behind, we are finally beginning to talk about it. One of our goals in Ohio is to be considered the state that graduates all its students. We hope that all of our students go on to post-secondary education and that when you think of Ohio, you will think of us as a state that made the greatest progress in closing achievement gaps.

When we began to disaggregate our data, we realized that we had schools in Ohio that were really defying the demographics and fulfilling Horace Mann's promise of a common school. In fact, we have schools that were over 50% poverty schools; these schools were meeting both our own statewide performance standards and the very hard federal requirements of Adequate Yearly Progress (AYP). We celebrate our Schools of Promise because when we do our case studies, we realize these schools have teachers of promise and very high expectations for our students. These are schools that have engaging curriculum—our teachers are not teaching to the test. These are schools where teachers track individual performance of students using diagnostic tools and take control over their own professional development. Most importantly, these are schools where principals and teachers care about our students. These are schools that have opened the schoolhouse door and used community resources to really make a difference.

We really have used this statewide as a way to teach and work with the profession so that we can make Ohio a state of promise. We have regional conferences. We have 17 schools in Appalachia and seven schools in the Cleveland Public Schools, which are Schools of Promise. Last week, we had 300 educators in seven Cleveland Public Schools being trained by teachers who are, in fact, making a difference.

We also think that the disaggregating of data has incredible implications for how we fund schools. The reality is that it costs more to educate some kids than others. We're working on a vision for school funding in Ohio where the money will follow the child. We will develop different costs for different types of children in response to No Child Left Behind. We actually like the notion of testing our children from grades three to eight because this will allow us to do value-added and to look at the data more reliably.

We very much like the notion of the accountability system. What we have done in Ohio is use No Child Left Behind as a way to rethink how we implement an accountability system. We have multiple measures where we not only look at schools and districts with regard to absolute performance, but we have also developed an index of improvement. We are also building a value-added component to our accountability system.

No Child Left Behind has allowed us to look at our data system, which was not very good. We are working on our new data exchange system to make it useful for teachers in the field and to get data to the classroom level for teachers to use to drive instruction.

We like No Child Left Behind because it forced Ohio and other states to consistently participate in the National Assessment of Educational Progress (NAEP). When we look at school funding and NAEP scores, we see a dilemma. Mississippi is held to the same standard of accountability as Connecticut, but Mississippi is only funding $5,000 a year while Connecticut is funding between $12,000 and $14,000 a year; I think this should spark policy discussions about how we fund schools to rethink a partnership among federal, state and local levels.

We want to encourage the U.S. Department of Education to allow for flexibility. I'm hoping that from the state perspective, the federal government will hold me accountable for results, and for results on the NAEP, but not for processes. I think we need to move away from a federal policy that dictates processes and toward one holding us accountable for results with a stronger state, federal and local partnership. Thank you very much.

Ken James

Good morning. How many practicing superintendents are in the room? Not too many. Well, I'm going to talk to you in my new role as state director of education, but I've also been a practicing superintendent for 11 years. Let me say upfront, that I'm a supporter of No Child Left Behind's high standards and accountability. I have no problem or issue with those things. I think I speak on behalf of a lot of the superintendents in Kentucky, and I also have a good sense of the superintendents in Arkansas in terms of what their feelings are on No Child Left Behind. One of the biggest concerns we have had with No Child Left Behind is the 1,178 pages of legislation. I think that we've probably taken on too much, too quickly. The law was passed in January; we then put it into effect in July. Schools put it into place in August. There is very little turnaround time there, in terms of being able to do some things systematically and making sure that we had the infrastructure in place. I think that's one of the issues we have all confronted as we've encountered some problems with No Child Left Behind.

When I moved to Lexington, Kentucky and took over the Fayette County Public School System (about 34,000 students), we had four schools that were on school improvement and had just finished a set of tests in April. When we test in April, we get results back in July and August, which puts a massive burden on transportation systems. Parents want to know in March; they were asking me, "Why can't you tell us what the choice schools are going to be next year?" I had to reply that we did not have the test results back because we were testing at the time, and we wouldn't get them back until the end of July. Hopefully, we would know the first week of August, although we started school in the middle of August. Those are some of the issues that have been imbedded with the quick rollout of No Child Left Behind that we need to work through and have good conversations about. I know that we are in the process and those are things that can be worked out.

One of the questions Lew asked our opinion on was, "Are the requirements realistic?" I think they're realistic and I think they're admirable goals. We want all of our students to achieve. I think the disaggregation of data, which has already been mentioned, is a key component. In a lot of systems across this country this was not being done in the fashion or to the level that it needed to be accomplished. I think that has brought the kinds of items that we really need to examine and focus on to the fore-front.

I also think one key component is that success depends not only on testing the students, but also on having the infrastructure in place to make sure that all of that happens. Further, we must couple that with resources as we go forth with the process. Another one of the questions Lew asked was, "Is there sufficient money at this point in time for No Child Left Behind?" I think most of us in the room would say, "Yes, at this point in time, we think there is sufficient money."

One concern I have is that as we continue to identify more schools in each and every state that need help, is there going to be enough money? As that list grows—and each and every one of us clearly understands that the list is going to grow—it's going to get broader. Are the resources at that point going to be sufficient to do it? Right now, all of us are dealing for the most part, with small numbers, and as those numbers escalate, are we going to have the resources to be able to do the things we need to do as we roll out No Child Left Behind?

Statistically, we also need to come to grips with the fact that some schools depending upon what plan they have in the state and what has been developed, (may not get off of this list.) That, is something that we probably haven't talked about a lot, but we must accept it. We have a benchmark and we have targets to reach by 2014.

In Fayette County School District in Lexington, Kentucky we had 25 targets to meet. Kentucky has a very comprehensive accountability system that has been in place for several years. Every one of our schools already had targets. We were already moving in that direction, and a lot of No Child Left Behind is based on the progress made in Kentucky. I had schools in Lexington, Kentucky that were meeting 15 out of 16, 12 out of 15, some even 95% of their targets. Those same schools were on rewards from the state of Kentucky, but if they meet only 15 out of 16 of their goals next year, they are going to be on school improvement. We've got to disconnect in terms of what our parents understand. The question becomes: Is the Kentucky accountability system not what it needs to be? I don't believe that; I think the Kentucky accountability system is probably one of the most far-reaching systems across the country. Many are looking at the Kentucky accountability system as we move forward.

As we continue to have dialogue about No Child Left Behind, those are some of the kinds of things that we have to make sure to relay to our community, so they understand clearly. We have to work with the media and say, "Okay, yes, X High School only missed one goal. Let's focus on the positive." I think those of us in the business are sincerely trying to do that. As we work with media outlets, we should say, "Let's look at this school that reached 15 out of 16 goals; if they do that again next year, they're on school improvement. What kind of message can we come together on to stress the positives instead of the negatives?"

We heard it said yesterday that there was never any intent for a school that is on school improvement to be considered a failure. That may not have been the intent, but we as practitioners clearly understand that, depending upon the media markets, it may be misconstrued and printed that those schools are failures. It is a mischaracterization and it's not fair to those schools. Those are things that I think we have to work on collectively, roll up our sleeves and say, "How are we going to do a better job of getting this message across?"

It goes back to what I said initially: It is a good law but it is trying to do too much, too quickly. I think some of the strategies need to be tweaked, but I think it's all fixable. I think we all stand here and say that we need more accountability. We need to make sure that each and every subgroup in our schools is performing at the highest level. None of us are arguing about that. I support accountability in standards, and I don't plan to change. From a practitioner's standpoint, we need to understand that there are some issues and concerns we need to talk about.

Supplemental services, is another area of concern that I think all of us have experienced. I know that in both states I've been in, one of the issues with supplemental services is that we had a lot of vendors signing up to be providers, but when we figured out who could provide those services for kids, that list really dwindled.

I think we have some disconnects and as we move forward, we need to have some more consistent approaches to this situation. I think we all understand that one size doesn't fit all. We've heard that comment throughout this conference in a variety of different venues. Using the Kentucky example again my district had 25 targets, but other school districts had six targets. Because of the various populations, is it going to be more difficult for those school districts that had 25 targets to meet No Child Left Behind standards, than it is for a school district that has five or six targets to meet? Undoubtedly!

One other mistake I made in Kentucky when I got there was when I said, "If Tubby Smith wins 14 out of 16, that's pretty good." Well, they quickly corrected me when I got to Kentucky. They said, "Tubby Smith has to win all of them." The point I was trying to make is that we cannot make the mistake of calling a school that's meeting 14 out of 16, or even 15 out of 16 of their goals and targets a "failure." That's incumbent upon each and every one of us, and we need to work with the media to not do that.

There are other concerns that I would like to briefly mention. I know our district superintendents in the state have identified a series of concerns including the Limited English Proficient (LEP) population, special ed population, and highly qualified certification in middle schools and high schools. However, I'll end my remarks, and hopefully we'll have time for questions.

Jay Mathews

I'm delighted to be here amongst educators who've been so patient over the last 20 years, explaining to me how things actually work inside schools. It's also delightful to be with all these very high powered educators on the panel. Actually, these are the kind of people that I've learned over the years to try to stay as far away from as possible. For 20 years I was sort of a stealth education reporter at the *Washington Post*. My assignment was not to cover education; I was trying to write books about high schools that interested me, while not telling my editors where I was from day to day to avoid getting into trouble. Over time I realized that what goes on inside classrooms is really so vital, so interesting, and so different than what you often read in the newspapers about education that that was going to be my job.

Over the last several years, once I finally got to be a full-time education writer for the *Post*, I have had the great delight of developing an online column, which people can very easily find all around the country. More importantly, they can very easily email me back and tell me how wrong I am. I'm too old and feeble for the *Post* to send me out on breaking news stories anymore, so I get time to wander around schools, get inside classrooms, talk to teachers, and see what's going on.

I'm going to give you a very quick summary of what I'm seeing inside classrooms. What are people telling me from around the country as to the impacts of No Child Left Behind on their classes? Let's start with testing. I don't think anybody can see a viable alternative to regular testing. We complain about it. Nina is the great idea-meister of the current education administration, and perhaps she can find a way to give a waiver to schools that are attempting a Deb Meier experiment, not with tests, but with portfolios and annual oral examinations, as a way to assess how kids are doing. I'd be fine with that, but testing is something that we really need. I don't see anybody showing a viable alternative to it.

Funding—are there sufficient funds? There are never going to be sufficient funds. Anybody who lives in this town knows that everybody is going to want more money than they have. We've got more money going into schools than we ever have before in this country, and I think most of the educators I talk to appreciate that. That's a good mark for whatever we're doing right now.

Disaggregation, the subgroups and breaking down our data into different racial and economic groups—nobody disagrees with that. Everybody knows that is a good idea. It is helping us in a lot of ways, such as sanctions requiring schools to pay for tutors and requiring schools to pay for transportation. I'll discuss one of those sanctions that is becoming a problem in some schools: We all know that the disaggregation of statistics, which we all can agree is a great thing to have, was mandated 10 years ago by the federal government, and lots of school districts out there just shrugged at it. There was no bite in the law, so they weren't going to push it. States were violating the law, and nobody was sending any superintendents to jail for not disaggregating their statistics. That's where we were.

Adequate Yearly Progress (AYP) and setting the deadline of 2014 for everyone becoming proficient—in the real world, that's insane. Interestingly enough, when you talk to really intelligent and experienced politicians in Washington who wrote this into the law, it makes sense to them. In the political world it makes sense because, even if they put the year 2014 in this law, these politicians don't really believe in it. They know that some time down the road, probably after the next presidential election, we will go back to that law and fix it. That's the way we do things. The 2014 deadline is really a fantasy land. It's a goal. It makes sense to politicians, so let them have their little fantasy. We're going to continue to work on each individual school and make things better.

So what's going on inside schools? I recently sent out an email, contacting as many people as I could, saying that I've heard the arguments for and against No Child Left Behind. I know the ideology and what you're upset about. Let's just focus on what's happening. Tell me what you're seeing inside classrooms as a parent, a teacher, or even as a student, that you think is good or bad. There was actually less response to that than I expected. I got a lot more response to a column I wrote yesterday suggesting that people should not let their high school children drink at home, than anything else I've written lately.

The response I did get suggested that number one, the transportation part of No Child Left Behind is a problem for some schools. There is sudden overcrowding in schools that have been designated as meeting the standards, and these schools are getting kids from schools that have not. Number two (and this is the one that was reflected most often), was the restrictions on recess, lunch, and field trips. That's something that makes parents and some principals very sad. Some schools are cutting back time for those, as well as cutting back time for subjects other than reading, writing, and math. That's something that people sense is a problem, although it's hard for me to see yet that it's a big problem. It's just something that people are sensitive to.

I'm seeing that good teachers, the ones that I've been following for years, do not see this as a problem. This is not a problem for good schools that I've been following for years, either. My favorite example is Wakefield High School in south Arlington, Virginia, where 73% of the students are Hispanic or African American and half of the kids are poor enough to qualify for federal subsidies. They are sort of making their targets, but as this goes along and as AYP continues, they will probably miss some targets. They don't care because they are one of the best schools in this region. They are the only public school in this region that requires all seniors to write a senior project as private schools do. Their participation rate in AP courses is way off the charts—they are in the top 3% of all American schools. They have something called the Cohort, in which they have designated minority males, Black and Hispanic kids. A total of 90 kids in this cohort meet with a special group of teachers every week; the teachers take them on college tours, get them into the fast-track courses and into the AP courses so they can show the brains that they've got. That's working. These students could have been overlooked since they're male and since they resist the kind of attention that will make them better students and eventually get them into college. Any parent who has a kid at Wakefield knows it is one of the best high schools that they will ever see, so they are not going to leave that school simply because their AYP takes a turn downward.

I think we have to put this in context. I think about No Child Left Behind, and I think about my own health. I'm getting old, and I'm getting fat. I used to sit around and just think that I was fairly healthy and that my blood pressure wasn't too bad. Then, I started to bike every other day, and that seemed to work. This is the way we do things in this country. We try stuff. We put it out there. This is a messy bill put together by a lot of people who are trying to make a compromise, and it's going to be a messy committee compromise, but at least we're doing something. That's a lot better than doing nothing. As we go forward, with each of you in your schools and districts helping kids and keeping the focus on kids and what's going on in the classrooms, I think we can only get better.

Richard Ingersoll

Over the last decade or so, I have done and continue to do research on teachers' supply and demand, and teacher quality issues. Lew had asked me if I would talk a little bit about what the data tell us about the prospects for the teacher quality portion of the No Child Left Behind Act.

No Child Left Behind does a very unprecedented, ambitious, and laudable thing. It sets the goal that within several years from now, all classes in the core academic subjects are going to be taught by teachers who are highly qualified. "Highly qualified" means they have a degree, a regular state certificate, and are competent in each of the subjects they are assigned to teach. This is a key point.

Well, where do things stand? The best national data we have on this are from the 1999-2000 school year, just before NCLB kicked in. What they tell us is that, first of all, the entire teacher workforce has a four-year college degree. In fact, half of them have a graduate degree, usually a master's degree. Furthermore, most of the workforce has a specialization—a concentration or a major in some field. There are very few teachers who have a generic degree, for instance, in curriculum or in secondary education. Most surprisingly, the data tell us that the vast majority of the teaching workforce has a full teaching certificate. These data tell us that over 90% of the elementary and secondary teachers in this country have a full, regular state certificate (Chart 9.22).

Now these data seem to go completely against the contrary conventional wisdom. We have been told that we have thousands of uncertified teachers. While it may be the case in certain urban and rural areas that significant numbers of teachers are uncertified, overall, this has been totally exaggerated.

Hence, on the face of it, the data seem to suggest that most of our teaching workforce do meet the NCLB requirements. Nevertheless, the

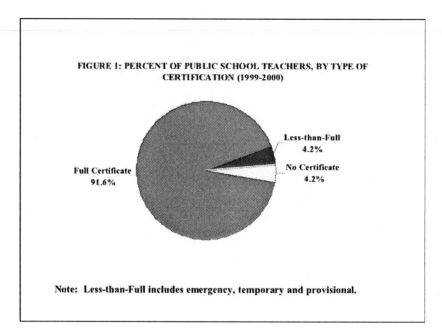

Chart 9.22

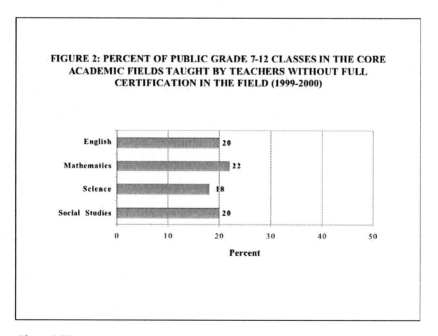

Chart 9.23

data also tell us that there are large percentages of classes out there taught by teachers who don't meet the bar at all. Please see Chart 9.23. This figure shows secondary level classes across the nation. It's grades 7 through 12. The data tell us that in each of the four core academic subjects, about a fifth of the classes were taught by teachers who did not have a teacher's certificate in that field. Now, this might seem odd. How can it be that over 90% of the teaching workforce is highly qualified, but we have around a fifth of the classes at the secondary level taught by people who don't meet the bar? Interestingly, you should also notice here that English and social studies are just about as high as math and science.

The answer to the question lies in the phenomenon known as out-of-field teaching. I know a bit about this myself, given my former experience as a high school teacher. I was a social studies teacher in both public and private schools for a number of years, and every semester I would teach social studies courses such as U.S. history, world civilization, civics, and world problems, etc. It didn't seem like there was a semester that went by where, in addition to my several history social studies courses, I was also assigned to teach a class or two in two other subjects—algebra, special ed., English, sex ed., etc. Needless to say, it's very challenging to teach subjects that you don't know well.

There are two separate problems here that are almost always confused and confounded. In the United States we have problems with the preservice preparation of teachers. Some teachers have had little preparation or what they have isn't very rigorous. We also have a different problem, one that's often overlooked: teachers are fully qualified, but once on the job, they are assigned to teach something that does not match their qualifications. The problem of out-of-field teaching and the distinction between these two sources of the problem of underqualified teachers is very important when it comes to prescriptions. Almost all of the prescriptions and reforms proposed, including No Child Left Behind, have to do with enhancing the training and evaluation, in-service, preservice, etc., of the teaching workforce. These are perfectly laudable things to do, but these alone will not solve the problem.

In plain terms, we can require all the teachers to have a PhD in some field, but if once they are on the job they're assigned to teach other subjects during part of their day, it really won't help us meet No Child Left Behind standards. The data suggests that we need to not just look at the training of teachers, but we also have to focus on how we treat, utilize, and manage these precious human resources once on the job. Think of the comparison with traditional professions. Except in an emergency, we wouldn't ask a cardiologist to deliver our baby. We wouldn't ask a rape lawyer to write our will. We wouldn't ask a chemical engineer to design a bridge. We wouldn't ask a sociology professor to teach English. Why not?

These are respected professions. We assume they take expertise. We assume specialization is good. It seems like these are precisely the things we fail to assume about high school and elementary teaching. That somehow it is okay to have the social studies teachers teach algebra. Yes, doing that may save some time and money for principals, schools, school districts, and ultimately for tax payers. However, I think we all recognize it is not cost-free to have the social studies teacher teach algebra. Thank you.

Nina Rees

I too, want to take this opportunity to congratulate all of the teachers who received the Milken Family Foundation Award last night. I also want to thank the Milken Family Foundation for hosting their event this year in Washington, D.C.

I am here to tell you a little bit about No Child Left Behind. I think that the panelists so far have done a nice job of telling you how they are implementing, or in some cases, studying the law. Before I comment on where we stand, I think it is also important for me to give you a backdrop as I'm sure Dr. Hickok and Ray Simon have already done in terms of why No Child Left Behind is in place.

Three quick facts: First and foremost, as Lew mentioned in his slides, we have a horrifying achievement gap in this country, just looking at the 12th grade test scores on the NAEP. Currently, only about 12% of African American 12th graders are performing at the proficient level in the area of reading. Only about 8% are performing at the proficient level in the area of math. When you look at the performance of Hispanics, the numbers are equally horrible. Fifteen percent are proficient in reading and 12% are proficient in math. If you continue to think about those facts and figures, I think you will understand why it was important for us to focus on the achievement gap at the federal level.

The other thing was when it comes to federal education spending, there is little correlation between federal spending and student achievement at the state and local levels. It is difficult when you spend a grand total of 7% to 8% of total funds in education to really draw direct correlations between what you're doing at the federal level and what is happening at the local level. The president and the secretary felt strongly that federal funds ought to leverage what states and districts were already doing in raising student achievement.

At the end of the day they ended up building on the standards-based reforms that were put in place back in 1988, and later on in 1994 with the reauthorizations of the previous Elementary and Secondary Education Acts. They also built largely upon a lot of the work that states and school districts were already doing to close the achievement gap. There's a lot of noise out there by the media—primarily, about how we have these new mandates in place. Really, what we did was build on what you have already put in place and simply firmed up some of the accountability measures that had not been enforced in previous administrations.

Another thing that's interesting about No Child Left Behind, which I have been noticing more and more as I travel to different schools that have successfully closed the gap, is that the same principles apply to these schools. I was at Harvest Prep Elementary in Minnesota yesterday, which is a charter school. A few weeks ago, the secretary visited the Amistad Academy in Connecticut. The key thing that the principals of these schools tell you when you talk to them, is about how they have successfully been able to close the achievement gap, and that their staff is focused on the goal of closing the gap. They are not making any excuses for the students they are bringing in. Having a mission that is focused on raising student achievement helps focus school systems, school districts, states, and us at the federal level on common goals. It is very important for us to continue to push the spirit behind No Child Left Behind, even though there are going to be some technical issues in different parts of the country.

What have we noticed so far? I think it's very early for us to point at results and draw too many conclusions, but there are already a couple of studies that I think are fairly encouraging in pointing us in the right direction. One of them is a study by the Council of Great City Schools, which demonstrates that the school districts they have represented are slowly showing a narrowing of the achievement gap. A lot of them are showing this because of the standards-based reforms that the districts and states had already put in place. The Council feels that No Child Left Behind is also contributing to the narrowing of this gap.

Another study that came out a week or so ago about Chicago, shows that after just 1 year of having the public school choice provisions of No Child Left Behind in place, the students who transferred to the public school of their choice have benefited. In addition, these students did not diminish the quality of the schools they moved to, despite public fears.

Ultimately, I want to convey a couple of key points about No Child Left Behind—one of which is that it's very important for us to build strong partnerships with individuals at the state and local levels, and practitioners at the school level, in order to make sure that this law is working effectively. It's also very important for us, as others have noted, not to pay too much attention to the hype that the media generates whenever the lists of schools in need of improvement come out. You are going to see a spike in the number of schools and districts that are in need of improvement. We need your help to make sure that the data and the reasoning for why these districts and schools have been labeled as such is apparent. We also need to make sure we are communicating as well as possible about what we are going to do to make sure that these schools and districts get off the needs improvement list.

I would like to touch upon school choice and supplemental services because that's my primary responsibility at the Department of Education. One of the things that we really would like to encourage districts and states to do is to encourage interdistrict school choice. It's not happening in a lot of places. I think that the quickest and best way to deal with some of the capacity issues the districts are facing is for states to offer incentives for interdistrict choice. Another option I'm sure all of you are familiar with is the creation of charter schools and finding ways to encourage education entrepreneurs to come into the business of education and create new schools.

I think that we are on the right track. I am extremely encouraged by what we have seen so far, but I think we need to work together more closely. If it is new flexibility options that we need to put in place for us to come into your districts and give you hands-on technical assistance to meet the requirements of the law, *we need to do this together.* Thank you very much.

Lewis Solmon

Let me impress people … please pull up Chart 9.24. This is the study that Nina was talking about. In Chicago, transfer kids posted 24% less than the expected gains in reading and 17% less than the expected gains in math. When they transferred, they gained roughly 8% more than expected on both tests, which is a very encouraging result.

The interesting thing is that people are talking about not being able to meet the highly qualified teacher criteria. However, when states were surveyed, 37 states indicated that 75% were already at or above the highly qualified level. Indeed 21 states were above 90% (Charts 9.25 & 9.26). Even in high-poverty schools, you can see those numbers are exceptionally high—and these are classes, not people. That means that either the states are lying or they are protesting too much. I think that might be an interesting question for somebody on the panel to explain to me.

I think that the panel has been really positive, but when you read and listen to the media, the program is getting bashed. There are many criticisms of No Child Left Behind that I've compiled, and some of them are listed on these charts (Charts 9.27, 9.28, 9.29, 9.30, 9.31, & 9.32).

Having provided the reasons for criticizing NCLB, I would like to comment on the charge that there is not enough money available (Chart 9.33). Ken didn't say that, but he did say that maybe there wouldn't be

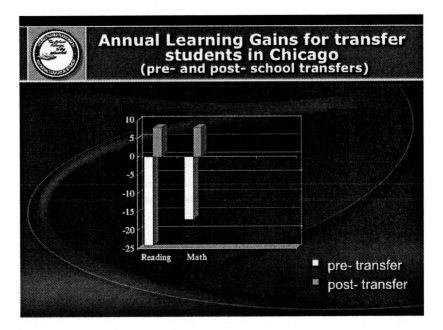

Chart 9.24

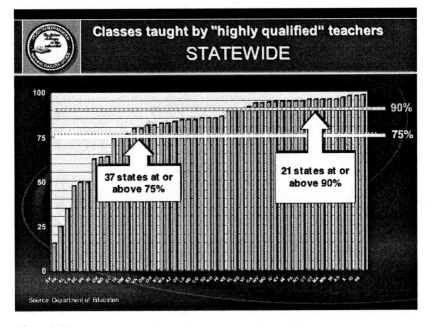

Chart 9.25

Chart 9.26

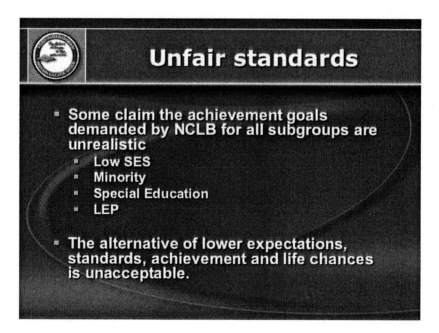

Chart 9.27

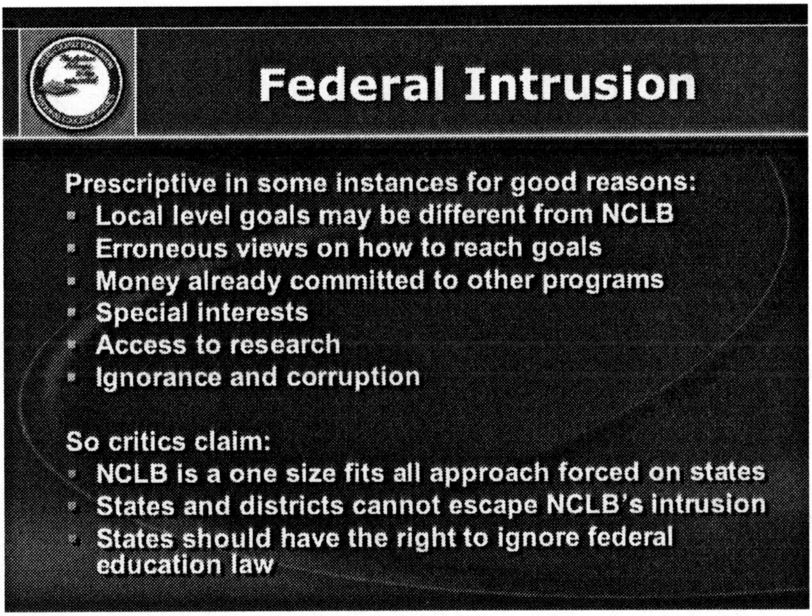

Federal Intrusion

Prescriptive in some instances for good reasons:
- Local level goals may be different from NCLB
- Erroneous views on how to reach goals
- Money already committed to other programs
- Special interests
- Access to research
- Ignorance and corruption

So critics claim:
- NCLB is a one size fits all approach forced on states
- States and districts cannot escape NCLB's intrusion
- States should have the right to ignore federal education law

Chart 9.28

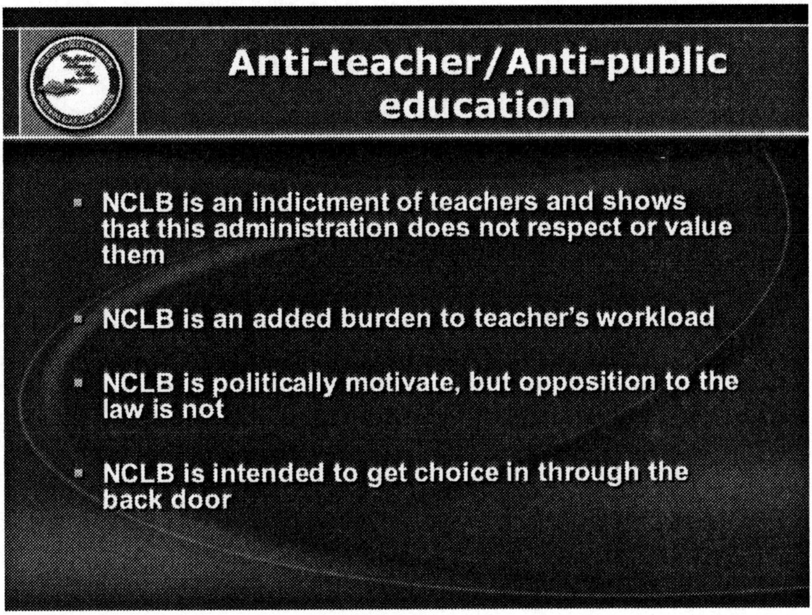

Anti-teacher/Anti-public education

- NCLB is an indictment of teachers and shows that this administration does not respect or value them

- NCLB is an added burden to teacher's workload

- NCLB is politically motivate, but opposition to the law is not

- NCLB is intended to get choice in through the back door

Chart 9.29

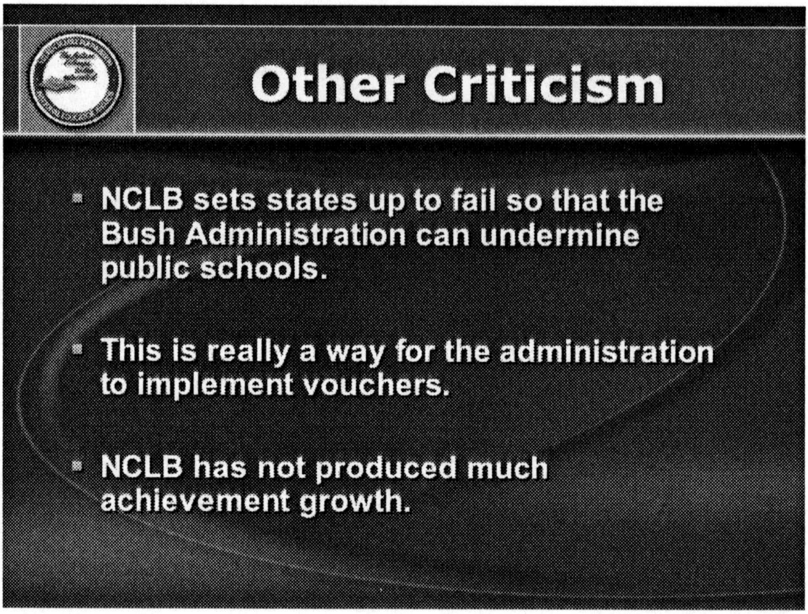

Other Criticism

- NCLB sets states up to fail so that the Bush Administration can undermine public schools.

- This is really a way for the administration to implement vouchers.

- NCLB has not produced much achievement growth.

Chart 9.30

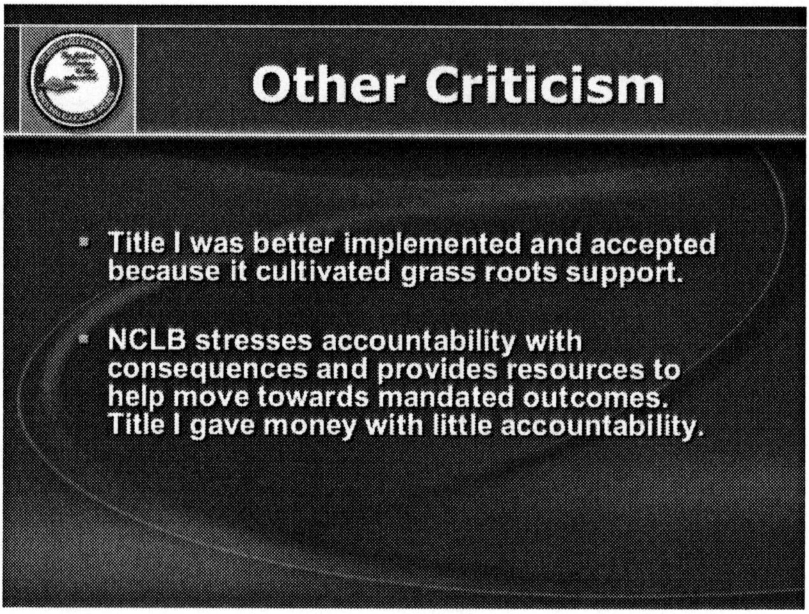

Other Criticism

- Title I was better implemented and accepted because it cultivated grass roots support.

- NCLB stresses accountability with consequences and provides resources to help move towards mandated outcomes. Title I gave money with little accountability.

Chart 9.31

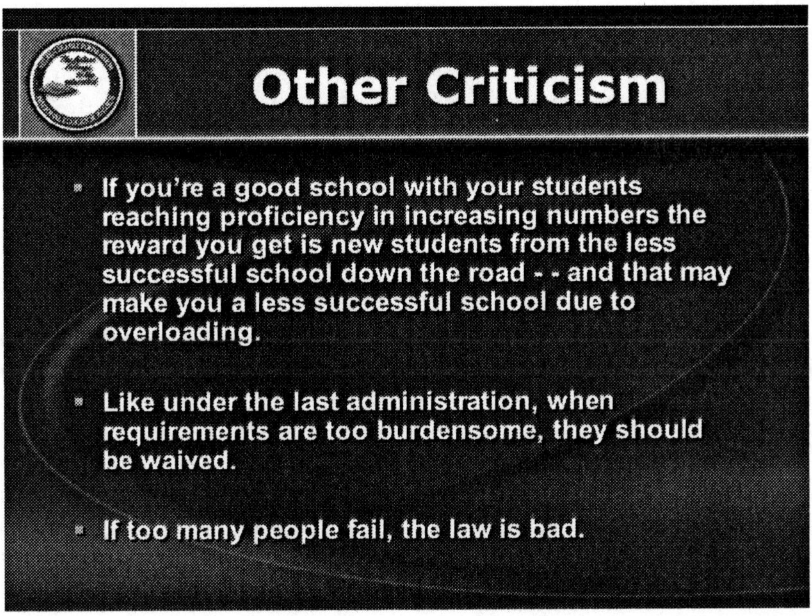

Other Criticism

- If you're a good school with your students reaching proficiency in increasing numbers the reward you get is new students from the less successful school down the road - - and that may make you a less successful school due to overloading.

- Like under the last administration, when requirements are too burdensome, they should be waived.

- If too many people fail, the law is bad.

Chart 9.32

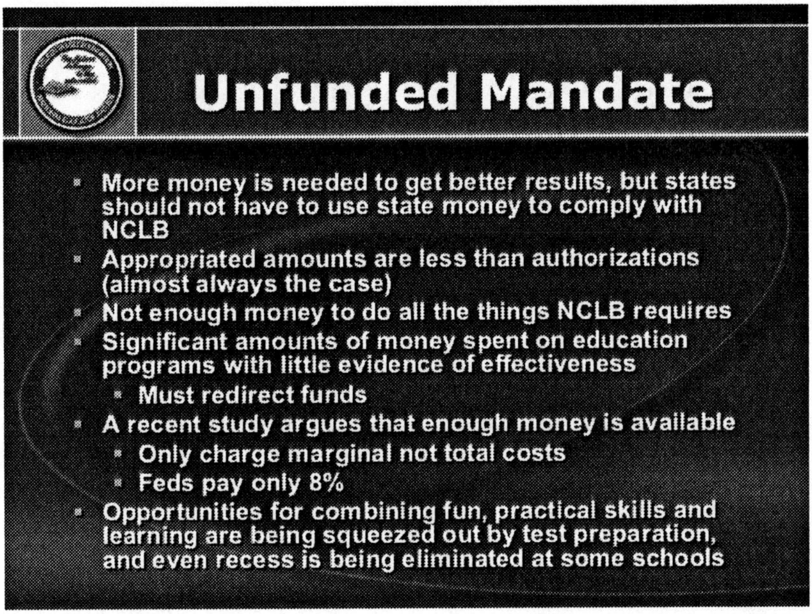

Unfunded Mandate

- More money is needed to get better results, but states should not have to use state money to comply with NCLB
- Appropriated amounts are less than authorizations (almost always the case)
- Not enough money to do all the things NCLB requires
- Significant amounts of money spent on education programs with little evidence of effectiveness
  - Must redirect funds
- A recent study argues that enough money is available
  - Only charge marginal not total costs
  - Feds pay only 8%
- Opportunities for combining fun, practical skills and learning are being squeezed out by test preparation, and even recess is being eliminated at some schools

Chart 9.33

enough money in the future. Maybe there won't. In my readings I have observed a number of things. First of all, there has been more money every year since the law was passed. Secondly, apparently some states have not even spent all the money they were entitled to. Finally, there have been a number of studies that have shown that the mandates are indeed paid for. I think that is in part, a definitional problem. If testing is required and you are already testing in every other grade, and then you are suddenly required to test every grade from three to eight, you cannot claim that all this testing should be paid for by the federal government. It's the incremental cost, not the total cost. In order to get student achievement up as an economist, it would be clear to me that you can't say, "All costs of instruction should be paid for by No Child Left Behind, because it requires improved achievement." The Feds, as Nina mentioned, only provide about 8% of spending.

The other thing I've observed over the years is that nothing is ever closed down in education. When a new program comes in, you say, "Well, we need more money because we're doing all these other things, and now we've got to do something else." What has to eventually happen is that people will look at programs and determine which ones are working and which ones are not. They will have to reallocate the money from the ones that are not working to try new things or to implement programs that work. I think the strangest, most surprising criticism on the basis of money has been that the amount authorized is not the amount appropriated. Now, my reading is that in the history of bills being passed, it is rarely the case that the amount appropriated is the amount authorized. The amount is always lower, but some people are shocked that in the case of No Child Left Behind the amount appropriated is not the amount authorized. Sort of like a scene from the movie *Casablanca*:

> "How can he close me up?" says nightclub owner Rick Blaine to the Major.
>
> The Major then answers, "I'm shocked, shocked to find that gambling is going on in here."
>
> Yet, a waiter comes over and says to the hypocritical Major, "Your winnings, sir."
>
> "Oh, thank you very much," he replies and in the same breath orders, "Everybody out at once."

Susan Zelman

The real issue is whether or not we have enough money in the education system, in general, to do the job we really need to do to make sure all kids are successful. Right now we have 26 states in litigation over their school funding issues. We have a nation which really relies heavily on the property tax. Maybe we should say that this is becoming a national problem and that one of the things we have to do is to look at this issue from a different type of partnership or distribution of funds from the state government, the local government and the federal government. When more than half of our states are in litigation, something is wrong with our system.

We only get 8% of total education dollars from the federal government. Yet, the reality is that we have this incredible variability in performance and how we fund education as a country. We know now, in a knowledge-based economy, that education is more important for our democracy and national security then any time in our future. Maybe we should look at this as a more systematic problem and come up with better solutions to fund our schools in general and stop quibbling about whether this is a funded or unfunded mandate.

Nina Rees

I agree with Susan, but as Lew mentioned, it's true that most of the time in federal lawmaking, the authorization level tends to be higher and is treated as a ceiling to stop us from overspending. Appropriations are usually lower. As all of you know, we could always use more money at the school level, in particular to raise student achievement. I think more than anything, it is important for us to work with states to better align federal spending with state and school district spending. We need to work at getting rid of the disparities in education spending, especially in center city school districts. Again, this is really a state issue and not something that the federal government can address.

Lewis Solmon

I think we are past the days where the federal government is going to give money and not require anything in return, which I think is good. Wouldn't it be the case that if the federal government gave more, people would say that you are intruding? You're violating state's rights?

Nina Rees

I just want to toss out another statistic that the secretary mentions a lot. If you just add up the total amount of money at the federal, state, local and private sectors, we're spending around $500 billion on education. A lot of money is being invested in education, but I am afraid it is not always being targeted at the right kinds of reforms.

Richard Ingersoll

One of the criticisms Lew mentioned is that the legislation is anti-teacher. I think there's some truth to that in the teacher quality provisions of the legislation. Underlying one provision is the assumption that the major source of low-quality teaching lies in teachers themselves. This provides a teacher deficit perspective and suggests that the sources of the problem lie in teacher's training, ability, competence, motivation, etc. It says the way to fix schools is to fix teachers.

In my own research, as I was laying out earlier, I found that, yes, low-quality teaching exists. However, sometimes it has nothing to do with the teachers themselves and everything to do with the way the school operates. If you take teachers qualified in one subject and assign them to teach something else part of the day, you can make them underqualified. Then, if you end up holding teachers accountable for that, in a sense it is really akin to victim blaming. It's not just a matter of switching the blame over to schools. Somehow we need to address the fact that the teachers are not necessarily the problem here. I think the legislation, if it is to have any chance of succeeding, will need to do that.

Lowell Milken

I'd like to direct a question to Richard because I happen to share his assessment here. You showed us statistics that showed there was around 20% of "out-of-field" teaching in those four disciplines we just saw. However, we know in high-poverty schools that those percentages probably range from 30% to 64% in science. I'm very perplexed to see how we are going to have any opportunity to meet the mandate, especially for the more challenging subgroups we're dealing with, until we come to the reality that we cannot have teachers teaching subjects that they do not have knowledge in. I am sure we have all experienced a case where a gym teacher was assigned to teach physics, which wasn't a rewarding year for our students.

What do you think the solution is? Do you think we should actually have a mandated law that does not beg the question of whether someone is qualified, per se, to be teaching, but mandated that you are not permitted to teach any individual class unless you have shown X amount of subject matter knowledge in that particular subject? What really is the solution to that? We are never going to improve the scores in our high-poverty schools until we deal with the teacher quality issue in those schools.

Richard Ingersoll

The No Child Left Behind legislation already does that, in a sense. The legislation says that for every class in core academic subjects, the teacher of that class must be highly qualified *in the subject taught*. The last three words are key. Furthermore, a number of us argued back in the late 1990s, in front of the House Education Committee, that there needs to be a parental right-to-know clause. I thought the most brilliant part of the legislation was that if your child is taught 10th grade math by a teacher who is not highly qualified in math, a note is supposed to go home to the parents informing them of this matter.

Now, compliance is another issue. I am not quite sure how many districts are now actually doing this, but the legislation is there. The bar has been set and it is laudable. To me, the real issue is how to get from Point A to Point B. We have a situation where the data are telling us about a fifth of our classes are taught by people who do not have a certification in the subject taught. How do we get that number down to zero? This is where the legislation does not give us any clues. It does not discuss strategies at all other than enhancing the training of teachers, which as I tried to point out earlier, is fine. This alone will not solve the problem. So, it really calls for us to rethink how we utilize these people called "teachers." That's going to be difficult because, as far as we can tell, the practice of out-of-field teaching has been going on for a century and the public never really knew about it. Though certainly, school people always did.

How do we change that? I don't know. I was thinking that the *Parental Right-to-Know* clause in No Child Left Behind might provide impetus. I can provide the national data documenting the problem. We have been doing that for awhile and everyone is really shocked. The data tell us how much of this is going to the nation and how much to each state. What I cannot tell you is how many classes in your kid's school are taught by people who do not even have a certificate in the field. When that information comes out, and the legislation is demanding that it come out, I am hoping that will be the impetus.

We will have to wait and see because there is also a devil in the details of NCLB, as we have seen. Just to give you one example, let's take the fields of science and social studies. These are broad amalgam fields comprised of six disciplines each. Does the teacher teaching physics need to have a background in physics or just in any science whatsoever? If we define it as any science whatsoever, immediately the problem is not nearly as big because it turns out we have many biology teachers teaching physics and vice versa. Right now, the legislation seems to be kind of murky, although it seems to say the latter is ok. Of course, if you ask any physics or biology teacher, they will tell you that those two fields are really different. If you're really good in biology, you may not have a clue how to teach physics and vice versa.

Lewis Solmon

I have a question for Nina also. The answer I was going to give to the question of how you fix it is: you tell the parents. However, one of the strange things in No Child Left Behind is that if you have teachers out-of-field, you are obligated to send a letter to the parents saying, "If you want to know whether your teachers are out-of-field, you can ask us." It seems to me, you should just say, "We'd like to tell you."

Nina Rees

That's a fair point, but I do want to target another question that you had up there. I think of all the criticisms that you listed, the one that's probably the most disturbing to those of us who believe in the mission of No Child Left Behind, is the one where some individuals feel that the students simply cannot learn. I was in Little Rock recently and had a great meeting with their school district officials. I asked them, "How do you deal with some of the teachers and principals who simply don't believe that all kids can learn?" Their answer to me was a very good one: If they are new teachers, you quickly take them to schools that are closing the achievement gap to demonstrate to them that it can be done.

I think that is something we need to do more of at the national level. I don't mean for this to come across the wrong way. Unfortunately, most of the people who do not believe all kids can learn happen to be in districts that do not have a lot of minority children. As a matter of just winning this debate in the court of public opinion, we need to do a better job of showcasing and highlighting those schools that are closing the gap. I hope that the media pays more attention to that as well.

Lewis Solmon

Thank you. Let's go to the audience.

Audience Question

I teach in Bismarck, North Dakota. In my experience, I think there is this huge assumption that the layers of leadership communicate well and effectively, that the U.S. Department of Education, the state legislature, the state department of education, the local school districts, and the local buildings are all on the same page. However, there is an institutionalized schizophrenia in the classroom, and we are tugged in 80 different directions by people who are not talking to each other. My question is: How can we combat this so that we are getting messages that are on the same highway, rather than all kinds of different messages from all kinds of special interests?

Ken James

I think it is the state and federal issues that you are addressing. As I tried to indicate, I think we need to have a lot more dialog. This is the bottom line with a lot of issues with No Child Left Behind. It was too much, too quick. It's 1,178 pages of stuff, lots of powerful stuff. The timeline in which it was rolled out created some of these communication issues. In addition, as it was being rolled out, the regulations and those kinds of things were being developed. School districts and state departments were trying to figure out what they were going to have to do.

It goes back to the simple fact that I think it was too much, too quick—the expectation for it to be rolled out in its completeness at that early stage, although that might not have been the objective. But that was what the community expected. In other words, you are doing this to us, moving our kids, and doing X, Y, and Z. We want some clear-cut answers. Well, there were a lot of times in that spectrum where there were no clear answers.

Lewis Solmon

But I thought there were 12 years to roll it out.

Ken James

We did not have 12 years to roll out choice. Those are the kinds of issues, problematically, that I am talking about that have created a PR nightmare in terms of the community situation. Yes, we have 12 years to roll it out, but some of this kicked right in depending upon when your baseline was, how many years that you were given and how many schools automatically jumped to year two. We started choice in the Little Rock School District in January. Now, is the elementary level a good time to move any kid from any school to another school, from an emotional standpoint? At that point, parents did not feel that it was, because most of them did not exercise a choice option. That is what we were obligated to do, and that is how quick we were obligated to do it.

Audience Question

Richard Ingersoll, you have refined the question with your data. I wanted to follow up on that. The school and staffing surveys have a column that shows "certified but lacking major or minor in a subject area field." In history and physics, in particular, those figures are apocalyptically bad. Now, the figures you gave show that there seems to be a very good, high proportion of certified teachers. So, is the question one of bad distribution and management at the school level or a supply problem that we simply do not have the people with those qualifications to begin with, or some combination of the two? The one suggestion that I was going to make is that No Child Left Behind prescribes a rigorous subject area examination to demonstrate that a teacher has the expertise to qualify as highly qualified in a given subject area. That could indeed be used as a way of making sure that we've got the supply.

Richard Ingersoll

One of your questions concerns the source of the problem. Is it a supply-side problem, that we just simply do not produce sufficient numbers of qualified teachers, or is it more, as I am arguing, mismanagement at the school level? Well, everybody assumes that the source of out-of-field teaching is shortages, and that it is a supply problem. This view holds that student enrollments are going up and teacher retirements are going up. Principals simply can't find sufficient numbers of people, so they cut corners. For instance, they assign a social studies teacher to teach a couple of classes in algebra. There is certainly some truth to this view.

However, remember my chart (Chart 9.23), where it showed there is just as much out-of-field teaching in social studies and English, which are surplus fields, as there is in math and science, which are supposedly shortage fields. What I find in the data is that there are lots of schools and school districts out there that do not have hiring difficulties; they do not suffer from so-called shortages. They have waiting lists of qualified individuals applying to new teaching openings, yet they still have out-of-field teaching. This gets to Lowell's earlier question. There is a larger issue here. Over the last 50 years we have done nothing but ask more of schools. If you look at a catalogue of courses from a 1940 high school and compare it to a current one, it is about 10 times as big. Schools have the same number of hours, the same number of days in the year and a limited teaching staff, but the demands on schools are greater. My own hypothesis is that this tension between demands and resources is part of the problem. We ask principals to staff an ever increasing array of courses, electives and programs, etc. So, with a limited staff and a limited part of the day, they cut corners.

Audience Question

Good morning. I'm Henry Johnson, the superintendent in Mississippi. In over a decade of work at the State Department of Education in North Carolina, I'm convinced that substitutive and comprehensive alignment among curriculum, assessment, professional development, and teaching will produce outstanding results in student learning. Jay, I would like for you in particular to respond to what I am going to say next. I think this issue of the timeline of 2014, while we may not reach it, is probably more realistic than one might first imagine.

My sense of student improvement is that if we really focus on the core, the basics of reading, writing, and math, that instead of a purely linear progression in achievement, at some point we are going to hit a critical mass for a vast majority of students. The improvement will be more curvedly linear, more geometric than asymmetric, and if we really do this well, it is going to be possible, if not by 2014, that we are probably going to be able to get nearly all of our kids proficient. We just stick to this and make sure that kids understand the basics first so they can learn and benefit from the broader curriculum experiences in schools and experiences outside of school. What do you think about this notion that we are talking about a curvedly linear versus a purely linear progression?

Jay Mathews

I think that is the most sensible comment anybody has made in this session. This is the spirit that brought all these teachers into this room. You are *primo* educators because you are looking to improve your kids every year. You are scratching, biting, doing whatever you can and finding new ways of getting kids up higher than they were before. The North Carolina system is blessed by its reigning philosophy.

You are looking at improvement year-to-year. There isn't so much of a worry about targets at the end. That is how we are going to get better. We will have targets, annoying regulations and administrators who you don't think are making any sense, but what you are doing is focusing on kids. All these arguments are often arguments about adults having issues with each other. The emphasis should be on what your state is focusing on to make kids better.

Susan Zelman

I agree with Henry's point. In education we focus a lot on programs. What No Child Left Behind does, and what we have done in some states, is to focus in on building a more rational system of aligning what we expect with how we teach and how we assess. Thus, if we fix the system, then we should get more than linear improvement; we should get geometric improvement.

Audience Question

I wanted to ask for a suggestion for what I feel is the frustration of my district in Carson City, Nevada. Over the past 5 years we have had a big migration of Hispanic students to our town. Many of them do not know their own language well, let alone English, so it is difficult for us to catch them up in English. Many times they leave for a month or two on vacation in the middle of the school year, so we do not even have the entire school year to help them catch up. Their subgroup, obviously, is not progressing as quickly as someone who already speaks English is progressing. This is a frustration because the new students are improving greatly, but not at the same rate; it is bringing that subgroup lower in our district. Are there any suggestions on how to deal with that problem?

Ken James

The whole Limited English Proficient (LEP) issue is one that we all have to attempt to get our arms around better than what we have in the past. I think the research tells us very clearly that it takes 5 to 7 years to master a language. Therein lies some of the issues, in terms of youngsters coming to the system then taking an assessment and being able to perform well on that assessment. Needless to say, we have to do some tutoring, much more engaged tutoring than what we have done in the past.

I think we also need to understand that youngsters are going to have difficulty in terms of assimilating and acquiring the mastery level of the language. In terms of being able to perform adequately on some hard-core assessments, we need to understand this going into the process. This does not mean we give up on that. It does not mean we do not put resources toward that. I think we need to understand that the research tells us that five to seven years is what we're looking at in terms of mastery in most languages.

Nina Rees

It also depends on what grade-level they are coming to your school system from. Are you talking about elementary or high school or a mix of both?

Audience Question Continued

I teach in middle school, but I guess it's throughout the whole grading system, K-12. Like you said, we're aware that it takes 5 to 7 years for full mastery. They are being tested as our English speakers are, but their subgroup is not progressing as adequately each year as the native English speaker.

Lewis Solmon

They could be progressing even if they don't reach the bar.

Ken James

They could be progressing, but if they are not making the level of progression that is expected in terms of what your state plan is, you are still going to be on school improvement.

Audience Question Continued

Right, exactly right.

Ken James

That's the kicker; that's the key. I'm not trying to be anti-No Child Left Behind, but I think we need to understand those pieces. Yes, you could be making progression. It is just the same analogy as when you are "below basic" to "basic." That is a big jump for some youngsters; it is lot of progression to be made in 1 or 2 years. Now you have to get to the proficient level in terms of being able to be where you need to be. I think one of the things that we have talked about at the superintendent level deals with the kind of recognition we can bring into this conversation about moving kids from one level to the next, before they get to proficient. I think we need to understand that it is a big jump for some youngsters who come in and test initially, then score below basic. If they jump in 1 year's time up to the basic level, then they have made some clear progression. There is no recognition of that at this point in time.

Susan Zelman

In Ohio's accountability system, we use multiple measures. We give our school districts credit for kids who move from below basic to basic. They move through a four-point or a five-level system, which is built into our accountability system. One of the things we need to do here is to really look at the whole issue of multiple measures and get a more robust picture of how we categorize schools, before we label them in school improvement.

Nina Rees

I need to defend the federal law and the intent here. As someone who moved to this country in high school, with English as my third language, I honestly do not think it takes 5 to 7 years to raise these kids' achievement levels and make sure that they are proficient. Depending on what kind of backgrounds they have and how involved their parents are, I think you can probably do this a lot faster. The sad part of it is that we do not have a lot of good research in this area for us to tell you what kinds of programs to use to bring them up to grade level.

I think it is very important to work very closely with the students and their parents. We should make sure their parents are more engaged and that they are not taking the kids out of the school system for 2 months in a row. Probably one of the best parent involvement programs that I know of, though this is not scientifically based research, is a program called

PIQUE based in California. I would encourage you to involve some of the groups that are engaging parents and making sure they are more involved. Do not give up and just assume that because the federal law is saying you have to test them and measure their progress, that somehow this is just an impossible task.

The secretary would really like for anyone who has any question about No Child Left Behind to call us directly. We have a 1-800 toll-free number: 1-800-USA-LEARN. If there is ever a misunderstanding or confusion about what is going on with the law, please give us a call. In the instances where I have personally been involved with school choice and supplemental service situations, in different cities, we have really helped the districts to come up with common sense solutions, but we need to hear from you in order to come up with the solutions. So give us a call.

Lewis Solmon

Thank you all for your participation and insights.

PANEL CONTRIBUTIONS

CHAPTER 10

THE TEACHER ADVANCEMENT PROGRAM (TAP) AND NO CHILD LEFT BEHIND

Lewis C. Solmon

While our country seems lost in what has become a labyrinth of debates about education reform, No Child Left Behind (NCLB) is taking most of the heat. TAP is an example of how a productive school reform effort that departs from the status quo will be met with criticism and resistance, and how that resistance can be overcome.

NCLB is predicated on the belief that, with proper support, all children can reach high standards; and relying on scientifically-based research, NCLB ultimately demands high levels of achievement from all students. Similarly, TAP has as its goal increased student achievement. Because teacher quality is the single most important school-related factor affecting student achievement, the TAP approach is to attract, motivate, develop, and retain high quality teachers, and reward them (in part) for the increases they obtain in the achievement of their students. NCLB also

Improving Student Achievement: Reforms that Work, 241–246
Copyright © 2005 by Information Age Publishing
All rights of reproduction in any form reserved.

This chapter originally appeared in *What's On TAP*, Volume 2, Issue 1, Spring 2004.

recognizes the centrality of teacher quality to its goals. According to NCLB, each year a larger percentage of all students, as well as students in every racial and income subgroup, and special education students must reach proficiency.

Even if the targeted share of all students combined reaches the proficiency bar, if all subgroups do not make growth, the school may still be designated as "needing improvement." Since schools are used to looking at totals, not subgroups, this is an alien concept. But being judged only by totals can lead schools to focus on those most likely to get over the bar, rather than on those students who need more help. Many argue that this focus on higher achieving students is a reason why the achievement gap has grown, or at least has not narrowed, over the years.

One inconsistency cited by some NCLB critics is the situation where a school's student achievement rises markedly, from, say, the 30th percentile to the 65th percentile, but is still designated as needing improvement. This is a huge amount of growth, either overall or for a subgroup. In contrast, TAP teachers are given performance pay based on how much their students learn, so such growth could lead to significant bonuses, even if this growth does not result in the number of students achieving proficiency that is required by the school's plan. We can reconcile rewarding teachers and schools designated by the U.S. Department of Education as needing improvement, because they are rewarded for progressing toward a goal, even if they have not yet reached it.

There are ways schools can make Adequate Yearly Progress (AYP) even if the percentage of students and the percentage in each subgroup in the school do not meet the statewide proficiency goal for the year. The school will make AYP if it reduces the percentage of students or percentage of a subgroup below the proficiency bar by 10% from the previous year. This policy, known as "Safe Harbor AYP," recognizes progress even when "enough" students are not achieving the state goal.

TAP, on the other hand, measures value-added for all students in a classroom or school, and does not consider value-added for subgroups. Due to statistical requirements for the value-added calculations, subgroups generally are too small to enable reliable calculations of value-added. NCLB may well have deflected some criticism had it given credit for improvement as well as looked at the percentage who reached the proficiency bar. However, NCLB's focus on subgroups precluded that.

Some claim the achievement goals for all subgroups demanded by NCLB are unrealistic because those with low SES (socioeconomic status) students should not be held to the same standards as teachers serving nondisadvantaged students. However, such assertions reflect a lack of confidence in what schools, and especially teachers, can do to make students learn. The alternative of lower expectations, standards, and life chances for the disadvantaged students is simply unacceptable. It may be more challenging to make disadvantaged students proficient, since they lack the out-of-school resources that others might have. If teachers matter, and research shows they matter a lot, then the challenge is to get the best teachers to the students having the fewest resources. This is an important goal for TAP, and we are already seeing migration of teachers from high SES, non-TAP schools to low SES TAP schools. This trend reversal augers well for growth in achievement by low SES students.

The NCLB requirement that all teachers in the basic disciplines be "highly qualified" causes much consternation from both ends of the policy spectrum. Some argue that the federal definition of "highly qualified" is not what superintendents and principals say they need. We all know that certification may be neither necessary nor sufficient to be deemed highly qualified, and that a high quality teacher means more than this credential. A high quality teacher knows her discipline, is constantly learning and up-to-date, knows teaching techniques and has different instructional strategies to deal with different students, can make students learn, is aware of state standards and uses them to guide instruction, has conflict mediation and classroom management skills, shares knowledge with colleagues, is passionate about her subject, is a hard worker, is intellectually curious, and can communicate with and involve parents. However, research has shown that teacher verbal ability and subject-matter knowledge are the most important measurable teacher-related factors that help students learn. These are the focus of NCLB.

Nevertheless, TAP rubrics evaluate teacher performance on this broader range of skills.

NCLB provides local education agencies (LEAs) with the definition of alternative criteria by which experienced teachers may demonstrate competencies (other than degrees in the fields in which they teach or passing grades on subject tests). The law allows states to establish a "high, objective uniform state standard of education" (HOUSSE) for experienced teachers to demonstrate a sufficient level of competency to achieve the status of "highly qualified." HOUSSE options may include credit for college coursework, teaching experience, certain types of professional development, or professional activities such as presenting research papers. However, if the opportunity to demonstrate subject matter knowledge by taking a test seems onerous, we must ask whether a teacher who cannot pass a test on the subject she is teaching is someone we want teaching our children?

Traditional educators fear that the "highly qualified" mandate is impossible to meet in the expected time frame. The requirement that all teachers be highly qualified by 2006, it is charged, has led many states to institute quick and dirty solutions for credentialing teachers under the

HOUSSE option, including short-term weekend classes or Web-based certification programs, despite lack of any evidence that these work. The charge is leveled even though there is little evidence that traditional credentialing/certification options allow teachers to better help students achieve.

The U.S. Department of Education recognized the need for flexibility in the requirements for highly qualified teachers even beyond the HOUSSE alternatives. Recently, the Education Department provided three new areas of flexibility for teachers to demonstrate that they are highly qualified. Often, teachers in rural areas are required to teach more than one academic subject. Under this new policy, teachers in eligible, rural districts who are highly qualified in at least one subject will have 3 years to become highly qualified in the additional subjects they teach. They must also receive professional development, intense supervision, or structured mentoring to become highly qualified in those additional subjects. TAP's mentoring and professional growth opportunities can help here.

Next, science teachers are being provided additional flexibility to demonstrate that they are highly qualified either in "broad field" science or individual fields of science. Finally, states may streamline their HOUSSE evaluation process by developing a method for current, multisubject teachers to demonstrate through one process that they are highly qualified in each of their subjects and maintain the same high standards in subject matter mastery.

It has become clear that states haven't been taking full advantage of this flexibility already at their disposal through NCLB. States must therefore accelerate alternative certification and do more to attract, retain, motivate, and develop high quality teachers, even though doing so might step on the toes of certain interests who oppose many performance pay plans, alternative certification methods, or new approaches to professional development. Alternatively certified teachers may need strong mentoring from experienced teachers in their first few years; but all new teachers should get this, as they do in TAP.

An overarching complaint is that there is not enough money to do all the things required by NCLB. This is similar to the claim that TAP is too expensive. A significant amount of money is now being spent on education programs that have been operating for years with no evidence that they improve student achievement. Part of the NCLB funding comes from such programs. If states and districts insist on continuing every failed program now on the books, charges of inadequate funding for NCLB (and TAP) have some merit. States and districts must redirect existing funds from ineffective programs to effective programs like TAP that are consistent with NCLB. Title II and recent noncompulsory regulations contain language that make TAP an encouraged use of these funds. The problem for TAP has been that much of the Title II money is the old class-size-reduction money that has already been committed to hiring new teachers. Research seems to indicate that small increases in class size would have no effect on student achievement but would provide substantial money to increase teacher quality.

Contrary to popular criticism, a recent study argues that there is enough money in NCLB for everything that the states are required to do. This becomes an issue of semantics. If NCLB requires testing, and testing is already occurring in a state, the state cannot attribute all testing costs to NCLB. Rather, it can only charge the incremental costs. Moreover, many states have not used all the money that has been provided for NCLB, and federal education funding has increased every year since NCLB was passed.

Yet another criticism of NCLB is a proliferation of testing in schools. TAP also requires annual testing for good reason. Whereas students used to be tested two or three times during their K-12 years in many states, NCLB now mandates annual testing in grades three through eight and at least once in high school. Let's put aside the arcane psychometric babble about the reliability and validity of achievement tests. They can all be dealt with. There may well be other valid measures of student learning, and standardized or state tests do not measure everything students learn. However, the tests used by states today do provide good indicators of how well students are achieving. Much of the antitesting rhetoric is residual from a time when educators were reluctant to be held accountable for student learning. That time has passed.

Now we hear that tests are not aligned to the curriculum. So let's align them. Tests are expensive. NCLB provides money to pay for testing, if states and districts choose to use the money for that purpose. Critics fear teachers will teach to the test, but this is great if we are testing what we want students to know. Parents like testing. Testing removes some of the subjectivity inherent in teacher grading, or at least confirms teacher judgments. It enables comparisons across states, schools, and teachers. It enables teachers to get feedback on what students are or aren't learning, and on how effective their teaching methods are. Testing provides valuable data when used properly, and as such is a prime element of TAP.

Another charge is that NCLB has not produced much achievement growth. There are programs that have been operating for decades, like Comprehensive School Reform, National Board Certification, and class size reduction, that have not been shown to have a great impact on student achievement. Yet educators advocate continued and greater funding of these programs. NCLB passed only 2 years ago, and in some states has only just started to be implemented; yet results are demanded already.

This is an ongoing problem in education, where results for programs that challenge the status quo are required before they have a chance to take hold; whereas programs that are comfortable, but do not necessarily show results, are allowed to go on forever. Nevertheless, the short-term results of NCLB are already encouraging, just as they are for TAP.

There are many ways to develop education policy. The simplest, albeit most ineffective, is to give the education system more money to do what has always been done. This approach will minimize protest from supporters of the status quo, BUT NOTHING WILL CHANGE. NCLB, like TAP, takes a new approach by focusing on student achievement; insisting on standards; holding states, districts, and schools accountable for teachers and students meeting those standards; providing resources to help meet standards; and then, having consequences for not meeting them. Many teachers, parents, and administrators support such efforts. Inevitably there will be protests from some, but we believe these efforts will lead to growing student achievement.

CHAPTER 11

DEPROFESSIONALIZING THE TEACHING PROFESSION

The Problem of Out-of-Field Teaching

Richard M. Ingersoll

The failure to ensure that the nation's classrooms are all staffed with qualified school teachers is one of the most important problems in contemporary American education. Over the past decade, dozens of reports and national commissions have focused attention on this problem and numerous reforms have been initiated to upgrade the quality and quantity of the teaching force. Reformers in many states have pushed tougher certification standards and more rigorous academic-coursework requirements for teaching candidates. Moreover, a host of initiatives and programs designed to recruit new candidates into teaching has sprung up. Among

Improving Student Achievement: Reforms that Work, 247–254
Copyright © 2005 by Information Age Publishing
All rights of reproduction in any form reserved.

This chapter was drawn from the author's (May 2001) longer article, "The Realities of Out-of-Field Teaching," *Educational Leadership, 58*(8), 42-45. Reprinted by permission from the Association for Supervision and Curriculum Development. All rights reserved.

these are programs designed to entice professionals into a mid-career change to teaching; alternative certification programs; and Peace Corps-like programs, such as Teach for America, which are designed to lure the "best and brightest" into understaffed schools. There have also been interest and action at the federal level: Presidents Clinton and Bush both made teacher quality a key part of their education agendas.

Although staffing our nation's classrooms with qualified teachers is among our most important issues, it is also among the least understood. Like many similarly worthwhile reforms, these efforts alone will not solve the problem of underqualified teachers because they do not address some of their key causes. One of the least recognized of these causes is the problem of out-of-field teaching—assigning teachers to teach subjects that do not match their training or education. This is a crucial issue, because highly qualified teachers may actually become highly unqualified if they are assigned to teach subjects for which they have little preparation. There has been little recognition of this problem, however, largely because of the absence of accurate data—a situation remedied with the release, beginning in the early 1990s, of the Schools and Staffing Survey conducted by the National Center for Education Statistics, the statistical arm of the U.S. Department of Education. Over the past 8 years, I have been analyzing these data to determine how much out-of-field teaching goes on in this country and why (for a summary, see Ingersoll, 1999).

My interest in this project originally stemmed from my previous experiences as a secondary school teacher. Out-of-field teaching was commonplace in my schools, both public and private. My field was social studies, but hardly a semester went by in which I was not assigned a couple of classes in other fields, such as math or special education or English. Teaching a subject for which one has little background or interest is challenging, to say the least. It is also, I quickly came to believe, very detrimental to the educational process.

My experiences left me with a number of questions: Were my schools unusual, or was this a common practice across the country. If so, why? Later, after leaving secondary teaching, and completing a doctorate, I got the opportunity to investigate these questions in a large-scale research project. The results of this research, which have generated widespread interest, have been featured in numerous major education reports, including those issued by the National Commission on Teaching and America's Future and *Education Week's* annual supplement *Quality Counts.* Notably, others have reached the same conclusion—that there is an alarming level of out-of-field teaching in American secondary schools.

As a result, the problem has become a real concern over the past several years. The findings have been disseminated in the national media and frequently cited by lawmakers in support of various teacher training and recruitment initiatives. However, despite a growing awareness of this problem and its importance, out-of-field teaching remains widely misunderstood.

HOW WIDESPREAD IS OUT-OF-FIELD TEACHING?

Research on the extent of underqualified teaching is difficult because there is surprisingly little consensus on how to define a "qualified teacher." Few would argue that teachers ought not to be qualified, and, moreover, there exists substantial evidence that the qualifications of teachers are tied to student achievement (see, e.g., Greenwald, Hedges, & Laine, 1996). But there is much controversy concerning how much education and which kinds of training teachers should have to be considered qualified in any given field (Ingersoll, 2001a). After using a number of measures (see Ingersoll, 2001c), I find the most compelling to be: How many secondary school teachers have neither a major nor a minor in their teaching fields?

Of course, some observers, questioning the necessity of even these prerequisites, argue that a good teacher should be able to teach anything, regardless of preparation. Moreover, a college minor guarantees neither quality teaching nor a qualified teacher. But the main assumption underlying my research is that adequately qualified teachers, especially at the secondary school level and especially in the core academic fields, ought to have at least a college minor in the subjects they teach. My assumption was that for most teachers, it is difficult to teach well what one does not know well. I also assumed that few parents would expect their teenagers to be taught, for example, 11th grade trigonometry by a teacher who did not have a minor in math, no matter how bright the teacher.

However, I found that situation all too commonly the case. For example, one third of all secondary school math teachers have neither a major nor a minor in math or such related disciplines as physics, engineering, or math education. Almost one quarter of all English teachers have neither a major nor minor in English, or such related disciplines as literature, communications, speech, journalism, English education, or reading education. Even worse, teachers in such broad fields as science and social studies are routinely required to teach any of a wide array of subjects outside of their discipline, but still within the larger field. As a result, more than half of all secondary school students enrolled in physical science classes (chemistry, physics, earth science, or space science) are taught by teachers who do not have either a major or a minor in any of these subjects. Similarly, more than half of all history students are taught by teachers without a major nor a minor in history. The actual numbers of students affected are not trivial. In grades 7-12, English, math, and history, are taught to over 4 million students apiece by teachers without a major or minor in the field.

Out-of-field teaching also varies greatly across schools, teachers, and classrooms. Recently hired teachers are more often assigned out of field. Low-income schools have higher levels of out of field teaching than do schools in more affluent communities. Particularly notable is the effect of school size; small schools have higher levels of out-of-field teaching. Junior-high-level classes are also more likely to be taught by out-of-field teachers than are senior high classes. There are also differences within schools: lower-achieving classes are more often taught by teachers without relative a major or minor than are higher-achieving classes.

No doubt some of these teachers may be qualified despite not having a major or minor in the subject. Some may be qualified by virtue of knowledge, gained through previous jobs, life experiences, or informal training. Others may have completed substantial college course work in a field but not obtained a major or minor. In some states, because accreditation regulations require at least 20 hours of college credit (about four courses) in a field to teach it, many of those assigned to teach out of field probably do have some background. However, my premise was that even a moderate number of teachers lacking the minimal prerequisite of a college minor signals the existence of serious problems in our schools. And the data clearly indicate that out-of-field teaching is widespread. In any given year it takes place in well over half of all secondary schools—both rural and urban, affluent and low-income—in the United States.

No matter how the problem is defined, the data show that levels of out-of-field teaching are alarming. I found, for example, that similarly high numbers of teachers do not have teaching certificates in their assigned fields. Indeed, when I upgraded the definition of a "qualified" teacher to include only those who earned *both* a college major and a teaching certificate in the field, the amount of out-of-field teaching substantially increased. For example, only 65% of those teaching 7th-12th grade math met this criteria. Moreover, out-of-field teaching does not appear to be going away; I found that levels of out-of-field teaching have changed little over the past decade.

The negative implications are obvious. Is it any surprise, for example, that science achievement is so low given, that *even* at the 12th grade level, 41% of public school students in physical science classes are taught by someone without either a major or a minor in either chemistry, physics, or earth science? The crucial question, and the source of great misunderstanding, is why so many teachers are teaching subjects for which they have little background.

THE CAUSES OF OUT-OF-FIELD TEACHING

Many assume that out-of-field teaching is a problem of poorly educated teachers and can be remedied by more rigorous standards for teacher education and training. Typically, those subscribers to this view assume that the source of the problem lies in teacher's lack of academic coursework on the part of teachers that can be remedied by requiring prospective teachers to complete a "real" undergraduate major in an academic discipline or specialty.

My own case provides an illustration of just how misleading this view is. I graduated magna cum laude from the University of California with a bachelor's degree in sociology. Several years later, I returned to school to take part in an intensive year-long teacher certification program in social studies. None of this background, however, precluded my regular assignment outside social studies.

The data clearly show that the typical out-of-field teacher has experience; a bachelor's and a master's degree; full certification; and substantial course work in an academic specialty. The source of out-of-field teaching primarily lies not primarily in teacher's amount of education but in the lack of fit between their training and their teaching assignments. Many teachers are misassigned by their principals.

The implications of this distinction for reform are important. The efforts by many states to toughen entry criteria, enact more stringent certification standards, and increase the use of testing for teaching candidates will not eliminate out-of-field teaching assignments and, hence, alone will not solve the problem. Mandating more rigorous coursework and certification requirements will help little if large numbers of teachers continue to be misassigned.

A second, and also popular, explanation of the problem of out-of-field teaching blames teacher shortages. This view holds that shortfalls in the number of available teachers, caused by a combination of increasing student enrollments and a "graying" teaching force, have led many school systems to resort to lowering standards to fill teaching openings. The data show, however, there are two problems with the shortage explanation. First, it cannot explain the high levels of out-of-field teaching in areas, such as English and social studies that have long had surpluses. Second, in any given field, even when the rates of student enrollment were peaking in the mid 1990s, only a minority of schools experienced trouble filling their job openings with qualified candidates. For example, less than one tenth of secondary schools had any difficulty filling their openings for English teachers in 1993-1994, but in that same year, a quarter of all public school English teachers were uncertified in English. Likewise, in that year only one sixth of secondary schools reported problems filling their openings for math teachers, but a third of all math teachers had neither a major or minor in math. The data also indicate that about half of all misassigned teachers in any given year were employed in schools that reported no difficulties finding qualified candidates for their job openings that year (Ingersoll, 2001b).

DEPROFESSIONALIZING A PROFESSION

The data point in another direction, away from deficits in qualifications and quantity and toward the way schools and teachers are managed. Allocating teaching assignments is usually the prerogative of school principals. The latter are charged with overseeing an ever-widening range of programs and courses with limited resources and limited staff. Principals' staffing decisions are constrained by teacher employment contracts, which stipulate, among other things, that full-time teaching staff in a typical secondary school must be assigned to teach five classes per day. But within those constraints, principals have an unusual degree of discretion.

As in traditional professions, teaching is subject to an elaborate array of state licensing requirements designed to assure the basic preparation and competence of teaching candidates. However, there is little regulation of how teachers are employed and utilized once on the job. Teacher employment regulations are weak or rarely enforced and, finally, most states routinely allow local school administrators to bypass even the limited requirements that do exist (Robinson, 1985). For example, in many states teachers are counted as out-of-field only if they are misassigned for more than half their classes per day. Because most misassignments amount to less than that, the problem is effectively defined out of existence. In this context, principals may find that assigning teachers to teach out of field is often not only legal but more convenient, less expensive, and less time consuming than the alternatives.

Rather than hire a new part-time science teacher to teach two sections of a newly state-mandated science curriculum, a principal may find it more convenient to assign a couple of English and social studies teachers to each "cover" a section in science. If a teacher suddenly leaves in the middle of a semester, a principal may find it faster and cheaper to hire a readily available, but not fully qualified, substitute teacher rather than conduct a formal search for a new teacher. When faced with the choice between hiring a fully-qualified candidate for an English position or hiring a less-qualified candidate who is also willing to coach, a principal may find the latter more convenient. The degree to which a school is faced with problems of recruitment or retention may shape the extent to which the principal relies on these options, but the data show they are available to almost all schools and used by many.

The comparison with traditional professions is stark. Few would require cardiologists to deliver babies, real estate lawyers to defend criminal cases, chemical engineers to design bridges, or sociology professors to teach English. The commonly held assumption specialization requires a great deal of expertise. In contrast, underlying out-of-field teaching is the assumption that school teaching require far less expertise than these traditional professions; hence, specialization is assumed less necessary.

Of course, teaching may, indeed, be less complex than some kinds of work. But those who have spent time in classrooms know that high quality teaching requires a great deal of expertise and skill and that teachers are not like interchangeable blocks. Good teaching entails a complex combination of art, craft, and science that the best contemporary research has begun to illuminate insightfully (Shulman, 1986). In short, the managerial choice to misassign teachers may save time and money for the school, and the taxpayer, but it is not cost free.

EDITOR'S NOTE

The Association for Supervision and Curriculum Development is a worldwide community of educators advocating sound policies and sharing best practices to achieve the success of each learner. To learn more, visit ASCD at www.ascd.org.

REFERENCES

Greenwald, R., Hedges, L., & Laine, R. (1996). The effect of school resources on student achievement. *Review of Educational Research, 66*, 361-396.

Ingersoll, R. (1999). The problem of underqualified teachers in American secondary schools. *Educational Researcher, 28*(2), 26-37. Available: www.aera.net/pubs/er/arts/28-02/ingsoll01.htm)

Ingersoll, R. (2001a). Misunderstanding the problem of out-of-field teaching. *Educational Researcher, 30*(1): 21-22.

Ingersoll, R. (2001b). Teacher turnover and teacher shortages: An organizational analysis. *American Educational Research Journal, 37*(3).

Ingersoll, R. (2001c). *Measuring out-of-field teaching.* Manuscript submitted for publication.

Robinson, V. (1985). *Making do in the classroom: A report on the misassignment of teachers.* Washington, DC: Council for Basic Education and American Federation of Teachers.

Shulman, L. (1986). Those who understand: Knowledge growth in teaching. *Educational Researcher, 15*, 4-14.

CHAPTER 12

HOW NO CHILD LEFT BEHIND HELPS PRINCIPALS

Jay Mathews

Washington Post Metro page columnist Marc Fisher last week used the stories of two excellent elementary schools to trash, once again, the No Child
Left Behind Act. I was delighted to read his columns because they were
not only well-written, but gave me a chance to expose, once again, Marc's
ill-considered bias against giving kids standardized tests and making the
results have some consequences for the school.

Marc and I both mourn the passing of that era in journalism when col-
umnists picked fights with each other all the time, if for no other reason
than to have easy topics they could type up fast and get to their favorite
taverns before noon. So let's start:

Marc's first column was about Bailey's Elementary School for the Arts
and Sciences in Fairfax County, a well-run magnet school where 54% of
the 912 students are poor enough to qualify for federal lunch subsidies
and 77% are from immigrant families. Marc congratulated the principal,
Jean Frey, for sending a letter to parents last spring saying that even if the

school failed to meet its No Child Left Behind achievement targets this year, she would not, as Marc puts it, "shutter her science lab, pull the plug on theatrical productions or tell teachers to scrap a literature discussion to drill kids on test facts."

The second column introduced readers to Anthony Fears, the principal of Anne Beers Elementary School in the Hillcrest section of Southeast Washington, who worries that his good program may be swamped by too many students transferring from less successful schools. Under No Child Left Behind, if a school is labeled "needs improvement" for failing to raise test scores sufficiently, it can be forced to provide tutoring to students who ask for it and let students transfer to better-performing public schools.

I spoke to both Frey and Fears and was happy Marc spotlighted such fine educators who are doing so much for their students. Frey is serving not only immigrant families in the school's neighborhood, but 200 out-of-boundary students, mostly from English-speaking middle class families, who have chosen Bailey's because of its good programs, and some middle-class families in the neighborhood who have stayed for the same reason. Fears, who used to be an assistant superintendent in Baltimore before deciding to get closer to kids, has given a once poorly disciplined school new focus and energy with firm rules and lots of love.

Marc is right to point out that No Child Left Behind is a clumsy instrument. Some schools have reduced arts classes to make more time for reading and math. Some schools have been hurt by getting too many transfer students from low-performing neighbors. But Bailey's and Beers are not those schools. Nor do there appear to be many schools in the Washington area suffering from these alleged bureaucratic outrages. If anything, both Bailey's and Beers have been helped by the new federal law because its accountability rules give good principals such as Frey and Fears power they never had before.

Many critics of No Child Left Behind hint darkly of monstrous educational practices about to devour the best schools. But when asked to point them out, they have trouble coming up with examples. Marc says in the Bailey's column that "many schools hack away at the arts to focus on test-taking skills." I am willing to buy him a new Washington Grays baseball cap if he can find any such schools in Fairfax County, a very well-run system whose principals and teachers have been preparing students for the new tests without wringing the joy out of learning.

Frey herself acknowledges that Bailey's teachers would spend time reviewing and assessing with or without the worries of No Child Left Behind, because they know that review is a vital part of the learning process and that a variety of assessments are invaluable to ascertaining what parts of the lesson have or have not been absorbed. All she wants is an assessment system that gets results back to her more quickly, and a reduction in the number of tripwires in the federal law so Bailey's isn't labeled as "needing improvement" just because a few too many of her Spanish-speaking students could not pass their English tests. When Congress tries to revise the law next year, such good suggestions are likely to be heeded.

As for Beers Elementary, the most interesting story there is not transfers flooding in because of the new law. Fears admits there were only 20 of them this year, in a school of 402 students. What has actually happened is a 23% reduction in the size of the student body, from 525 to 402 kids, since Fears arrived 3 years ago.

The Beers principal said he found a school that was not enforcing many rules, including those limiting enrollment by students from outside the neighborhood. Previous principals seemed to think that the more students they had, the better off they were, since that meant they could hire more staff. But Fears thought the crowding was hurting the learning, and began to deny many transfer requests.

How was he able to do that, and why has he been able to keep the number of transfers this year to 20? Part of the answer is No Child Left Behind. Fears was recruited by former D.C. superintendent Paul Vance, who knew from the administrators grapevine what talent Fears had. And Fears, an adept office politician from his years as a headquarters administrator, knew that the emphasis on achievement under the new law meant that if new policy threatened his test scores, he could say no. His math scores are up to 18th place in the district, and he is working on similar progress in reading, where the scores are in 44th place. As long as student achievement gets better, few people are likely to try to mess with him.

When you look at the actual numbers, you discover the threat of massive transfers from the district's many underperforming schools is a non-issue anyway. *Post* Staff Writer Sewell Chan reported Oct. 10 that "of an estimated 25,000 to 33,000 students eligible to change schools, only 106 applied for transfers, and 68 of them were accepted." People still prefer their neighborhood schools, a phenomenon educators throughout the area have noted.

Frey, for instance, said she had little fear that her immigrant families would transfer out of the school if it did not meet the No Child Left Behind requirements. She just wanted to assure the middle class parents who knew of the law that, no matter what they heard, their kids were doing well. And in the end, Bailey's reached its testing targets after all.

No Child Left Behind is not the best accountability system ever invented. But, most policymakers and educators say, it has the right idea. Learning should be measured with tests. Standardized tests are in many ways better than the teachers' tests that have ruled schools up to now, because teachers can quietly decide not to test concepts that they have failed to teach well. Other forms of assessment, such as collections of work and conversations with teachers, have potential, but nobody has yet shown a way to make them work well with elementary school children from low-income homes.

Good educators such as Frey and Fears need a standard to guide them, a target to shoot for, so they can convince teachers to spend more time helping struggling students, convince parents to make sure homework is done, and convince administrators at headquarters not to choke them with red tape.

To borrow an example from the little world Marc and I inhabit, many people at *The Post* are concerned about the recent drop in circulation. Everyone is talking about finding more subscribers. You may have noticed our new advertising campaign. But what Marc and I don't do is brag about our energetic reporting and deft metaphors and denounce the whole idea of measuring our sophistication as journalists by something so mundane as how many copies of the paper are sold.

Helping kids learn requires knowing each year how much they haven't learned, and using those numbers to do something about it. The educators at Bailey's and Beers know that, and I suspect the skeptics out there, particularly those as smart at Marc Fisher, will figure it out soon enough.

CHAPTER 13

FIRST STEPS TOWARD STANDARDS-BASED EDUCATION IN OHIO

Susan Tave Zelman

Education, then, beyond all other devices of human origin, is the great equalizer of the conditions of men—the balance wheel of social machinery.... It does better than to disarm the poor of their hostility toward the rich: it prevents being poor.

—Horace Mann[1]

As state superintendent of Public Instruction in Ohio, from time to time, I reflect on why my career shifted from the insular world of collegiate academia to the transparent fishbowl that is government and public service. Reflection often comes when I awaken to unnecessarily hostile education headlines or we find ourselves in an unending uphill battle against budget cuts for schools.

During those reflective moments, I remember educational reformer Horace Mann and his concept of the common school in the nineteenth century—an educational system where *all* children have access to a high quality education, no matter where they live, no matter how much money their families make. I recall that as a college professor, I grew weary of talking to students *about* Horace Mann; I wanted to *be* Horace Mann.

Improving Student Achievement: Reforms that Work, 259–272
Copyright © 2005 by Information Age Publishing
All rights of reproduction in any form reserved.

And so I entered the world of public service in education, taking me from Massachusetts to Missouri to Ohio, where I have tried to put into practice this theory of education as the great equalizer. Every day as state superintendent, I continue to refine the early work of Horace Mann, hoping to improve Ohio's system so that *all* children receive the richness of education they deserve in a democracy. We are not there yet as a state or a nation, but we are on our way.

FIVE YEARS AGO IN OHIO

In March of 1999, when I came to Ohio after being deputy superintendent in Missouri, I faced both state and federal challenges. We had pieces of an educational system that had not gelled together as a system. Ohio had a high school graduation test based on eighth-grade competencies. Assessments and publication of test results in elementary and middle grades began in the mid-1990s in reading, writing, and mathematics. Ohio had begun to assess in social studies and science in the late 1990s. A system of rating districts had just been implemented. A number of initiatives to improve reading instruction had started.

Ohio did not collect student-level data at the state level, so there was no way to measure and track the real achievement or improvement of students' performance. More alarming—with the publication of state and local report cards, we could see then that less than half of our fourth-graders (47.7%) were passing the reading portion of the state proficiency test. Yet, there was no true accountability for student performance, other than to blame students for their poor performance and label school districts as effective, continuous improvement, academic watch, or academic emergency. State law also prevented us from publishing any disaggregated data by race, even though we had it. Then, only 19% of our African American fourth-graders were passing the reading test, but this was unspoken information not discussed in the public arena. Student performance in our urban cities hit rock bottom with all of the eight major cities in academic emergency and more than half of our inner-city youth not even graduating from high school.

At the same time, we faced a legal challenge about the constitutionality of Ohio's school funding system because of inequities across the state, a thorny problem that plagues Ohio to this day, 12 years after the litigation began. The physical conditions of many of Ohio's school buildings had deteriorated, especially in our rural and inner-city school districts. Additionally, Ohio was out of compliance with the federal 1994 Improving America's Schools Act because it did not have the required system of academic content standards, assessments, and accountability.

We did have a proficiency testing system in Grades 4, 6, 9 and 12, although it was not based on clear academic content standards. Because Ohio is a local-control state, school districts created their own curricula based on state minimum competencies. The quality and consistency of curriculum and instruction varied from school district to school district, from school to school, from classroom to classroom. Additionally, I inherited the voucher and charter school movements, which I viewed as potential school choice options for families, but which wrought a slew of lawsuits over Ohio's charter schools and eventually, involvement of the U.S. Supreme Court in the constitutionality of the Cleveland Scholarship and Tutoring Program.

Internally, we needed direction and change. While staff at the Ohio Department of Education worked hard, the agency's focus was more on compliance than student achievement. Basically, programs and projects functioned in isolation, randomly, with no clear accountability about whether the department was making a difference in the achievement levels of Ohio's students. We needed to improve Ohio's educational system, but first we had to improve ourselves.

FIRST STEPS TO EDUCATION REFORM

Our first strategy was to build an internal leadership team with expertise from Ohio school districts and state government. We hired a school district superintendent with more than 30 years of experience as our deputy superintendent of Public Instruction. Our chief of staff came with more than a decade of service at the Office of Budget and Management. A school district treasurer with a CPA and local political experience headed up finances. A school district superintendent who ran large districts in both Ohio and North Carolina oversaw curriculum and assessment. We held onto our organizational history with key leaders in early childhood education and the teaching profession, but we brought in a university professor who specialized in literacy. We pulled from educational organizations for a legislative liaison and chief legal counsel. Eventually, over the years, we would go beyond Ohio to hire national experts in assessments, closing achievement gaps and federal programs, but in the early days, we concentrated on culling strong Ohio leaders.

At the same time, we brought in an outside management team that conducted audits and a study to determine where we needed organizational change. The consultants helped us create the management structure internally as well as the strategic plan for the state,[2] which set the framework for all of our goals and initiatives. In short, our vision was to become the most improved state education department in the nation by

2005. Our mantra became: Raise the bar, close the gap, accept no excuses. We had three missions: (1) to raise expectations for all students by setting clear and high academic content standards for what all students should know and be able to do; (2) to build the capacity of schools and school districts with both fiscal and human resource systems; and (3) to improve results and hold everyone accountable for student performance. We were on the road to standards-based reform.

Even though we were building strong internal leadership, we knew we could not accomplish this vision alone. With the support of our State Board of Education, our second strategy was to collaborate with Governor Bob Taft, key legislative leaders, and the education community in the state, including top union officials. Fortunately, I had come to a state where the governor had already made a conscious commitment to make education his top priority.

When he came into office in January 1999, the governor and his wife, Hope, spotlighted literacy by creating OhioReads, a program that provides funding to schools for literacy programs, specialists and materials.[3] By 2004, the OhioReads program brought more than 45,000 business and community volunteers into Ohio classrooms and close to $130 million into the schools. Additionally, Governor Taft's first education budget[4] increased funding for Ohio's Education Management Information System and provided the department with the ability to collect and analyze non-identifiable student-level data. This was a key tool necessary to begin analyzing student performance, measuring achievement gaps and planning for improvement. Also, under the governor's Rebuild Ohio school facilities program,[5] the state committed $10.2 billion over 12 years to build and repair Ohio schools. By 2003, more than 190 school districts had projects in design, construction, or completion with $3.6 billion committed to rebuilding Ohio schools. This continues today.

The governor also embraced the strategies needed to create high expectations for students and build the human and fiscal capacity of schools to meet those expectations. In April 2000, he formed the Governor's Commission for Student Success, a 33-member group of parents, educators, students, employers, school board members and legislators. Their charge was to recommend what Ohio could do to create an aligned system of high academic standards, rigorous assessments and accountability for results.

OHIO SENATE BILL 1

In response to the commission's recommendations, the legislature, under the direction of Ohio Senator Bob Gardner (R-Madison) and former Ohio

Speaker of the House JoAnn Davidson, passed Senate Bill 1 in 2001, the Student Success Bill. This legislation set Ohio solidly on the road to standards-based reform. Because of this sweeping legislation and the commitment of the State Board of Education, we now have academic content standards in English language arts, mathematics, social studies, science, technology, foreign languages, and fine arts. In January of 2004, Education Week's *2004 Quality Counts Report* gave Ohio an "A" grade for our system of standards and accountability.[6]

Once we had reading and mathematics standards, we moved forward with intensive concentration in professional development around these standards, starting with literacy. We crafted the state's vision for literacy with the State Board of Education, using the National Reading Research Panel's five components of literacy: phonemic awareness, phonics, vocabulary, fluency, and comprehension. We then conducted Summer Institutes for Reading Intervention (SIRI), which to date have trained more than 45,000 teachers in the latest research and techniques in reading instruction.[7]

Our literacy initiative laid the foundation for a clear concentration on the preparation and professional development of teachers in reading. We required all new elementary and middle school teachers to complete 12 semester hours in reading diagnosis, instruction, and assessment. We created strong professional development programs in conjunction with federal funding provided by the Reading Excellence Act, and today, the Reading First Act. Eventually, we would realize the fruits of our labor—reading scores today are higher than they have ever been in Ohio. Today, we are planning to place the same emphasis on mathematics that we did on literacy, and we have launched an initiative to link the state mathematics standards with online professional development and curriculum.

While we were working on new academic standards in other subjects areas, we also developed online curriculum models for teachers in English language arts and mathematics. This online system helps them both model and create lesson plans, and we continue today to build curriculum models aligned to those standards. By the summer of 2004, we will have these online models in social studies and science. We will continue to build on this Web-based system in all seven core subject areas.

The passage of Senate Bill 1 also set in motion a more refined assessment system with a timeline for the phase-in of new tests. Our goal was to provide a system of assessments from kindergarten through high school that would provide teachers with both diagnostic and achievement information about their students. We designed the system to ensure that no students fell though the cracks, that students needing additional help would be identified early in their schooling, and that teachers had the information they needed to make sound instructional decisions.

Senate Bill 1 created a strategic statewide plan for education in Ohio. Standards would drive curriculum and instruction. Assessments would measure student achievement of the standards. And finally, schools and students would be held accountable for meeting the standards. We also wanted to ensure that schools and students would be provided with training, support, and intervention to help them meet those standards. The bill mandated continuous improvement planning, provided for school building as well as district performance ratings, and mandated sanctions for low-performing schools.

In addition, Senate Bill 1 redressed requirements of the 1994 Improving America's Schools Act for which Ohio was out of compliance. These areas included inclusion of students with disabilities and students with limited English proficiency in statewide assessments and accountability results, and the need for a test that measured high school level expectations. The legislation also rectified other problems. Most importantly, it allowed us to disaggregate data based on poverty, race, gender, and disability status. We could now openly publish and discuss data concerning achievement gaps.

Senate Bill 1 was an omnibus reform package for education in Ohio. It took tremendous collaboration to get the bill passed. Through the strong support of the governor, legislative leadership and the business community, the legislature passed an historic package of statewide standards, new assessments and accountability for results.

THE CHALLENGES OF FEDERAL LEGISLATION

Then, just as we thought we were heading in the right direction, the enactment of the federal No Child Left Behind Act of 2001 (NCLB) presented both challenges and opportunities for Ohio. When President George W. Bush came to Ohio with the bill's sponsor, Rep. John Boehner (R-West Chester), to sign the act into law on Jan. 8, 2002, this generated the political momentum for Ohio to step up to the plate at the national level. We already had laid a solid foundation for an accountability system with this aligned system of standards, curriculum, and assessments.

With the passage of NCLB in 2002, Ohio's legislature was not anxious to reopen the state education statutes in the wake of the energy it had taken to secure a majority vote on Senate Bill 1. There was much concern that the coalition that won passage of Senate Bill 1 would not be able to muster support for revising Ohio code to conform to new federal requirements. Revision of Ohio law to meet the requirements of NCLB required consensus among educators in Ohio, the legislature, the State Board of

Education, and the U.S. Department of Education about a plan that made sense for Ohio and met the requirements of the federal statute.

Our greatest challenge was to figure out how to implement NCLB in a way that was true to the spirit of the legislation, but also would be viewed as fair and achievable by school leaders. Our first action step was to go directly to education leaders around the state to seek their input on options for an NCLB-compatible accountability plan. We met with superintendents, administrators, teachers, parents, school board members, educational associations, and the business community. After more than 70 meetings and focus groups, we used the feedback to create a plan that was responsive to the concerns of superintendents and educators across the state.

We heard loud and clear: They wanted a unitary accountability system that combined state and federal accountability requirements. Among the features that educators valued—and that we incorporated into this system—is greater sensitivity to levels of achievement than simply measuring the percent of students who are proficient and higher. Schools wanted credit for improved student achievement. The system finally adopted by the State Board of Education, the U.S. Department of Education, and the Ohio legislature, subsumed the federal Adequate Yearly Progress (AYP) requirement within the larger state accountability system. The AYP measurement is one of four measures that are the basis for sorting schools and districts into five designations from excellent to academic emergency.[8]

As we settled on the design that addressed the federal requirements and listened to feedback from Ohio educators, we began to engage the U.S. Department of Education in the discussion of our plan. We perceived that leading up to the first anniversary of the passage of NCLB, federal officials were anxious to identify states whose accountability plans met the requirements of the federal law to use as examples for those who thought the federal law was unworkable. During November and December of 2002, we held several face-to-face meetings and numerous telephone conferences with federal officials as we negotiated the details of our plan. We found the U.S. Department of Education to be reasonable in exploring what was allowable under the federal law. The department did a credible job of upholding the requirements of the statute while honoring our state's individual context and plan established under Senate Bill 1.

On Jan.8, 2003, President Bush and U.S. Secretary of Education Rod Paige announced Ohio as one of five states that had won early approval of the accountability plan. We think our strategy of being one of the first was a good one because we were able to win approval of virtually all features of our plan that we felt were essential. We ended up with what we believe is a fairer and more credible gauge of student and school district performance and improvement than ever before. For the first time, this system requires everyone to focus on the proficiency and achievement rates of diverse groups of students, including those from the major racial and ethnic groups, students who are economically disadvantaged, those with disabilities and students with limited English proficiency. Most importantly, this new accountability system seems fairer to districts, schools, and students because it provides multiple measures for schools and school districts to show both the achievement status and improvement.

We continue to monitor two areas of concern that we tried to address through our accountability design. The first is accountability for the performance of students with disabilities. We believe that too often, educators have placed an unwarranted ceiling and low expectations for what students with disabilities can accomplish. So, we believe accountability for the performance of these students is appropriate. However, the challenges of reengineering the system so that students with disabilities participate in the general curriculum are enormous. We will continue to tackle the task of fairly assessing the performance of students with disabilities while giving schools the fiscal and human resources they need to ensure these children reach their highest potential.

The second concern is the potential for overidentifying schools needing improvement. We addressed this concern by subsuming AYP within the larger state system and differentiating school effectiveness based on four measures of performance. While we hope that our plan appropriately addressed these areas, we continue to be diligent in monitoring them.

Another formidable challenge in implementing Ohio's new accountability system was securing legislative approval. After all, we were revising a system that had just been enacted and implemented throughout the state, and again, we had to convince the Ohio General Assembly that we were preserving the state structure they had embraced, while also trying to meet the federal requirements. This presented its own set of challenges. A number of legislators viewed the new federal law as unwarranted and unfunded federal intrusion. More than one member of the legislature referenced the 10th Amendment to the U.S. Constitution[9] when urging colleagues to vote against the bill. The bill passed the House and the Senate but to everyone's surprise, in the final week before the legislative summer break of 2003, the bill failed to get concurrence, due to a last minute amendment unrelated to accountability issues. The Ohio General Assembly recessed without enacting the accountability system. Under threat by the U.S. Department of Education to withhold Ohio's federal Title 1 funds, the legislature convened a special session in August 2003 and passed House Bill 3.

Throughout this experience, we had our fair share of public criticism. Some Ohio educators took us to task for being one of the first states to comply with the federal accountability legislation. The field, legislators, media, and even liberal Democrats had railed against NCLB as federal interference. When we altered the accountability system, we felt some backlash. The year had been a difficult one, especially the summer of 2002 when all states scrambled with interpretations of the law while simultaneously trying to comply with it. The timeline for implementation had been quick—seven months after the bill passed, states and districts needed to implement major provisions of the law, including school choice, supplemental services and the highly qualified teacher provision. Often, the requirements for the timeline for implementation came before the U.S. Department of Education had issued guidance.

We faced numerous challenges along the way. We tried to comply with the federal mandate to identify schools in "school improvement" status by the beginning of the school year of 2002. Because school improvement status is based, in part, on the results of student testing from the spring, we did not have enough time to verify data with school districts. The window from May to July 2002 for test data verification was, quite simply, too narrow. In the past, Ohio school districts had more than 6 months to verify test data, so they were not used to a rapid turnaround time, and our fragmented data system was ill-equipped to handle the task.

In our haste to let schools, districts, and parents know which schools were in improvement status so they could exercise the school choice option of allowing parents to transfer their children to other schools, we released preliminary data in July. Ohio public records law does not protect preliminary data, and it generally becomes a matter of public record. We had an overwhelming number of public information requests from both state and national media for the list of schools that needed improvement under NCLB. After we released the information, we found that we had made an internal error in the calculation of the formula we used to identify schools, and we ended up overidentifying schools. The media and schools both came down on us hard, and I publicly apologized to school superintendents for the damage done. We learned from that mistake, and today we have an Educational Data Advisory Council comprised of business experts and educational leaders familiar with large-scale information data systems. They are helping us develop a data exchange system that will provide useful data to school districts and meet our requirements for reporting at both the state and federal levels. We hope, in Ohio, that eventually we will rectify these data problems.

In the meantime, it also took some time to determine who would be supplemental service providers. If school districts were required to provide these services to students by September 2002 in schools needing improvement, the state had the responsibility to determine who qualified as a provider. The process for reviewing providers took time, and the more time it took, the more confusion reigned for both school districts and parents. Eventually, we did set up a system for both the identification, and now, the evaluation of supplemental service providers.[10]

THE IMPORTANCE OF QUALITY TEACHERS

Long before NCLB hit the horizon, we knew from both national and state statistics that we had a teacher shortage in key subject areas—mathematics, science and special education—and we knew the quality of teachers differed from district to district. We needed a major effort to prepare, recruit and retain high-quality teachers, especially in hard-to-staff schools, especially in our poorest school districts. There is nothing more important to student success than the quality of the teacher in the classroom, and I vowed that Ohio schools would have a competent, caring teacher in every classroom when I first became state superintendent. In November 2001, Governor Taft convened the Commission on Teaching Success comprised of 46 teachers, principals, superintendents, school board members, parents, faculty, higher education representatives, state legislators, and business and community leaders. Through December 2002, this group convened seven times, made recommendations, conducted 13 regional community meetings with 1,126 people giving responses to those recommendations, and then finalized their report in February 2003. Their recommendations set the stage for teacher requirements in Ohio that already were becoming more stringent.

Fortunately, Ohio already had a history of strong teacher quality provisions. We had teachers striving for National Board Certification, and we made sure that we provided the funding to pay them an annual stipend for this rigorous certification. Today, we are sixth in the nation for nationally certified teachers. At the state level, we also eliminated the generalist elementary education certificate and required teachers to have strong preparation in their content areas in Grades 4 through 12. In addition, we had a state-level program that funded entry-year teachers with the training, mentoring, and performance assessments they needed as beginning teachers. We also were concerned about recruitment. Today, we have multiple teacher recruitment initiatives, including alternative routes to licensure and funding for mid-career and minority teacher candidates. Under federal funding, we also have expanded our Troops-to-Teachers initiative so that Ohio can benefit from the expertise of our veterans. Our latest initiative is to require colleges and universities to align their teacher education programs with Ohio's academic content standards.

Yet again, the federal NCLB "highly qualified" teacher provision provided the momentum to push this work forward and codify it in law. It took us a longer time than the federal legislation required to comply with the identification of highly qualified teachers in Ohio schools, but the process we went through involved thorough research in the field, field testing of rubrics to determine teacher qualifications, and finally, by September 2003, a quality product teachers and schools could use to determine their qualifications. Educators and the Ohio legislature felt it was extremely important for veteran teachers to be identified as "highly qualified." We created a rubric for alternative ways to qualify, giving teachers credit for professional development opportunities and years of experience. The process worked well. In September 2003, we reported to the U.S. Department of Education that 82% of our teachers were highly qualified.

In Ohio, we believe that we must not only ask what we want our students to know and be able to do, but also what we expect our teachers to know and be able to do. When the Ohio General Assembly approves Senate Bill 2 in 2004, we will put into motion the recommendations made by the Governor's Commission on Teaching Success. We will have clear standards for teachers and principals that are aligned to the student academic content standards. Equally important, we will have standards for professional development to ensure that teachers get training that is meaningful, constructive, and job-embedded. We are on our way to ensuring there is a competent, caring teacher in every classroom.

RESULTS: FIVE YEARS LATER

Are we making improvements? Yes. Five years later, the hard work of educators has paid off. Historically, Ohio had been "stuck in the middle" in both our statewide student achievement scores and national comparisons. When we looked at last year's data, however, our performance index shows that over the past 3 years, the averages of our students' scores on proficiency tests increased from 73.7 to 83.1 points (100 points would mean, on average, that Ohio students are at the proficient level.) We also found that the new accountability system gave a more sensitive picture of improvement. Four of our eight urban school districts pulled out of academic emergency, and more than 40% (262) of our 612 school districts are rated as excellent or effective.

At the national level, our fourth- and eighth-graders continue to outperform the national averages on the National Assessment of Educational Progress in reading and mathematics. We did better than our neighboring states, and it is gratifying to see some of the benefits of our state's reform efforts paying off.

Can we do better? Absolutely. We still have unacceptable gaps in the achievement of minority and economically disadvantaged students when compared to students from largely White, wealthy school districts. Five years ago, only 19% of our African American students passed the fourth-grade proficiency test. In 2003, 61.9% of our African American students passed. While we have made progress, it is not good enough.

We have instituted a "Schools of Promise" program where we are identifying schools that beat the demographic odds.[11] Over the past 2 years, we identified 64 schools where 50% of the student body comes from low-income families but more than 75% meet or exceed Ohio's 75% passage rate in reading or mathematics. In part, these schools reflect Horace Mann's common school, a place where students receive a high quality education, despite family income or background. We found schools in our largest urban district—Cleveland— that are showing promising practices. Also, we found schools in our poorest Appalachian counties that prove children from low-income communities can achieve. Today, we are setting up networks, meetings and school visits so these schools can share what is working with other school districts. The challenge ahead will be to see if these schools can maintain high performance under state and federal guidelines. We think so.

NCLB spurred this kind of recognition nationally, too. Over the past 2 years we have nominated 15 low-income, high-performing schools to the U.S. Department of Education's No Child Left Behind-Blue Ribbon Schools program. Personally, I would like to see more. But remember, 5 years ago in Ohio, this would not have happened. We needed a shift in thinking that we should not be awarding just the best schools in Ohio, we should be honoring those that have broken the mold.

MORE STEPS TOWARD REFORM

While we have experienced growing pains and setbacks as we tried to implement this federal legislation, I still believe that NCLB ignited the national flame for standards-based reform in our country. While some of the logistics of the legislation still need improvement, the spirit of the law is quite simply the right thing to do for our children and our nation. In Ohio, the possibilities for improvement are endless.

As state superintendent, I feel positive about the creation of a coherent system of standards-based education in Ohio. We now have clear academic content standards in seven core subjects that we can align to curriculum models. We are developing new achievement tests aligned with standards, and the first of those tests are being given this year in third-grade reading. We now have a year of accountability under the new system. We are looking forward to implementing a value-added calculation into the system with the help of the business community, so we can assist administrators and teachers in tracking the individual progress of each and every student. We now have student-level data to inform instruction.

Are we still faced with challenges? Yes. The school funding issue in Ohio remains unresolved. The governor has created a Blue Ribbon Task Force on Financing Student Success, which we hope will spark better and more innovative ways to rectify the inequity in funding school districts throughout Ohio. At a time when we are holding schools, school districts and states more accountable for the performance of their students, we are faced with a declining economy, budget cuts, and in Ohio, an uncertain tax base and economy.

My hope is that the use of NCLB as a political football at the state and national levels will cease. How can anyone argue with a law that asks that we, as a country, make sure that every child is learning and succeeding? The harsh reality is that as a nation, we have not served all populations of students well. For too long, states have failed children of color, children who are poor, children with disabilities, children with limited English skills. For too long, educators, communities, public officials, and many others in the public have silently sent the message that because you are Black, because you are poor, because you have a disability, you cannot learn. As President Bush has said, we can no longer tolerate the "soft bigotry of low expectations" for any child in our state or in our nation. But we also cannot tolerate the hard reality that there are not enough resources in the educational system at the federal, state, and local levels to give our children the quality education they deserve.

We must not allow NCLB to be the death of common sense. We must work together as states and as a nation to ensure that the assessments of all children—especially those with disabilities—are fair and realistic. We must ensure that all of our children have access to an educational system that is coherent and not punitive—one that will truly help our children succeed.

Have we fulfilled Horace Mann's promise of education as the great equalizer? Not entirely. But today, both Ohio and the nation are making great strides so that every child in America has the opportunity to succeed and compete in a twenty-first century global economy. Together, we can ensure that *all* children receive the richness of education they deserve in a democracy. We are well on our way.

NOTES

1. Mann, Horace. Twelfth Annual Report to Massachusetts State Board of Education. 1848. 2 Feb. 2004. <http:// www.tncrimlaw.com/civil_bible/ horace_mann.htm>.

2. State of Ohio. Ohio Department of Education. *Strategic Plan*. 2 Feb. 2004. < http://www.ode.state.oh.us/centers/strategic_plan.asp>.

3.   State of Ohio. Ohio Department of Education. Office of Reading Improvement. *OhioReads*. 2 Feb. 2004. <http://www.ohioreads.org>.

4.   Amended Substitute House Bill 282. 123rd Ohio General Assembly. 29 June 1999.

5.   State of Ohio. Ohio School Facilities Commission. 2 Feb. 2004. <http://www.osfc.state.oh.us/>.

6.   *Education Week*. Quality Counts 2004: Count Me In: Special Education in an Era of Standards. *State Report Cards: Ohio*. 2 Feb. 2004. <http://www.edweek.org/sreports/qc04/rc/rcard_frameset.htm>.

7.   State of Ohio. Department of Education. Office of Reading Improvement. Ohio Literacy Initiative. 2 Feb. 2004. <http://www.ode.state.oh.us/literacy-initiative/>.

8.   State of Ohio. Department of Education. Office of Finance and School Accountability. Accountability-Ohio's Plan. 2 Feb. 2004. <http://www.ode.state.oh.us/Finance-School-Accountability/default.asp>.

9.   The 10th Amendment reads as follows: "The powers not delegated to the United States by the Constitution, nor prohibited by it to the States, are reserved to the States respectively, or to the people." Some asserted that, based upon this amendment, education was a province reserved to the states, and not an appropriate topic for extensive federal legislation, such as NCLB.

10. State of Ohio. Department of Education. Office of School Reform and Options. *No Child Left Behind*. 2 Feb. 2004. <http://www.ode.state.oh.us/esea>.

11. State of Ohio. Department of Education. *State Superintendent's Schools of Promise*. 2 Feb. 2004. <http://www.ode.state.oh.us/achievement_gaps/Schools_of_Promise/Default.asp>.

PART VI

WHAT WILL MY UNION SAY

CHAPTER 14

WHAT WILL MY UNION SAY?

Joan Baratz-Snowden

Joan Baratz-Snowden is the director of the Educational Issues Department, American Federation of Teachers (AFT). In that capacity, she assists the AFT in developing policy, programs and services to enhance the skills of members and to improve the institutions in which they work. Prior to joining the AFT, Dr. Baratz-Snowden was vice president for Education Policy and Reform at the National Board for Professional Teaching Standards (NBPTS) where she was responsible for addressing policy issues related to creating a more effective environment for teaching and learning in schools; increasing the supply of high-quality entrants into the profession with special emphasis on minority teachers; and improving teacher education and continuing professional development. Dr. Baratz-Snowden was also the vice president for Assessment and Research at the NBPTS. Prior to joining NBPTS, Dr. Baratz-Snowden worked at the Educational Testing Service where she was the director of the Policy Information Center.

Interest in the politics of education led her to studies of postsecondary, graduate and professional education, where her attention centered particularly on problems of access to education and on retention of minority students. She has conducted groundbreaking research concerning minority participation in medical education and the role of special programs in

Improving Student Achievement: Reforms that Work, 275–286
Copyright © 2005 by Information Age Publishing
All rights of reproduction in any form reserved.

increasing minority involvement in the health professions and in graduate education.

Dr. Baratz-Snowden is well-known for her early research on the language and cultural differences of Black children. In the 1960s she championed the notion of cultural differences and challenged the then popular perception that the behavior of Black Americans was defective and pathological because of economic and/or environmental misfortune.

Joan Baratz-Snowden

I was delighted when Lew asked me to speak, especially when he said, "Why don't you speak on 'What Will the Union Say?'" I thought that was a terrific title because when it comes to reform, very few people ask the union. All too often education reform is thrust upon the union. Leaders are summarily informed of the "reform du jour" that is to be imposed. Or, the union is the excuse for somebody else not doing something. They say "the union won't let us do it; the union doesn't want to do it." We end up taking the rap and appearing anti-reform. That's too bad because the AFT has lots of good ideas, and in many instances, especially in urban areas, the union is the only stabilizing force in town.

Superintendents and other policymakers come and go. I was in Kansas City not too long ago and discovered that they were looking for a superintendent while still paying off two superintendents who had "left prematurely." In a little under 2 years, the District of Columbia has had two superintendents and two "acting" superintendents. School boards are being taken over by mayors who come and go. Nonetheless, the union is there. Not only can we be useful in introducing the reform, but we are there to help keep the reform in place as others come and go. Thus, we need to be in the forefront, not an afterthought, of education reform.

I want to talk about three things today.

- One is role that the AFT has taken in efforts to improve schooling and particularly to improve teacher quality. I'm delighted to do this because most people have what Lew referred to as the "goon mentality" about unions and the idea that unions only say "no," that unions have no ideas. That's an antiquated view of unionism.

- Second, I want to discuss our position on professional pay, which TAP refers to as pay-for-performance. We think teacher compensation is part of improving teacher quality and professionalism. It is not the "be-all-end-all" of education reform.

- Finally, I want to evaluate TAP against our criteria.

THE ROLE OF THE AFT IN EDUCATION REFORM

The AFT was founded almost a century ago. Many of you may be unaware that John Dewey was one of our founding members. From its inception the AFT has been a forward-looking union. Today its mission is twofold: to increase the skills and effectiveness of its members and to improve the institutions in which its members work. Indeed, Al Shanker said, "It is as much the duty of the union to preserve public education as it is to negotiate a contract." The features of that contract should improve teaching and learning and assist in the professionalization of teaching. It's often been remarked that what is good for teachers and their teaching and working environment is good for students and their learning environment. The AFT has been prominent as a voice for reform, and I want to talk about our vision of teacher quality.

We view teacher compensation as only one piece of a larger picture of teacher quality. That larger picture also includes teacher preparation, teacher induction and professional development. Teacher preparation is important because if we do things like TAP and don't fix the front end, we are forever running to catch up. Before I get to teacher quality, per se, I want to point out that the AFT began worrying about these things long before No Child Left Behind. After the publication of *A Nation At Risk*, the AFT lead the way in calling for higher standards for all children. At that time, some in the civil rights community attacked the AFT, insisting that calling for these high standards was a racist idea because imposing such standards on poor children and particularly children of color before "opportunity to learn" standards were in place was unfair. Nonetheless, we pursued this; we published *Making Standards Matter*. We had, as my grandmother would say, the *chutzpah* to rate states on how well they were doing in producing high standards. Over time we got recognized as the critical judge in this area. To this day, when you get your *Quality Counts* from *Education Week* and see the rating of state's standards, the AFT is the group making the judgments.

High standards aren't the whole game. Teacher quality is a subject near and dear to AFT members. Our teachers know what recent research has affirmed: quality teaching is one of the most important *in-school* factors affecting student achievement. Our members want well-prepared and well-qualified colleagues because teachers know the consequences of poor teaching, not only for students, but for themselves. They know the work they must do to compensate for the learning that was lost, due in part to the practice of unprepared or poorly prepared teachers. Long before NCLB defined what I will refer to as "a peculiar definition of a highly qualified teacher," the AFT had called for professionalizing teaching by having higher standards for entry into teacher education—don't just let education be the major for anybody who's in college and can't figure out what they want to do. We need higher standards for those who want to become teachers.

We called for a rigorous liberal arts program for all teacher candidates. Some people think that political science is the undergraduate major for lawyers, and biology, or chemistry is for doctors; the AFT believes that a strong liberal arts program is very important in preparing teacher candidates. But, on top of that rigorous undergraduate preparation, we called for an academic major. We also called for training in a core pedagogy based on research. For example, teachers, through no fault of their own, often graduate without knowing how to teach reading, knowing nothing about assessment, and being unfamiliar with the recent exciting research on how children learn. This core knowledge is often not required in teacher preparation programs. It is no wonder beginning teachers feel ill-prepared. We must do something about that.

We want a rigorous core pedagogy and also a serious clinical program. How many of you remember your student-teacher days? For many of you, student teaching was the highlight of your teacher preparation programs. But all too often we find that student teachers are not placed with the best teachers. Instead they are placed with a teacher in a school that happens to be closest to where they live, or with whomever is most willing to take somebody into their classroom. We need to change that.

We also need a more demanding licensure test to enter teaching. One that not only has demanding subject-matter and pedagogy content, but also a rigorous cut score.

We need an induction program for new teachers, not just a buddy system. The AFT and its affiliates have gone out front in calling for peer assistance and review programs for all new teachers. Let's face it, in too many places, teachers are thrown into classrooms and left to sink or swim. Furthermore, the standards for earning tenure are often lax or nonexistent. Beginning teachers may sometimes earn tenure if they survive 3 years in the classroom and not too many parents complain. That's not a good standard. Peer assistance programs provide the opportunity not only to strengthen skills but also to judge teaching competence. In those AFT affiliates where such programs exist, the standards for remaining in the profession and earning tenure are higher than had previously been the case in the district.

AFT also called for eliminating emergency certification and not allowing unprepared people into the classroom. Had these reforms been taken seriously and put in place, we wouldn't have so many of the conversations we now have about "highly qualified teachers" and the "revolving door" of teacher employment.

Our view of improving teacher preparation keeps an eye on teacher professionalism. The current highly qualified teacher standard does not have teacher professionalism at its heart. It does call for teachers' knowledge of their subject matter, and we agree that teachers need to know their subject matter because you can't teach something you don't know. But content is not sufficient. If it were sufficient, we would all be giving plaques to our college mathematics professors for being the best teachers we ever encountered. We know that's not the case. There's more to teaching than knowing your subject matter and picking up a few tricks of the trade when you get into a classroom.

The union also recognized that most teachers did not have an opportunity to benefit from good professional development, so it developed standards for professional development long before NCLB and the Higher Education Act recognized the importance of professional development. We said professional development must address teachers' needs and be developed with teachers. It must be content-driven and research-based. It must be sustained and embedded in the teacher's workday, and it must be delivered within a collegial environment. This is what we are talking about when we refer to teacher professionalism. We also felt that it was the responsibility of teachers in the union to advocate for and collaborate with others to deliver that high-quality professional development. Teachers must have a voice in the decision-making process regarding both the content and process of their professional development opportunities.

Over 20 years ago the AFT worked with the University of Pittsburgh to create the AFT's Educational Research and Dissemination Program (ER&D). At that time, there was plenty of good research but it was inaccessible and incomprehensible to teachers. So the AFT worked with researchers and teachers to translate the research, and it created courses for its members. Today, hundreds of AFT affiliates across the country deliver ER&D courses to their colleagues in subjects as diverse as how to teach reading, how to teach thinking math, management of antisocial behavior, assessment, the use of data, and the like.

The AFT's New York City affiliate, the United Federation of Teachers, is responsible for all professional development of teachers. They deliver that professional development through teacher centers supported by the district, state, federal government, private foundations, and corporate grants. In Pittsburgh our teacher union uses union members' dues to pay for its professional development center. Many of our local affiliates, in partnerships with universities in their districts, also deliver professional development to their members.

Long before NCLB, we also recognized the need to improve the institutions where our members work and in particular, to transform failing schools. Sandra Feldman, the immediate past president of AFT, said,

"Those of us responsible for public education must never defend or try to perpetuate a school to which we would not send our own children." Instead, she said we must work to improve those schools.

We did not fight against change; we did not fight against the need for reform. We did fight against "reconstitution," what I call the "neutron bomb" of school reform. The "neutron bomb" kills everybody but leaves the buildings standing. Reconstitution was first practiced in San Francisco, where the administration moved everybody out—students, teachers and administrators—but left the buildings standing. Instead, the AFT proposed a productive, research-based approach to turning around low-performing schools. We wanted to be sure that when a district was going to change a school, they had a plan and the union participated in creating that plan. We believed that when embarking on school reform, it was first necessary to have high standards for students and the opportunity for teachers to work together to understand what those "high standards" were. How are they substantiated in student work? What did shoddy work look like? No longer could a teacher say, "This is ok; this is an A for this poor kid," when such work was not an A on the other side of town. We wanted high standards for behavior. You can't have a learning environment if the disruptive kid is permitted to destroy the learning opportunities of all the other kids in the class. There had to be high standards of behavior, and there had to be clear, credible criteria for identifying low-performing schools. Teachers need to be involved in the reform process. That is part of the professionalism we called for. Indeed, teacher involvement in school reform creates new roles and responsibilities that a revised compensation system can address.

THE AFT'S POSITION ON PAY-FOR-PERFORMANCE

About the time that TAP was being designed, the AFT called for rethinking compensation systems. We believe we need a compensation system that has a competitive base pay and benefits for all—one that is forged through cooperative labor-management relations and includes multiple opportunities for teachers to advance along the pay scale, in addition to experience and education level. We need a system that moves beyond the rigid hierarchy of the traditional salary schedule. We believe that teachers should receive additional compensation for achieving National Board Certification. We believe that teachers should get additional compensation for teaching in shortage areas. We believe that teachers should get paid more for extra responsibilities and for taking appointments in hard-to-staff schools. But, we are very wary of merit pay systems because of past experience.

There's a reason that teachers and their unions are nervous when people wave performance pay in front of them. In the past, those schemes were underfunded—the pay associated with excellence amounted to trivial bonuses. Furthermore, the budgets were tight and when some other "reform du jour" appeared, the bonuses disappeared. The former pay-for-performance systems robbed Peter to pay Paul. They used quotas for determining quality. They had questionable or difficult to understand assessment procedures. They did not improve student learning or teacher performance, and they created morale problems stemming from unfair competition in a profession where collaboration and cooperation are valued.

I cannot stress enough that, in order to assure an adequate supply of skilled, qualified teachers and to retain those already in the profession, the base salary must be competitive with the salary of other professionals. If teachers are going to seek additional professional development opportunities, take on additional responsibilities and more difficult teaching assignments, or subject themselves to the rigor of the NBPTS process, there also must be meaningful financial incentives to encourage teachers.

Teachers also need to have credible, rigorous standards and measures of professional practice. When I became a vice president at the National Board, my job was to create an assessment to identify outstanding teachers. You can't develop a valid assessment without having standards upon which the assessment is based. I was shocked in 1987 to learn that there were no standards for excellent teaching that I could use. The absence of such standards made me understand why the teacher preparation system was so weak. As the Cheshire cat said, "If you don't know where you are going, any road will take you there." With no standards, anything goes and quality disappears.

Another reason it is critically important that we need high-quality teaching standards is that it helps define what excellent teaching is all about. One of the things I learned when I was at the National Board is that teachers often don't have a vocabulary to talk about teaching. Oh, they liked "this," and "that" seemed engaging. I was at my grandson's birthday party and the clown was engaging, but I don't think anybody learned anything. There is more to teaching than keeping order and amusing children!

Developing standards of excellent practice is very important because then credible measures of excellence can be developed and teachers can measure their practice against the standards. Credible standards and ways to measure the standards are critical to a differentiated compensation system. There must also be a clear opportunity to improve professional practice, combined with the necessary supports. Any viable compensation system must include well-developed and adequately funded professional development designed by those in the profession to help teachers achieve the necessary skills and knowledge to improve teaching. Finally, the incentives must be made available to all eligible teachers. There can't be quotas or a reduction of individual monetary awards as more teachers develop into the quality professionals we want. We need all the high-quality teachers we can get, not just what we can afford. We have to afford more.

HOW DOES TAP MEASURE UP TO THE AFT CRITERIA?

I've followed the progress of TAP over the years, and I believe the program has made great strides. I wasn't always delighted with TAP. I first encountered TAP when a brochure that had very fancy graphs and purported to solve education's problems with pay-for-performance caught my eye. TAP was billed as an incentive plan that would:

- get the good teachers to "produce" (as if teachers were "holding back" their services and only needed a bit of money to increase their performance),
- get rid of the bad teachers (presumably by starving them), and finally
- attract a new breed of teachers into the system with the promise of more money (but hardly enough to compete with salaries in other fields requiring comparable training and education).

This TAP miracle was going to be done largely by redistributing the existing money. Well, not to my surprise, TAP tried this and found almost immediately that "this dog wouldn't hunt." Change was more complex, more difficult, and more costly. Now the reason I got to like TAP was that, instead of blaming the system and moving on, TAP learned from its earlier efforts. Like excellent teachers, TAP creators reflected on their practice, and made the necessary changes. They are still doing that, which is why I am now a TAP supporter.

As it has matured, TAP has learned a lot and has become a program that addresses the needs of teaching as a profession. It has moved from an economist's model of reform to an educational one that recognizes the teaching professional. I think a lot of its controversies might go away if that were the case and if people understood the complexity of what TAP has become. It does have many of the elements we call for to assure teacher quality, of which compensation is only one piece.

So what does TAP do?

- It calls for compensation for a variety of roles. Good, we like that.
- It does not rob Peter to pay Paul. We like that too.
- It provides a number of ways to earn additional compensation, another check.
- It has clear standards for teaching performance.
- It has an evaluation system that involves teachers and requires trained evaluators, and that evaluation system is linked to professional development.
- It provides professional development opportunities, and the professional development activities appear to meet AFT criteria.

TAP pushes for meaningful levels of additional compensation, but it doesn't seem to get there. The compensation range that TAP suggests is modest but certainly a good step forward. But most financial rewards are below the TAP suggested targets. It seems to me that TAP needs to be sold for what it is: a whole school improvement program that is dependent on teacher professionalism, not merely as a new, souped-up compensation system.

Let me comment briefly on the way TAP changes the manner in which teachers are compensated. As you all know, the overwhelming way in which teachers are paid today, whether in regular public schools or in charter schools, is through the traditional salary schedule that was invented in the early part of the twentieth century. I emphasize charter schools because they were supposed to be the innovators, the future. Charter schools don't have any system they have to work within. They can create a different compensation system, but it appears the only charter schools that are doing so are the handful of TAP schools that are charters. Remember, the traditional salary scale was created as a reform measure in response to discriminatory practices. It eliminated such abusive practices as differential pay based on race, gender, or the level of students whom teachers taught, and replaced them with a salary schedule focused on years of experience and teacher knowledge as demonstrated by their college degrees and advanced credits.

We've had a lot of experience with this system, and while it has many virtues, it certainly has its limitations. It hasn't produced salaries that are competitive, given teachers' educational levels and the complexity of the work they do. We all know—and I think it may have even been reported in that original TAP brochure—that beginning teachers make about $8,000 less than those with similar educational backgrounds who enter other professions, and over time this gap increases geometrically. The longer you stay in teaching, the more it costs you. In addition, as implemented, the traditional system does not always reward the additional knowledge and skills that teachers acquire to benefit children. It doesn't provide an incentive for teachers to get additional endorsements or multiple licensures in shortage fields. Only recently have additional funds been provided for exemplary practice, such as for National Board Certified teachers. In general, the current compensation system doesn't provide additional money for teaching in extraordinary circumstances, like hard-to-staff schools, nor does it address issues of shortage areas. Furthermore, it does not include incentives for teachers to assume differentiated professional roles such as mentors, lead teachers, or curriculum developers.

There is no question that we need a change. There is no question that the public supports more money for teachers, generally, and the rewarding of excellent teachers. The AFT supports differential models of compensation provided they are implemented properly as part of a larger effort at improving teacher quality and professionalism. So the question for us is, what is the model and on whose back are you going to achieve it?

So What Are My Concerns?

I do have a few.

The first one is that TAP is a bit more of an enthusiast of value-added models for compensation than the AFT is at this time. The AFT is not against value-added models, but we are wary of how easily the term is thrown around and used without regard to the many technical issues concerning the tests, the data systems, and the capacity for analysis that must be present to build a valid and reliable value-added system. For example, TAP talks about rewarding teachers for student improvement. Students may fall along a wide range of achievement in your classroom. Each of them, from the lowest performing—perhaps two grades below "grade-level" to the highest—perhaps three grades beyond grade-level—have to demonstrate that they moved forward to earn a reward. Well, most of the current tests don't measure the full range of student performance in the classroom. They start at point X, but the kids may in fact be performing below point X when they reach the classroom. So if you move a kid who is way off the chart to just below where the test starts measuring, it looks like he made no progress in a year. Similarly, if you have a kid that is up there at the top of the test, it is going to be hard to show that he has moved because the test doesn't assess beyond where he was when he came into the class. Value-added cannot be done just by taking the ITBS or whatever test the school uses and saying we will now do pre- and posttesting so that we can have a value-added system. You need tests with specific characteristics. This discussion, of course, leaves aside whether the testing narrows the curriculum and whether the curriculum is aligned to the tests. In addition, I'm sure most teachers teach children lots of valuable things that are not on the test or really can't be measured in a quantifiable fashion, but nonetheless add value to students.

But the quality of the test is only one issue in thinking about value-added systems for rewarding individual teachers. You have to have a data system that has individual IDs for students and can account for where kids are as they move through school. Most district systems aren't there yet. Given the current technical capacity of districts, the AFT is more comfortable with systems that reward whole school performance than with those that purport to identify and reward individual teachers.

Another concern I have involves "going to scale." TAP has 75 schools and counting, which is terrific. TAP says it *only* costs $400 per kid, per year. We have 40 million kids in this country, so this is not a trivial amount of money if TAP is to be implemented across the nation.

I am also concerned that as you move to scale, the union needs to be involved and be more prominent in your efforts to sell TAP as a professional reform. TAP needs to be proactive. Don't just go to the state or district hierarchy. Seek out the union. Don't just wait for us to come to you. You come to us. You can get the cooperation of the unions when you convince them that you fit into their definition of teacher professionalism.

And you should use the union's structure to implement and sustain your reform. The building stewards and others can have a role, along with the masters and the mentors, in implementing TAP.

Lew indicated that compensation is part of a larger picture of teacher professionalism. As you expand into more places, you will run into two problems. One is that you are going to expand to places that are already ahead of you on teacher professionalism, and the second is you are going to expand into places that are Neanderthal. Both of these scenarios are going to give you different problems. There are those places that are already well into the game of teacher professionalism and reform, who have already negotiated professional teaching standards, peer review, mentor, career ladders, and the like. You need to be flexible enough to incorporate their programs into your programs and their terminology into your program. After all, you are building the compensation onto their current reforms. You are not replacing them. And, in places that are reluctant, you have to take the time to educate the teacher-leaders. Imposing TAP by administrative fiat—without leader buy-in—will doom the program.

TAP recognizes that reform is difficult. It's going to be harder in strapped districts. They may already know they want reform. But wanting it and being able to do it are two different things. You are going to have to work very hard to build the capacity to bring in the reform. It's going to be damn hard, if not futile, to bring in the reform and then run behind it to build the capacity.

In Conclusion

I am sure you can see that we at the AFT are serious about reform. We embrace reform, but not all reformers. We know it's hard, and we know that it takes time. We stand ready to work with you. More must be done to succeed, and greater investments must be made. One of our biggest problems is that as a society we do not invest seriously in the lives of children, most especially in the lives of poor children and children of color. It will take political will, resources, and a greater seriousness of purpose among all involved in the policy and practices related to the preparation and compensation of teachers if we are to ensure a highly qualified teacher in every classroom.

PART VII

EVALUATING REFORM

CHAPTER 15

PLANNING AND EVALUATION OF EDUCATIONAL EVALUATIONS

Herbert J. Walberg

INTRODUCTION AND OVERVIEW

The purpose of this chapter is to analyze the features of educational evaluations that facilitate causal conclusions about the effectiveness of K-12 educational programs. Since many factors in communities, homes, schools, and classrooms causally affect student-learning outcomes, it is no small matter to separate the unique effects of a particular program from other programs, conditions, and characteristics of students in schools. For example, socioeconomic status (SES) and present achievement can predict as much as 80% of the schools' subsequent achievement.

Failing to take only these differences alone into account can invalidate comparisons of schools. For instance, if 100 schools employing a new program were simply compared to 100 schools that did not and that also differed in socioeconomic status, no unequivocal causal inference could be drawn since any differences in achievement could well be attributable to SES differences. Neither would the intuitively appealing "matching" or pairing schools in socioeconomic status suffice since they undoubtedly

Improving Student Achievement: Reforms that Work, 289–327
Copyright © 2005 by Information Age Publishing

differ in many other respects such as student ethnicity, teacher effectiveness, curricular emphases, principal leadership, and staff interest and
willingness to participate in the new program.

Medicine may be a century or so ahead of education in regards to
insisting on basing practice on rigorous causal evidence yielded by experiments. Yet, the new U.S. Department of Education's Institute of Education Sciences has set forth guidelines that are requiring more rigorous
research methods. As discussed below, the National Academy of Sciences
and the National Institute of Child Health and Development have also
argued persuasively that research standards must be raised to sort out
what works and what doesn't work in the nation's schools.

Overview

This chapter covers much ground since its specific purpose is to cata-
log the various experimental and other designs for inferring causality and
providing case studies of successes and failures. After this introductory
section, the next section explains why randomized or "true experiments"
are now regarded as the gold standard of educational program evaluation, and the strengths and weakness of experiments and other research
designs are explained. The following sections present the chief experimental designs, related threats to validity, and special problems of educational evaluations. The next five sections illustrate design features
reflected in recent educational program evaluations including the
Teacher Advancement Program. The final section concludes and summa-
rizes the main points of this report.

Achievement Tests Count

This report assumes the overriding importance of student learning in
evaluating educational evaluations. In today's climate of opinion, achievement or learning outcomes are a *sine qua non* of school and program evaluation. Two decades ago, the famous report "A Nation at Risk" (National
Commission on Excellence in Education, 1983) alerted policymakers that
Americans students compared unfavorably with their peers in other countries. Subsequent surveys showed that U.S. students fell further behind,
the longer they are in school despite high per-student costs of American
schools (Walberg, 2001).

Scores on the National Assessment of Educational Progress (NAEP),
moreover, remained poor and stagnant despite steadily and substantially
rising cost-adjusted per-student expenditures and many touted educa-

tional reforms. These and other developments led to the present sense of deep concern among citizens, parents, and policymakers about how well students are learning, as evident in two controversies extensively covered in the media.

The federal No Child Left Behind Act, was overwhelmingly supported by Congressional Democrats and Republicans is taking strong hold in all 50 states. It requires increased achievement testing; and identification of schools that fail to meet Annual Yearly Progress (AYP) in helping increasing numbers of children to attain proficiency levels. Failing schools may be required to close or to allow their students to attend other schools. Many high-poverty schools in big cities are under AYP pressure.

Surprisingly, some formerly highly regarded suburban schools in high-wealth communities failed AYP standards and were required to write letters to parents declaring their failure. Unlike the past, they could no longer rely on their achievement status, much of which may have causally derived from parental socioeconomic status but had to achieve gains in the numbers of students that attain proficiency bars or actual "value-added" progress from one year to the next.

Similarly, in evaluating programs and policy innovations, it is important to consider apples-to-apples comparisons. For example, a recent survey by the American Federation of Teachers showed that several charter schools performed less well than regular schools (Nelson, Rosenberg, & Van Meter, 2004). A group of 31 scholars, however, pointed out that charter schools are typically concentrated in poverty areas of big cities, which would account for any differences between charter and other schools (Soifer, 2004). A more definite Harvard University statistically controlled analysis of nearly all U.S. charter schools showed charter schools achieved better than nearby regular schools (Hoxby, 2004). A previous Arizona study (Solmon, 2003) had also shown the strong appeal of charter schools to parents, and a single defective study should not be taken seriously.

The point is that evaluations that do not analyze achievement are unlikely to be influential on legislative policy and school decision making. Testing creates pressure on educators. Even so, parents, citizens, legislators, and business people want to know how their schools are performing. They rightly believe that the nation's and children's futures depend on how well students acquire knowledge and skills revealed on tests.

Other Indicators

None of this is to claim that learning as indicated on tests is the only consideration. Parental, staff, and even student attitudes and perceptions about their schools and their policies, practices, and programs are useful.

They can be indicative not only the value of program choices and improvement but also in discovering what factors account for roadblocks and successful implementation.

In addition, cost information should be considered since schools should employ their resources wisely and cost effectively. Though evaluations rarely provide cost information, ratios of the estimated outcome benefits to costs should be a prime consideration in economically rational policy and decision making. Even so, as discussed in the previous section, this chapter concentrates on learning outcomes.

CAUSAL INFERENCES

The short "golden age" of education research may have begun in 1963 with the publication of a chapter by Donald Campbell and Julian Stanley (1963a) in the *Handbook of Research on Teaching*. The authors showed how "true experiments" in which students were assigned at random to experimental and control groups produced more confident causal conclusions about program, curriculum, and teaching effects as compared to "quasi-experiments," which make use of statistical controls for pre-existing differences among groups in an effort to equate them. Psychologists refined this original statement and cataloged the various threats to the validity of experimental and other research. This culminated in Cook and Campbell's (1979) definitive work in the field, the ideas of which are the subject of much of the present report.

In the subsequent years, case studies and other forms of qualitative research became increasingly popular, and experiments became rare in mainstream educational research. Though many psychologists continued with experiments, they often focused on minute phenomena that educators questioned as to its relevance to the problems and decisions they faced.

New Emphasis on Experimental Rigor

Recently, however, experimentation and rigorous research standards have returned to education under the influence of other fields. Experiments have become the "gold standard" in medicine, and economists have increasingly made use of experimentation to establish fundamental economic principles of benefit, cost, and risk.

One group was particularly influential in emphasizing rigor. Established by congressional mandate to summarize research-based knowledge, and commissioned by the National Institute of Child Health and

Development, the National Reading Panel (2000) recently reviewed the enormous body of existing research on the teaching of reading.

The panel uncovered 1,962 articles on phonemic awareness (the child's recognition that written words are composed of distinct sounds, such as C-A-T), but only 52 articles were deemed scientifically rigorous. Probably one reason for the endless controversies in education is the host of causally uncertain studies without randomized control groups, as would be found in studies in agriculture, medicine, and psychology. In any case, the rigorous studies showed one of the largest effects ever uncovered in educational research, .86, which would place the average student instructed in Pennsylvania at the 80th percentile of control groups using other methods of reading instruction.

In 2002, the National Research Council of the National Academy of Sciences published an important volume, which points out the reasons for experiments, statistical controls, relevance of research to theory and practice, and compliance with rigorous research standards (Shavelson & Towne, 2002). The new Institute of Education Sciences that controls $400 million in funds for research seems unlikely to fund studies that fail to meet such criteria.

Assessing the effects of programs requires such evidence. To assess the studies that evaluate the program's performance, hopes, or claims, a framework detailing the strengths and weaknesses of experimental designs is necessary. This section lists, explains, and provides examples of the strengths and weaknesses of the study designs that can be employed to assess school programs. The valid and invalid features of the evaluation designs are highlighted. Made explicit, these features allow us to determine the scientific rigor or validity of any given evaluation. The greater the number of more rigorous study designs employed, the greater the confidence in the conclusions.

EVALUATION DESIGNS

Designs for research and evaluation can be usefully grouped into several categories: pre-experimental, (true) experimental, and quasi-experimental (see Table 15.l). This section explores the merits and practicality of each study design. Even more specific threats to validity are subsequently discussed.

Pre-Experimental Designs

Much, perhaps most educational research allows no causal inference. To avoid such designs, it is worthwhile to analyze their flaws.

Table 1. Evaluation Designs and Important Features

Design and Features	Frequency	Advantage
1. Experiment	Rare but increasing in view of recognition of efficacy	Causal confidence
2. Pre-experiment	Common	Easy (but untenable)
3. Quasi-experiment	Common	Realism
4. Statistical Control	Common	Increased confidence and precision
5. Pre-post without control	Common	Somewhat better than pre-experiments
6. Standardized tests	Moderately common	General and fair comparison
7. Developer tests	Moderately common	Measures EMO goals
8. Effect sizes	Rare until recently	Allows magnitude estimation

One-Group, One-Shot Case Study Design

The first of three common but flawed one-group, "pre-experimental designs" is the one group, one-shot case study. It relies on a single measurement of a single group after a "treatment," that is, a procedure, regimen, or program may have caused a change. Consider, for example, the new and rapidly growing number of charter schools, which are publicly funded but privately governed by nonprofit boards. If a charter board opened a new school, this design would measure its results at one point in time without regard to other nearby schools.

Unfortunately, according to Campbell and Stanley (1963b, p. 6), "such studies have such a total absence of control as to be of almost no scientific value." The major reason, of course, is that they yield no information of whether or not students have achieved more than they would have in the usual programs because they provide no basis of comparison.

Valid evidence, among other things, requires at least one comparison. In the charter school example, since only the new school is examined, it is almost impossible to tell whether the new school has promoted a desired effect, or whether achievement scores were caused by a host of other factors (e.g. brighter students, more motivated parents, better teachers, etc.). Since many factors could account for the scores, this evaluation design study tells us little about what is causing the effect, and thus, poorly informs on how well the school is actually performing.

One-Group, Pretest-Posttest Design

The second pre-experimental design is the "one-group pretest-posttest evaluation." Although widely used and better than the one-shot case study, the design is flawed because other factors may have caused the change in test scores. An example of this design examines a mathematics class with three parts. First, students are given a math test, then taught the class using a new textbook, and then given the math test again. If the students scored higher on the posttest than the pretest, one might conclude that the new textbook was the cause for the change in test scores.

Unfortunately, many other explanations could also explain a change in scores, and the study yields no information on how the gains compare to classes using a different textbook. The pretest itself, for example, could explain a gain in scores since students are known to do better on tests they take a second time even without a treatment. This is due to practice effects. If the study took place on a single day, a drop in posttest scores could be explained by the students getting bored or tired. In short, this type of study is not scientifically rigorous because many alternative explanations cannot be ruled out.

Static-Group Comparison Design

The third pre-experimental design involves matching or pairing and is called the "static-group comparison design." As the latter name suggests, one group that has experienced a treatment is compared to one which has not. An example of this type of study is comparing a charter school to a nearby regular school. While this may seem more defensible than the previous two study designs, there is no way to ensure that the two schools started on the same level.

If, for example, the charter school had an entrance requirement or lengthy application process, they might attract a more intelligent or motivated pool of students, thus attaining higher achievement scores even if everything else were equal. Even assuming this type of study started with identical students, if the charter school experienced higher student drop out rates from the program, average achievement scores would rise as the lower achieving students were weeded out. On the other hand, the charter school may have taken over a failing school with poorly prepared teachers and students. In summary, this type of evaluation does not allow a determination that the schools were the same except for the treatment.

True Experimental Designs

Properly designed and executed true experiments can allow valid inferences about school effects.[1] When cost is no object, they would normally be the first choice.

Pretest-Posttest, Control-Group Design

The first true experimental design is also the most often used—the pretest-posttest control-group design. In this design, students are randomly assigned to a treatment or a control group. Both groups are tested; the treatment group receives the treatment in question while the control group does not. Both groups are tested again and the posttest scores are compared. Notice that the random assignment of subjects to control and treatment groups increases the probability that both groups start on a level playing field, reducing or eliminating the weaknesses discussed thus far.

To study the effect of a charter school, for example, students would be assigned to the charter school or another school based on the flip of a coin (randomly generated numbers is another means for selection). The students at both schools would be tested prior to instruction. The students would then attend their schools, and subsequently undergo testing again at the conclusion of their studies.

Although this solves most of the problems raised so far, it also raises practical issues. For example, it might be difficult to find a community that would accept the random assignment of their children to different or untested schools, and furthermore, difficulties may arise during implementation if the schools were geographically distant (e.g. why should Jimmy go 10 miles to school X, when he lives a few blocks from school Y).

True experiments are difficult in education yet it may be argued that they are still more difficult and morally challenging in cases where recovery from disease or even death may depend on a coin flip. Yet, without proof of causal efficacy, it may be arbitrary and even unethical to assign uncertain treatments to patients. For this reason, modern medicine is increasingly insistent on the accumulation of results of true experiments. Does the same not hold true in education? And there are many reforms that do not require such huge manipulations as assigning students to schools.

Posttest-Only, Control-Group Design

The "posttest-only control-group design" is another type of true experiment. In this case, subjects are randomly assigned to two groups, and neither group is pretested. One group receives the treatment, while the other group does not. After the treatment, both groups are tested. Although the exclusion of pretests may seem counterintuitive, the use of randomization alone in large samples is likely to reduce or eliminate biases between groups. Pretests, however, can serve as a check to ensure that randomization worked and to increase the sensitivity of the evaluation to learning gains made during the study. Using this technique to compare a charter school with another school, students would be randomly assigned to either school and then tested at the end of the school year. Although this design suffers from the same practical problems discussed earlier, it may be the only option available when pretests are impossible, as when introducing completely new or original material.

In conclusion, it is highly preferable but admittedly difficult to randomly assign students with a flip of a coin to treatment and control groups, or to charters and other schools. Without such random assignment, there will be a degree of uncertainty about the causes of achievement differences between groups. As in rigorous medical and agricultural research, this is a "true experiment," and its strength is that there are few reasons that the groups differ other than the program and small random variations. Of the thousands of education evaluations, however, only a few have had this feature because children, teachers, and schools are not easily assigned in this way.

Limitations of True Experiments

True experiments are hardly foolproof and may not be cost effective. They may not even be definitive is ascertaining causality. The often-cited Tennessee experiment on class size, for example, was so flawed as to give little useful policy information (Hanushek, 1999). Because of "Hawthorne effects," moreover, experiments may tell us how educators and students do in artificially contrived circumstances rather than in ordinary circumstances, and the results may not generalize to other settings.

For these reasons, quasi-experiments are often a reasonable choice and have distinct advantages. Best of all, of course, is to compile large amounts of evidence from many experimental and quasi-experimental studies even though none could by itself be completely definitive. A good medical example is the case of the cigarette smoking-cancer link shown by many animal experiments as well as several large-scale epidemiological studies linking cigarette smoking and lung cancer.

Quasi-Experimental Designs

As the name suggests, these quasi-experimental techniques may employ elements of true experiments, such as who is tested and when they are tested. Although unlike a true experiment, the evaluator may not control who receives the treatment, determine the treatment delivery time, or randomly assign treatments. In this design, nonrandomly assigned treatment and control groups are compared, but they may have initially differed. For example, better-informed administrators and teachers or those in districts of higher socioeconomic status may have chosen to use the new program. Or, children having achievement or behavioral problems may more frequently transfer to charter schools. Thus, apparent program superiority or inferiority may be attributable to factors other than the program.

For similar reasons, a high success rate for a new form of bypass surgery on highly educated patients in university hospitals may leave open important rival explanations of success. Perhaps, for example, people that go to university hospitals get better nursing and surgeons. Despite these flaws, quasi-experimental designs can be worthwhile if we can assume that rival causes have been statistically rather than experimentally controlled. The disadvantage is that the factors to be controlled depend on assumptions and measures on which authorities may disagree and question. Should, for example, socioeconomic status be controlled? If so, is parental income, education, or household possessions the best measure? What follows is a description of single-group experimental designs, and then a discussion of multiple-group experiments.

Single-Group, Time-Series Design

The first quasi-experimental design used to study a single group is the time-series experiment. This design entails a series of periodic observations or measurements, the introduction of the treatment, then followed by another series of observations or measurements. An example of this technique involves the study of a 12-week political science class. The investigator or researcher would make daily or weekly classroom observations to establish a benchmark. Subjects receive treatment (e.g. new lesson plan, textbook, instructional technique, etc.) in the sixth week. The researcher would then continue to make periodic observations after the treatment.

This design suffers from the lack of control over outside events that affect learning. The terrorist attacks on September 11, or something as simple as spring weather, for example, could explain changes in students as readily as the treatment.

This type of study works well within institutional settings that already keep records. Specifically, many schools already keep attendance records; and attendance levels before and after the introduction of a new program to improve attendance could show a pronounced positive effect. While superficially similar to the pre-experimental one-group pretest-posttest design discussed earlier, the added observations before and after treatment of the time-series experiment is a more rigorous approach.

Recurrent-Treatment, Time-Series Design

Another quasi-experimental design for use with a single subject or group is the equivalent time-series design. The equivalent time-samples design is a recurrent approach which switches the treatment on and off at various intervals. This design compares the often behavioral results between episodes when the treatment is present to when the treatment is absent.

The time-series design is especially suited to treatment effects that may be short-lived or easily reversible. A classic example is the effect of music on industrial production. Music on an automobile assembly line is alternatively turned on and off for an hour. Car output with music and without is compared. To reduce the threat of other influences (e.g. beginning of the workday, the end of the workday, before and after lunch, employees on breaks, etc.) the music should randomly be turned on at different times during the day, week, and month.

The analogy in a charter school evaluation entails studying rates of gain of students who switch from school to school, a common occurrence in inner cities. A weakness in this design is whether the treatment, music in the automobile assembly line case, is causing the desired effect—more cars produced per hour. Or is it test itself, with employees knowing they are being scrutinized while the music is on, the cause? In addition, it is inappropriate to make the generalization that if productivity was higher when the music was briefly turned on, that leaving the music on all the time would lead to higher productivity. This type of study simply helps to validate the recurrent effect of turning the music on and off. Nevertheless, this study design has particular value in the classroom if a teacher wants to study the effects of lecturing versus quiet study, or perhaps student class participation during the presence of parent volunteers.

Nonequivalent Control-Group Design

The first quasi-experimental design for multiple group experiments is the common nonequivalent control-group design. This technique is similar to the pretest-posttest control group design mentioned earlier. This method, however, lacks the random assignment of subjects to control and experimental groups. Widely used in educational research, the nonequivalent control group design employs a pretest and posttest for both control and experimental groups although the treatment is not randomly assigned.[2]

This type of evaluation approaches the rigor of true experimentation discussed earlier if it can be assumed that this kind of pretest captures all of the factors that make the group differ outside of the treatment. However, if the subjects self-select themselves for treatment, the inferences that can be made are subject to uncertainty since the more motivated or the best-informed subjects may volunteer and these differences may not be taken into account. Although this design lacks the rigor associated with the random assignment of control and treatment groups, it can be the best available design in real-world settings where randomization is not possible.

Counterbalanced Control-Group Design

Counterbalanced designs, the second type of quasi-experimental design for multiple group experiments, improve precision by exposing all subjects to all treatments. Also known as "rotation experiments," each experimental treatment is randomly given in turn to naturally occurring groups such as classrooms. This design is useful to compare the effects of multiple types of treatments in comparison groups when randomization of individuals to treatment and control groups is not possible, for example, classrooms or schools that have already been established. The design, "gains strength through the consistency of the internal replications of the experiment" (Campbell & Stanley, 1963b, p. 52)

The weaknesses of this approach include the lack of randomization to treatment and control groups, which means the groups may initially differ and that important factors may not be controlled. Initial differences between the groups, not the treatment itself, could explain differences; and the sequence of multiple treatments could help explain an effect versus the treatment alone. The study of a foreign language, for example, could employ three different techniques in three different classrooms. One class could practice immersion with no English speaking allowed. Another class might focus on reading skills, and the last class might concentrate on writing. Every 2 weeks, students are tested and the treatments or teaching techniques would change until each class experienced every teaching technique and was tested at the conclusion of each treatment. Although similar to the previous nonequivalent control group design, this technique does not employ a pretest.

Separate-Sample, Control-Group Design

The third quasi-experimental design for multiple group experiments is the separate-sample pretest-posttest design. In this approach, randomly assigned subjects within the experimental and within the control group are each split into two groups—one that is only pretested before the treatment, and one that is only posttested after the treatment. Although both groups receive the treatment, the pretested group is never posttested, and simply serves as a comparison group. Also known as the "simulated before-and-after design," this design is ideal for large populations when random assignment to treatments is not possible, the experimenter has control over when and which subjects are tested, and when the treatment is likely to be exposed to the whole population.

The design is not inherently strong. But in some cases it may be the only feasible study, hence, worth doing. To test the effectiveness of anti-smoking advertisements, for example, half the subjects in the study could randomly be selected to assess their attitudes and beliefs about smoking. The TV ads against smoking could then be run, and the attitudes and beliefs of another randomly selected group would then be collected. A fundamental weakness to this approach is the competing causes that could also account for changes in the posttested group. Using the anti-smoking campaign scenario, other factors that could account for changes in attitudes include a major celebrity dying from emphysema, a massive advertising campaign by tobacco companies, or the introduction of new drugs and patches that fight nicotine addiction. Despite this shortcoming, this technique has the benefit of testing treatments in their natural rather than contrived settings, thus making the results more generalizable to other settings.

Multiple-Group, Time-Series Design

The final quasi experiment for multiple groups is the multiple time series design. In this approach a series of observations or measurements are made between two groups. A treatment is applied to one of the groups, and then another series of observations or measurements are made. This is similar to the previously mentioned nonequivalent control group design. But this design is more powerful since the effect is not only compared with the pretreatment observations or measurements of its own series, but also contrasted against a control group. For example, a study of attendance could be conducted by finding two similar schools and collecting weekly attendance results for several weeks; then randomly introducing, say, a parent involvement program at one of the schools. Then continue to collect weekly attendance records, finally looking for a large increase after the treatment introduction.

FOUR KINDS OF RESEARCH VALIDITY

Four types of validity in evaluations are statistical conclusion validity, internal validity, external validity, and construct validity (see Table 15.2 for an overview). Statistical conclusion validity concerns whether or not the presumed causes and effects covary, that is, vary directly or inversely with one another. Internal validity involves whether the experimental treatments cause the differences in the measured effect. External validity concerns the degree to which the results from a particular evaluation can be generalized to other populations and settings. Generalizations can only apply to a well-defined population from which the sample has been randomly selected. Lastly, construct validity weighs plausible hypotheses

Table 15.2.   Four Kinds of Validity in Experiments

A.   Statistical Conclusion: Do the presumed causes and effects covary?

1. Statistical Power: Is the sample size large enough to reject the null hypotheses at a given level of probability (or, as preferred, estimate coefficients with a reasonable small margin of error)?

2. Error rate: Does the "significant" effect occur on average in more than 1 in 20 studies?

3. Reliability of measures: Are the measurement instruments internally consistent or stable enough to detect changes during, or differences in, treatments?

4. Reliability of treatment implementation: Have the units in a treatment actually undergone the same putative conditions?

B.   Internal: Are there other plausible explanations of the covariation between causes and effects?

5. Maturation: Have factors within the units, rather than the presumed external causes, brought about changes or differences?

6. History: Have external factors within the units, rather than the presumed external causes brought about changes or differences?

7. Selection bias: Do preexisting differences among the groups account for later differences on the dependent variable?

8. Contamination and compensation: Do untreated control groups imitate or somehow gain the benefits of a treatment; or do they enter into competition and expend extra energies and therefore do better than they otherwise would?

9. Mortality: Do differential dropout rates in the treatment groups account for differences on the dependent variable obtained at the end of the experiment?

C.   External: Can the cause-effect be generalized to other times, units, and settings?

10. See text: Is the sample representative of the population not through random assignment but through random sampling?

D.   Construct: Are there other plausible hypotheses about both the cause and effect?

11. Operational irrelevancy: Does the treatment as administered contain Hawthorne, experimenter-bias, placebo, or other unintended causes or artifacts that actually produce the effects?

12. Time restrictions: Does the treatment produce "fade out" and "sleeper" effects?

Source: Adapted from Cook and Campbell (1979).

about both the cause and effect constructs. Each of these different types of validity are described in the following section.

Statistical Conclusion Validity

As indicated in Table 15.2, statistical conclusion validity asks whether the presumed causes and effects covary. All else being equal, larger samples enable evaluators to reject the null hypotheses of no group differences at a given level of probability (or, as preferred here, estimate coefficients with a reasonable small margin of error). The conventional level of significance is .05, meaning that the probability of the results is less than 1 in 20 if there is no difference between the population of experimental and control groups from which the study sampled. If the measures employed are unreliable or insensitive to the treatment, then an effect that actually took place may not be detected. Finally, have the experimental students in the evaluation actually undergone the program in question? A subsequent section treats further threats to statistical validity.

Internal or Causal Validity

According to Cook and Campbell, "internal validity refers to the approximate validity with which we infer that a relationship between two variables is causal or that the absence of a relationship implies the absence of cause" (Cook & Campbell, 1979, p. 37) In other words, did the experimental treatments make a difference sufficient to cause a change in the subjects or are there alternative explanations that are just as likely to have caused the change? Table 15.2 makes raises questions about five threats to internal validity and gives alternative causal explanations for academic gains or differences among experimental and control groups. Adapted from Cook and Campbell's comprehensive treatment, several threats deserve emphasis:

Testing
The mere act of taking a pretest may affect the scores of a second testing, irrespective of any treatment. In other words, the process of measuring may change that which is being measured. In a weight control study, for example, an initial weigh-in itself may be stimulus to lose weight even without treatment. A pretest may sensitize students in a special curriculum to what should be learned from the curriculum thereby giving them an advantage over control students who would not be exposed to the content.

Instrumentation Decay
Changes in physical measuring instruments, student fatigue over repeated testings, and changes over time in standards of classroom observers or test scorers may contribute to rising or falling outcomes.

Statistical Regression
Groups selected as having extreme scores, perhaps unreliably measured, may regress in later measurements toward their average. Initially

poor scoring groups may rise, and high scoring groups may fall, thereby confounding apparent effects if their initial status differs.

Sample Mortality

Teachers and students who remain in a treated group may be less mobile and more enthusiastic. For these reasons alone, the group that remains in the treatment may score higher on tests.

External or Generalizable Validity

As indicated in Table 15.2, external validity examines whether or not observed sample effects generalize to the population from which the sample was drawn and to other populations, settings, and times. Long ago, telephone surveys of voters, for example, were inaccurate in predicting election results because they excluded voters without telephones. Even today, a random sample or the entire population of North Carolina schools would not allow scientific inferences to the nation as a whole.

Drawing on laboratory studies, psychologists seem less sensitive than social scientists to address the need for drawing random samples and to the requirement of restricting generalizations to the populations from which their samples have been drawn. Psychologists, however, compensate for this usual disciplinary weakness with meta-analyses, which bring many studies of different populations and conditions together to measure overall effects. Meta-analysis can also be used to examine variations in implementation of treatments, experimental conditions, and the students in the studies.

Other generalizations may not be warranted. For example, it cannot be assumed that what worked in the 1960s will work in the same way decades later. What works for kindergarten girls may not work for middle school boys.

Construct Validity

Construct validity, as noted in Table 15.2, is concerned with determining whether there are alternative plausible hypotheses about both the cause and effect. In the prior example of music's effect on automobile production, one must consider if the music itself causes an increase in automobile output, or whether the workers are simply more productive because they believe they are being scrutinized or observed when the music is on.

The time restriction effect considers the longevity of the desired result. If, in our music example on automobile assembly lines, the output of cars increased while the music was on, one must consider how long the effect would last once the music was turned off, and whether leaving the music on all the time would incur the same benefit.

Analytic Validity[19]

As indicated in Table 15.3, the validity of evaluations may be threatened by additional problems of "analytic validity." Otherwise systematic treatments of validity (Bracht, & Glass, 1968; Campbell & Stanley, 1963a; Cook & Campbell, 1979) neglect some of these analytic threats except for power, error rate, and reliability (see Table 15.2). Perhaps the reason is that these works are addressed primarily to design rather than analysis. Statistics books also neglect them, and they are often neglected in published educational research. Subsequent paragraphs discuss these threats in greater detail; they can apply to both experimental and observational data. Since the present chapter focuses on evaluation design rather than analyses, the reader is referred to the cited original work for a comprehensive treatment of analytic validity.

DESIGN FEATURES PARTICULARLY RELEVANT TO EDUCATIONAL EVALUATIONS

Table 15.4 explains a dozen general accountability principles that, in addition to the design and analytic principles discussed above, have bearings on the specific value of information reported by states, school districts, and other groups. The first principle suggests that, other things being equal, independent evaluations of performance should be weighed more heavily than those evaluations performed by program developers.

As suggested by the other principles, evaluations are more valuable when they are focused on results, and are comprehensible and timely. Data for reports are more valuable if they are objective, fair, value added, and balanced. It may be highly useful to have disaggregated data, as called for in the federal No Child Left Behind Act, to detect the separate achievement gains of boys and girls and those in poverty and ethnic groups.

Value-Added Accountability

One of the principles in Table 15.4—value-added scores—is more technical than the others and deserves further discussion. Value-added achievement scores can also be called gain or progress scores in contrast

Table 15.3.   Threats to Analytic Validity

A. Expression

1. Leveling—grouping continuous measurements into levels such as high, middle, and low intelligence, thereby losing the original precision of the variable; or grouping measurements into high and low levels on a variable when middle values on the variable are associated with high or low values on another variable thereby concealing the curvature.

2. Compositing—stereotyping complex patterns of basic variables into a single variable or typology; for example, measuring psychological reactions to red and yellow instead of hue, intensity, and saturation; correlating children's IQ with a social-class composite rather than specific features of child-parent interaction; or analyzing the differences in student achievement of teachers above and below the median on a composite rating of effectiveness thereby concealing the magnitude and specificity of the covariations. (Specific covariations may be more generalizable to other units, conditions, environments, and times than covariations of preconceived or factor-analytically derived composites and classifications.)

3. Transformations—failing to transform independent and dependent variables to optimal covariations between them, thereby reducing the magnitude of apparent covariation or requiring collinear, unreplicable products and square terms in the regression equation.

4. Outliers—failing to detect and consider or remedy aberrant observations.

5. Constancy—failing to note that dependent variables with only slight variation an covariation (perhaps due to invalidity or unreliability) may not be sensitive to independent variables, or that independent variables with slight variation do not display the full possible covariation with dependent variables.

B. Cluster

6. Measures—failing to note possible artifactual linkages or covariations between contaminating errors of measurement between independent and dependent variables.

7. Colinearity—entering many correlated variables, some of them perhaps coindicators of a common theoretical construct or unknown pattern of cluster, into equations and concluding from the inflated errors of the regression coefficients that none or only a few covary significantly with dependent variables.

8. Units—choosing an inappropriate level of aggregation; analyzing nonindependent units such as students within a class whose behavior affects one another rather than independent units such as cliques, classes, or school, to meet the independence assumptions of analysis; or generalizing relation coefficients at one level of analysis to another when the magnitude and sign may actually differ at the level of intended generalizations; or falling to attribute the sources of covariation to appropriate levels of aggregation.

C. Multiplicity

9. Multiple and multivariate exploitation—isolating as significant, without appropriate tests, several covariations between independent and dependent variables from many examined.

10. Incompleteness—failing to include the full sets of independent and dependent variables.

Table 15.4.   Twelve Accountability Principals

Independence	To avoid bias and conflicts of interest, information should be sought from other than staff and institutions being evaluated.
Results focused	Though indexes of inputs and processes may be useful, the chief focus of accountability should be on the attainment of intended and measured results.
Comprehensible	Written and oral accountability reports should be readily understandable.
Timeliness	Other things being equal, accountability value is proportional to how quickly it can be reported.
Incentive driven	Consequences, preferably prespecified, should follow good and bad results.
Objective	Quantifiable information such as examination results should be preferred over anecdotes, public hearings, and the like.
Fair	Prespecified goals and content and curriculum-based external examinations should be favored.
Value-added	Accountability should include progress or gains in learning as well as end results.
Balanced	The scoring of multiple indicators should reflect the intended range and priority of subjects, topics, and skills.
Expressive	Success and failure should be displayed in ways that are readily comprehended by those responsible for policies and decisions.
Disaggregated	Results should be reported for girls and boys, poor and not, and various ethnic and language groups of concern.
Consumer informed	What citizens, parents, and others are concerned about, and their opinions about the quality of provided services should be included in accountability indicators.

Source: Walberg (2002).

to status scores for which student test results reflect one point in time. In their simplest form, value-added scores are the gains from one test administration to another, say, over the span of 1 year.

Value-added scores are important for several reasons. Status scores may be deceptive since they may be attributable to only recent education experiences, say, of only the past year. They could also be determined by earlier schooling and extramural experiences including those in early childhood and peer groups. Thus, schools serving children in poverty may make excellent value-added progress even though their status scores are poor. Similarly, status scores in rich neighborhoods may oversuggest school effectiveness, particularly scores that may have been largely determined by social advantages.

Despite such obvious appeal, value-added scores are not without controversy. Value-added scores, for example, require tests on at least two occasions. But some educators resist increased testing, and tests for preschoolers require special efforts and expense. Scholars, moreover, do not completely agree on how they should be calculated and employed. They may be a somewhat unreliable indication of a school's or a teacher's progress. Even so, "the perfect should not be the enemy of the good." In science and practical affairs, an approximate answer to the right question is better than a precise answer to the wrong question. In holding institutions and personnel accountable, it is useful to know both their status and their progress, even though neither indication is precise.

Selection Bias as Special Considerations

Previous sections describe general threats to the validity of evaluations and illustrate these with examples of charter school and other research. In addition to these, several issues are particularly important in the evaluation of most educational programs and deserve special consideration.

With greater concentrations of population, cities are likely to have sufficient numbers of families that desire distinctive educational experiences for their children. Large cities are more likely than elsewhere to have sufficient demand for college preparatory programs. Families that send their children to these schools may provide more academically stimulating home environments. Because of such differential selection, charter school superiority may be ambiguously attributable to initial and continuing differences in families, the superior programs of the charter school, or both.

On the other hand, some charter schools may attract students who are failing or who are having behavior problems in regular schools. The causes of such students' failure in a charter school may be similarly ambiguous. Random assignment, statistical controls, and a multiplicity of studies may help to diminish such ambiguity, but a measure of uncertainty is probably inevitable.

ADDITIONAL DESIGN CONSIDERATIONS

Nationally Standardized Tests

The Stanford, Iowa, and Metropolitan tests are examples of widely used tests employed to assess students, schools, districts, and programs. Although less than perfect, as are nearly all measures in psychology and the social sciences, they are used throughout the United States to assess achievement in reading, mathematics, science, and other subjects. Their manuals contain test information relating to scope, validity, and reliability. Their "norming" is based on national random samples. This allows expressions of scores such as percentiles in relation to all U.S. students rather than a local, convenience, or "grab" sample.

Such scores are crude approximations of physical measures; a mile or kilometer is the same distance in California and Maine. A grade equivalent gain on a well-standardized test has similar universality but less precision.

Calibrated Developer Tests

Scores on developer tests but not on nationally standardized tests may be available. In such cases, developer tests alone might be considered at least for the initial statistical controls and evaluation. In this case, it would be highly desirable to show that the developer's test correlates substantially with nationally standardized tests. In addition, the tests should be calibrated so that the scores can be expressed on national scales such as grade equivalents.

Such calibration or equating is easier said then done. In addition, developers' tests may favor their own programs. Ideally, multiple tests including national standardized test would be used, and educational consumers might be more impressed if a developer's program did better than randomly assigned control groups on all tests.

Effect Sizes

For several decades, evaluators and other researchers sought to determine whether program groups scored significantly higher or lower than control groups on outcome measures. It is more informative to know how much better. Effect sizes[4] express this difference. Effect sizes allow rough comparisons of program effects under different conditions and with various samples of students, even though tests of different lengths and difficulties may have been used.

Multiplicity of Results

No matter how large and well designed, a single evaluation is unlikely to be definitive. Known or unrecognized differences, other than the program, may have made experimental and control groups differ. Thus, consistent results from many studies provide the best evidence. Experiments, for example, provide the most rigorous probe of causal efficacy, but quasi-experiments are less disruptive and may give a better indication of efficacy in less contrived settings. Using more of both types leads to greater confidence in the conclusions.

Again, meta-analyses can lead to definitive conclusions by systematically synthesizing the multiple studies and weighing the more rigorous studies more heavily. Comparing the overall effects with costs of programs can even be telling since policymakers and educators should be concerned with both benefits and costs, or "bang for the buck."

SINGLE-SUBJECT EVALUATIONS OF EXTRAORDINARY PROGRAMS

Most of the better educational programs and methods of teaching only confer a small effect on learning (perhaps a few percentile points on achievement tests) and require elaborate procedures, as described in this chapter, to detect them. If programs, however, have extraordinarily beneficial effects, there would be little need for the many threats to validity discussed here. Two such programs and their evaluations are worth considering.

Archival Analysis of the O'Donnell Foundation Incentive Program

Despite the powerful effects and widespread use of incentives in many walks of life including employment, many educators appear reluctant to employ them with teachers or students. Incentive effects, however, were so large in a recent evaluation that a more elaborate study seemed unnecessary. The O'Donnell Foundation of Dallas initiated a large-scale trial of monetary incentives for public school teachers and students that made use of the Advanced Placement examinations, the only national tests that provide external, objective, and rigorous standards for high school students. Over half-million, high school students take AP exams on the content of more than 25 college level courses. Over 2,500 colleges grant course credits for passing grades, allowing students to graduate early or take more advanced college courses. The O'Donnell Foundation began the Incentive Program in response to widely voiced concerns about poor academic performance in Texas, a state becoming less dependent on agriculture and oil while competing more with other states and nations in increasingly technical industries. Yet, of the typical 100 Texas students who entered kindergarten in 1981, only 72 graduated from high school in 1994. Only 36 of the original 100 entered higher education, and only 18 were expected to finish college in 1998. Test scores for students in the Dallas Independent School District, where the trial took place, were lower than elsewhere, and African American and Hispanic American students showed large disparities in academic performance when compared to their caucasion peers. Beginning with the 1990-1991 school year, the Incentive Program paid students $100 for each passing Advanced Placement examination score in English, calculus, statistics, computer science, biology, chemistry, and physics. The program also provided a reimbursement for the cost of taking the exam. Additionally, it gave a $2,500 stipend to each teacher undergoing training to teach advanced courses in these subjects. They also received $100 for each subsequent passing AP examination score of their students. In the nine participating Dallas schools, sharply increasing numbers of boys and girls of all major ethnic groups took and passed the AP exams. The number rose more than 12-fold from 41 the year before the program began to 521 when it ended in 1994-1995. After terminating, the program continued to have carry-over effects. In the 1996-1997 school year, 2 years after the program ended, 442 students passed, about 11 times more than the number in the year before the program began. Though these numbers speak for themselves, interviews with students, teachers, and college admission officers revealed high regard for the Incentive Program. They felt that even students who failed AP exams learned better study habits and the importance of hard work to meet high standards. In addition, the program had other benefits. Students could take more advanced courses in college. Those that passed a sufficient number of AP courses could graduate from college early. This saves their families' tuition and relieves taxpayers subsidies. Those who passed AP courses also had a better chance for merit scholarships and entry into selective colleges.

Thus, the program was not only extraordinarily effective but also very cost effective. Unfortunately, incentive programs remain rare in schools.

Formative Evaluation of Headsprout

Air travel has transformed modern life. Yet the Wright brothers did not employ experiments or quasi-experiments in the way they are described here. They made minute changes in airframe and wing design until they got things right for the maiden voyage at Kitty Hawk. In the same way, wind tunnels were subsequently used to simulate the effects of various aircraft design features. Clear goals, the capacity to change design features easily, and measure their effects can lead to impressive progress. Can education programs demonstrate such clear results?

Headsprout Early Reading exemplifies the Wright principles. An Internet-based reading program, it teaches the essential skills and strategies required for reading success. Experienced educators and learning scientists made use of years of classroom experience and scientific research in developing the product. The program was extensively tested with children, and has taken years and millions of dollars to research, develop, test, and refine (Layng, Twyman, & Stikeleather, 2003; Twyman, Layng, Stikeleather, & Hobbins, in press, see also www.headspout.com).

On the surface the program appears to the child as an interactive cartoon. Underneath is a patented technology that systematically teaches phonemic awareness and the phonics skills to sound–out words and begin reading with understanding. The program was so rigorously developed and tested that Headsprout offers schools a full product refund for each kindergarten or first grade student who is not at or above grade level upon completing the Early Reading program.

The keys to the Headsprout success were:

- a complete and detailed specification of the skills such as individual letter recognition that children need to become effective beginning readers,
- continuous repetitive revision of the program based on millions of children's actual responses, and
- the precise monitoring of each individual child's responses so that rewards and correctives can be instantly administered over the Internet with a speed and appropriateness that could not be achieved even by a skilled tutor.

Because the child's progress is continuously monitored, mastery of the initially specified skills can and is guaranteed. Using the same principles, Headsprout follows phonemic awareness and phonics with vocabulary development, fluent oral reading skills, and reading comprehension strategies.

EXEMPLARY NATIONAL RANDOMIZED
CONTROL-GROUP EVALUATIONS

To my knowledge, there have been exactly two national randomized educational evaluations—Harvard Project Physics for high school and the School Health Curriculum Project for middle and upper grades. Since these evaluations employed random assignment to experimental, control groups, and national samples, they addressed questions of both internal and external validity, that is, causality and national generalizability. They originated in basic and applied "hard science": Being sponsored respectively by the National Science Foundation and the U.S. Public Health Service Center for Disease Control that insisted on rigorous national experiments. The present writer was fortunate in collaborating with physicists and health policy experts in planning and conducting both evaluations (Errecart et al., 1991; Gold et al., 1991; Walberg, Connell, Turner, & Olsen, 1986; Welch & Walberg, 1972).

Although both evaluations focused on outcomes, they included considerable supplementary information. Data on the degree and conditions of implementations revealed the optimal arrangements for maximum achievement. Student attitude data revealed important information about how students' views toward physics and health changed.

Harvard Project Physics

Partly in reaction to abstract and overly quantitative physics, which appeared to diminish the already low enrollments in high school physics, Harvard Project Physics (HPP) featured elective qualitative and qualitative components to awaken students' understanding and appreciation of physics and scientific methods. Thus, the course materials provided a rich array of laboratory experiments, scientific history, concise biographies of famous physicists, the contribution of physics to economic development, and the relations of ideas in physics to those of other disciplines.

Though it was recognized that very few high school students would become physicists, the developers believed that citizens should have an understanding of hard science methods and the contributions of physics and other sciences to modern life. Accordingly, the evaluators developed psychometric instruments to measure student attitudes toward their physics classes, voluntary behaviors related to physics that the students may have engaged in as a result of their course experiences, and attitudes toward physics, toward science in general, and the need for scientific methods that test hypotheses and theories.

A national random sample of teachers was randomly assigned to HPP or their usual course materials. The evaluators' brought the experimental group to Harvard to discuss the course philosophy and materials. To counterbalance or minimize the possible "Hawthorne" or "hothouse" effect" of being in the group singled out for the program, the control group teachers spent the summer at Harvard studying physics with leading professors.

In addition to tests to measure the distinctive content featured in HPP, the evaluators employed standard tests of high school physics. The results indicated that HPP students exceed control students in both kinds of achievement measures as well as on the attitudinal and behavioral measures.

School Health Curriculum Project

The School Health Curriculum Project (SHCP) was sponsored by several U.S. federal agencies: the National Clearinghouse for Smoking and Health, the Bureau of Health Education, the Center for Health Promotion and Education, the Center for Disease Control, and the Public Health Service. SHCP was first developed in 1969 and consists of lesson units of health instruction designed for students in Grades 4 through 7. It was specifically designated for evaluation because it was used in over 400 school districts in 40 states.

Unlike the Harvard Project Physics evaluation, which randomly sampled from a list of physics teachers in the United States, the SHCP evaluation relied on paired samples of cooperating districts, one of which was randomly assigned to SHCP.

Like HPP, however, the SHCP evaluation measured not only outcomes such as achievement and attitudes, but also their mediating conditions. These measures allowed a richer analysis of causal influences and conditions that raise or lower treatment efficacy; analysis of them showed that the more SHCP units covered, and the greater the teachers' fidelity to the program requirements, the better the outcomes. Similar to HPP, SHCP employed pretests to increase the sensitivity and power of the evaluation in detecting effects. Furthermore, and also like HPP, SHCP employed reported behaviors since health education goals emphasize healthy behavior in addition to the usual cognitive and affective outcomes.

A QUASI-EXPERIMENT: CORE KNOWLEDGE

Core Knowledge (CK) is a primary and middle grade curriculum that emphasizes the liberal arts and sciences. It was designed by E. D. Hirsch, Jr., professor emeritus at the University of Virginia and author of many acclaimed books including *Cultural Literacy: What Every American Needs to Know* and *The Schools We Need and Why We Don't Have Them*. The Milken Family Foundation conducts research on its curricula, develops books and other materials for parents and teachers, and offers workshops for teachers. It also serves as the hub and certifier of Core Knowledge schools.

The Core Knowledge Foundation commissioned an independent evaluation to determine the comparative effectiveness of the curriculum and the degree to which schools followed implementation and training recommendations (Walberg & Meyer, 2004). North Carolina turned out to have the best conditions for a quasi-experiment because the state can link individual students state test scores from one year to the next. Unlike school aggregate information, detailed data allows the analysis more precision and restricts analyses to only those individual students that were in experimental and control schools on both test dates.

Tests Measuring State Standards

The North Carolina state test also seemed a good choice for evaluating school policies, practices, and curricula for several reasons. Tests, particularly national commercial tests, may vary greatly in the degree that they reflect the goals of a given school's curriculum and instructional emphases. For example, because schools may adapt their curricula to the commercial tests they use, such as the Metropolitan Achievement Tests, they are likely to do better than other schools on the tests they have chosen. Tests required by states, however, put schools on an even footing, and reflect what political representatives in the state think is important.

Moreover, because of the federal No Child Left Behind (NCLB) legislation, new state requirements, wider availability of school "report cards," and the pressures of accountability and choice, many schools in the nation are increasingly under pressure to perform well on the state tests. Along with the National Assessment of Educational Progress, state tests are becoming "the currency of the realm." Under NCLB, poor progress on state tests can mean that the principal must inform parents of their children's school failure and students may use part of their schools' funds for tutoring elsewhere. Repeated poor progress can mean that the school may be closed or carry on under new management and staff.

Finally, all regular schools in each state are required to participate in state testing programs. Hence, the complete universe of schools can be analyzed rather than a small sample of "matched schools." Now, the state database allowed for contrasting the performance of 1,592 CK students with that of the other 533,919 students in non-Core Knowledge schools.

Modern Statistical Analyses

Initial analysis of the 1,592 eligible Core Knowledge students' test results showed that the much of the variation in their scores, about 80%, is attributable to differences among students rather than differences among the Core Knowledge schools. As many studies have shown, achievement is a continuously accumulative process, and variations among schools in any given year make for relatively small differences in student achievement compared with their previous experiences at home and, in the later grade levels, in school. During the first 18 years of life, for example, only about 8% of the student's time is spent in school. For this reason, variations in the quality of schooling and particular school features and practices are often dwarfed and difficult to detect compared to family influences on intellectual development and achievement (Walberg, in press). Because the majority of the variation was attributable to differences among students, the analysis was designed to take into account the variations among them. Specifically, during the analysis, "value added" gains from the 2001-2002 to the 2002-2003 school year were calculated. As explained further below, the analysis also took into account the poverty and minority status of each student. Only students with complete information for both school years were included in the analyses.

In addition, the initial analyses confirmed that the data were correlated or statistically clustered within schools, the consequences of which are explained below. Clustering could be expected since students are influenced by features and conditions within their schools and communities that tend may tend to make them similar to one another and different from students in other schools; a given student's achievement is likely to be correlated with another student's achievement within the same school. For example, a highly effective principal or school board may confer higher test scores on students within their purview, which sets them apart from control students in other school locales.

The consequence of such "clustered" or "correlated effects" is that the student scores within a school are not independent of one another as required for statistical inference. Thus, the basis of estimating school effects is a combination of the number of schools, the number of students in a school, and the underlying correlation structure (i.e., how the test scores of students in the same school are correlated with each other). Even though the sample of students, numbering 1,592 for the evaluation, was seemingly very large, the valid sample size is dependent on the number of schools. This more conservative number avoids coming to misleading positive or negative conclusions that have often characterized previous studies of school effects. To account precisely and simultaneously for such individual student variations and clustered school effects, generalized linear models were employed.

Summative and Formative Results

Summative Results

The evaluation of CK showed that, on average, Core Knowledge schools in North Carolina excelled the other schools in the state in achievement progress in 8 of 10 comparisons of reading and mathematics in the five grade levels available for analysis. Although not all comparisons were significant, the probability of 8 of 10 positive flips is highly significant. These findings are based on individual pretest-posttest, value-added scores, conservative statistical estimates, and the entire population of eligible students in Core Knowledge schools and those in the rest of the state.

Formative Results

Formative information on implementation factors was also analyzed. The staffs of CK schools that wished for their schools to remain certified users filled out the "Official Core Knowledge School Renewal Form 2003-2004." The form requires such detailed information as participation in the CK annual conference, planning and implementation of CK procedures, and use of CK curricular materials.

The evaluation showed that the CK schools, with over 90% compliance, had implemented the required CK features and requirements. This finding may deserve celebration since it suggests adherence to Core Knowledge implementation ideals and because such adherence was thought to increase achievement. From a research point of view, however, it means that schools without these ideals were unrepresented in that implementation effects could not be detected.

Perhaps a physical analogy may be useful: Each of a variety of training effects would be difficult to detect among runners uniformly well trained. Similarly, no implementation effects on outcomes were detected. This does not mean that a different sample would lead to different results. Larger samples with greater variations in implementation of Core Knowledge principles might show large and significant implementation effects on achievement progress. It seems likely, for example, that if true implementation effects exist, that a sample with many schools with percent implementation rates that vary between 10 and 100% would differ significantly in achievement progress.

On the other hand, the tail should not wag the dog. It is better to have an effective program for students than to discover that the program's components and degree of implementation account for degrees of varying success. In other words, knowing that program generally works has more important action implications than knowing under what conditions it works best, although of course the latter is also valuable.

WHOLE SCHOOL REFORMS

Like the "whole child," the "whole school" reform idea was perhaps ill defined but still generated great enthusiasm and considerable change. It seemed reasonable that the piecemeal reforms du jour would not work and that a cohesive, overall approach might be an improvement. From today's perspective, however, the big question is, "Do whole school reforms yield learning improvements by object standards?" Two of the best known of these reforms give illustrative answers about the results and quality of the evaluations.

Coalition of Essential Schools (CES)

This coalition

> Promotes a vision of schooling in which students engage in in-depth and rigorous learning. CES schools select a small number of core skills and areas of knowledge that they expect all students to demonstrate and exercise broadly across content areas. While all students are expected to achieve the same goals, teachers strive to shape instruction in order to meet individual students' unique strengths and needs. This approach to teaching and learning—setting high standards while personalizing instruction—results in increased student achievement and equitable outcomes on a variety of measures.[5]

Despite the report's title and last sentence if its organization's description above, in an anonymous self-evaluation, CES reported:

> The percentage of students in CES CSRD schools passing state achievement tests increased substantially from the initial year of testing.

> CES CSRD schools are making significant progress in closing the gap between the percentage of their students who are passing and the state average of students passing the tests. On four tests in two states, CES CSRD schools not only narrowed the gap but also surpassed the state averages.

Even at face value, both findings are of course pre-experimental, which allow no scientific inference for the reasons explained and illustrated in early sections of this chapter. Among other things, the report makes no claim of measuring value-added or gain scores to attempt to put the schools on a fair footing, and CES schools could have differed in unknown ways from the state averages. In addition, the report fails to provide a detailed description of the 22 schools, the achievement tests involved, and the means of analysis.

In addition to these findings, the CES

> research team also interviewed "coaches"—CES regional staff people working with individual schools—about changes they observed in the schools' practices over the course of the CSRD grants. In addition, we collected a

wide range of documents from the schools that further demonstrate how the schools changed classroom practices, leadership practices, school design features, and relationships with the community in order to improve outcomes for student."

Reported in anecdotes and quotes, these "vignettes" for Ohio, Maine, Michigan, and Massachusetts produced results that are difficult to evaluate. An unspecified number of interviews were conducted and no specifications were given for selecting the quotes and anecdotal findings to report. Such problems are magnified when an organization subjectively and exclusively evaluates itself.

National Center on Education and the Economy (NCEE)

According to its Website, this center is dedicated to "providing the tools and technical assistance the nation needs to lead the world in education and training."[5] The president's message states that the NCEE was launched in 1989 to meet the challenge of

> giving our young people the world-class skills they need to compete in a swiftly integrating world economy.

Therefore,

> the common goal of the programs is to build the capacity of the people and organizations we work with to create powerful, coherent, standards-based education and training systems.

As stated in the *Results* report, the conclusions unique to NCEE's chief program, America's Choice, are:

1. A 2004 study of America's Choice elementary and middle schools in Rochester, New York, by the Consortium for Policy Research in Education (CPRE) at the University of Pennsylvania that found students in 16 America's Choice schools learned "significantly more than students in other Rochester schools in both reading and mathematics."

2. A CPRE study of America's Choice schools in Plainfield, New Jersey reported that students of teachers who more fully implemented the America's Choice model learned more than students of teachers who implemented the model less completely—powerful evidence of the strength of the America's Choice model.

Even though NCEE was founded in 1989, these are apparently the only studies available or worth singling out as the general conclusions on results. The first conclusion refers to "a forthcoming study" even though it is only one of two studies done since the NCEE founding in 1989. Were there other studies that NCEE decided not to mention? Even taken at face value, the study is apparently pre-experimental in that no mention is made of pretests and socioeconomic status, which leaves doubts about the equivalence of NCEE and other schools in the district.

The second study actually has little bearing on the program efficacy since better results in some NCEE schools may derive from a superior school's capacity to implement programs rather than the NCEE program itself. In either case, the conditions and student populations in the eastern cities of Rochester, New York, and Plainfield, New Jersey may differ from those in other American cities.

Like the Coalition for Essential Schools results report, much of NCEE's derives apparently from a self-evaluation, although no investigators are actually named as authors. The report mentions the names of schools and districts and briefly recounts anecdotes. It also contains participants' quotes and many pictures of children. But there is next to nothing about study methodology in either of the two conclusions that would enable a disinterested investigator to judge the validity of the two conclusions.

Evaluative Syntheses of Evaluations of 24 Schoolwide Programs

Huge amounts of money have been spent on the schoolwide reform programs, which are also known as "whole school," or "comprehensive" approaches for improving achievement. The U.S. Congress supplemented expenditures of $8 billion per year with a special allocation of funds schoolwide to be used for entire schools in which 50% or more of the children were in poverty. These programs are well known to many educators and policymakers and include Accelerated Schools, Coalition of Essential Schools, High Schools That Work, High Scope, Paideia, Roots and Wings, and Success for All.

Six professional organizations contracted with the American Institutes of Research to review 24 major schoolwide programs (quoted in "Dear Colleague" letter in unnumbered preface, American Institutes for Research, 1999). These organizations included the American Association of School Administrators, the American Federation of Teachers, the National Association of Elementary School Principals, the National Association of Secondary School Principals, and the National Education Asso-

Table 15.5. Evidence of Positive Effects on Achievement In 24 Evaluations of Schoolwide Reforms

Rating	Number of Evaluations
Strong	3
Promising	5
Marginal	6
Mixed or weak	2
No research	8

ciation. In a preface to the report, the leaders of these organizations concluded as follows about the evaluations:

> This review found that only a few approaches have documented their positive effects on student achievement. Several approaches appear to hold promise, but lack evidence to verify this conclusion.

Table 15.5 shows how the evaluations of the programs were rated by the American Institutes of Research. Only 3 of the 24 were rated as having "strong evidence," and none of these would meet high standards of causal inference and generalizability described in the present report.

A later but similar synthesis (RAND Corporation, 2002) of decade-long research on six schoolwide programs, originally funded by the New American Schools foundation, revealed similarly weak achievement evaluations and inconclusive findings. Among other problems, it was unclear that the schoolwide programs had actually be implemented as designed.

THE TEACHER ADVANCEMENT PROGRAM

The initial readers of this report are likely to be familiar with the Teacher Advancement Program (TAP), but it may be useful to review its features. The program is explained as follows:

> The Milken Family Foundation created the Teacher Advancement Program (TAP), a bold new strategy to attract, retain, motivate and develop talented people to the teaching profession.
>
> TAP's goal is to draw more talented people to the teaching profession—and keep them there—by making it more attractive and rewarding to be a teacher. Under the TAP system, good teachers can earn higher salaries and advance professionally, just as in other careers. And they can do it without leaving the classroom, where they often are needed most.

At the same time, TAP helps teachers become the best they can be, by giving them opportunities to learn better teaching strategies and holding them accountable for their performance.

According to TAP reports (Milken Family Foundation, n.d.; Schacter et al., n.d.; Schacter, Thum, et al., n.d.), the program "costs $415 per pupil, approximately 5% of the average cost to educate a child." The program has four chief elements:

- Multiple Career Paths
- Ongoing, Applied Professional Growth
- Instructionally Focused Accountability
- Performance-Based Compensation

By combining these elements in an effective strategy for reform, TAP is working to turn teaching from a revolving-door profession into a highly rewarding career choice. The real reward will be the outstanding education available to each and every student in the country.

The TAP evaluations made use of individual-level, value-added scores and showed that TAP schools outperformed comparable schools by about 13% over a 2-year period. Reflecting such results, greater proportions of TAP than comparison teachers achieved learning gains.[7]

In the nomenclature of classic research design philosophy, the evaluation would be categorized as a pretest-posttest, control-group quasi-experimental design. It is an excellent choice since it is more practical and less expensive than a true experiment but still makes use of a comparable control group of schools. Plus, it equates the TAP and comparison schools with respect to their beginning test scores.

The study employed before-and-after individual-level student data, which means that the students were in the school for both pretests and posttests given a year apart. Thus, neither TAP or control schools would not be advantaged or penalized by systematic changes in their composition. The quasi-experimental design required less disruption in the schools while minimizing the "hothouse effect" sometimes induced by true experiments.

Supplementary analyses showed that:

1. Greater TAP implementation was associated with greater learning gains, and that
2. The teachers had generally favorable attitudes about the five TAP features.

The first finding supports the idea of using resources and special efforts, and possibly systematic teacher monitoring, to advance full and authentic TAP implementation. The second finding complements the achievement results, and though the most important conclusion shows that the program promotes achievement, it is also encouraging that teachers generally favored the five program components.

As indicated in Table 15.6, the TAP quasi-experimental evaluation compares very favorably with previous schoolwide evaluation with respect to internal validity or the confidence that can be placed in the causal inference about its causal effects even though, like other schoolwide evaluations, the sampling is limited.

Thus, from the standpoint of internal validity, the TAP evaluation is state-of-the-art. Though it lacks a national or large state sample of randomly assigned TAP and non-TAP schools, the evaluation does control for

Table 15.6.   Some Features of Example Evaluations

Program Evaluated	Evaluation Design	Causality (Internal Validity)	Generalizability (External Validity)	Comment
O'Donnell Foundation	Decisive single subject	++		Confined to Dallas
Headsprout	Decisive single subject	+++	++	Many varied students
Harvard Project Physics	Experiment	+++	+++	Random national sample
School Health Curriculum	Experiment	+++	++	National sample
Core Knowledge	Quasi-experiment	+	+++	All North Carolina schools
Coalition of Essential Schools	Pre-experiment		+	Many varied students
National Center on Education and the Economy	Pre-experiment		+	Many varied students
Schoolwide Reforms	Mostly pre-experiments		+	Many varied students
Teacher Advancement Program	Quasi-experiment	++	+	Varied students

Note: The number of positive signs indicates the degree of confidence that can be placed in causality and generalizability.

pre-existing achievement. This strengthens the power of the analysis without the intrusiveness, difficulty, expense, and "hothouse" (Hawthorne) effects of being in a possible singled-out winner's circle.

CONCLUSION:
THE RIGOR AND FEASIBILITY OF EVALUATION DESIGNS

Evaluating educational programs is hardly a simple matter. As explained and illustrated above, many things can go wrong with research in basic psychology and the social sciences. In applied evaluation research, the difficulties multiply and intensify. Yet questions of program efficacy are urgent.

The body of the present report sets forth the criteria for "evaluating evaluations." Table 15.6 provides a simple summary of the strengths and weaknesses of evaluations reviewed in this chapter. Obviously, much more definitive evaluations are needed if education is to become more like medicine in basing policy and practice on definitive evidence.

In further summary, when program results are debatable or insufficiently obvious to detect, three types of design are used in educational research: pre-experimental, true experimental, and quasi-experimental. Although common in educational research, pre-experimental designs are the easiest experimental designs to implement, but they provide no scientifically defensible causal information. The true experimental designs are the most rigorous, but they are rare because they are both very costly and difficult to implement. Finally, quasi-experimental designs represent a balance of feasibility and rigor.

The use of experimental and quasi-experimental designs should be assessed on a case-by-case basis to determine which is best suited for a given application. Within each category, as pointed out in the body of this report, further decisions are required. Of top importance for any educational evaluation, regardless of the experimental design, are the questions of validity, generalizability, and special problems of educational research explained and illustrated in previous sections.

NOTES

1.   Because experiments are difficult to execute, quasi-experiments are reasonable to employ and are discussed in a subsequent section.
2.   Regression, analysis of covariance, and other techniques can help remove pre-existing differences among the groups.
3.   This section draws chiefly on Walberg (1984).

4. A conventional way of calculating effect sizes is to divide the difference between program and control group means by the standard deviation of the control group. For pre-post designs, the gain in test scores may be divided by the pretest standard deviation. The underlying scores should be raw scores, normal curve equivalents, or other equal-interval expression.

5. Available from Coalition of Essential Schools, *Students Thrive in Schools that Promote Intellectual Rigor and Personalize Learning*; the "Results of Kids" page of the CES Website lists this report as "Study of School Achievement: http://www.essentialschools.org/pub/ces_docs/about/results/csrdstud.html

6. See http://www.ncee.org/index.jsp;jsessionid=a7cz23xFc7i7?setProtocol= true; see also *Results: From Schools, Districts, and States Using the America's Choice Design* on the NCEE Website.

7. During the second year of implementation, the teachers on average had less favorable attitudes toward accountability and performance pay, but the report notes that these aberrations may have been mainly attributable to teachers in only schools that received less than expected compensation because of cuts in the state budget.

REFERENCES

American Institutes for Research. (1999). *An educators' guide to schoolwide reform.* Arlington, VA: Educational Research Service.

Bracht, G. H., & Glass, G. V. (1968). The external validity of experiments. *American Educational Research Journal, 5,* 437-474.

Campbell, D. T., & Stanley, J. C. (1963a). Experimental and quasi-experimental designs for research on teaching. In N. L. Gage (Ed.), *Handbook of research on teaching.* Chicago: Rand-McNally.

Campbell, D. T., & Stanley, J. C. (1963b). *Experimental and quasi-experimental designs for research.* Chicago: Rand McNally.

Cook, T. D., & Campbell, D. T. (1979). *Quasi-experimentation: Design and analysis issues for field settings.* Chicago: Rand McNally.

Errecart, M. T., Walberg, H. J., Ross, J. G., Gold, R. S., Fiedler, J. L., & Kolbe, L. J. (1991). Effectiveness of teenage health teaching models. *Journal of School Health, 61*(1), 26-30.

Gold, R. S., Parcel, G. S. Walberg, H. J., Luepker, R. V., Portnoy, B., & Stone, E. J. (1991). Summary and conclusions of the THTM Evaluation—The expert work group perspective. *Journal of School Health, 4,* 39-44.

Hanushek, E. A. (1999, Summer). Some findings from an independent investigation of the Tennessee STAR experiment and from other investigations of class size effects. *Educational Evaluation and Policy Analysis, 21*(2), 143-163.

Hoxby, C. M. (2004). *A straightforward comparison of charter schools and regular public schools in the United States.* Cambridge, MA.: Harvard University and National Bureau of Economic Research.

Layng, J., Twyman, J. S., & Stikeleather, G. (2003). Headsprout early reading: Reliably teaching children to read. *Behavioral Technology Today, 3,* 7-20.

Milken Family Foundation. (n.d.). *What is the Teacher Advancement Program?* Santa Monica, CA: Author.

National Commission on Excellence in Education. (1983). *A nation at risk: The imperative for school reform.* Washington, DC: U.S Government Printing Office.

National Reading Panel. (2000). *The National Reading Panel Report: Teaching children to read.* Washington, DC: U.S. Department of Health and Human Services, Public Health Service, National Institute of Health, National Institute of Child Health and Human Development.

Nelsonm, F. H., Rosenberg, B., & Van Meter, N. (2004). *Charter school achievement on the 2003 National Assessment of Educational Progress.* Washington, DC: Ameriocan Federation of Teachers.

RAND Corporation. (2002). *A decade of whole-school reform.* Santa Monica, CA: Author. Available: http://www.rand.org/publications/RB/RB8019

Schacter, J., Schiff, T., Thum, Y. M., Fagnano, C., Bendotti, M., Solmon, L., Firetag, K., & Milken, L. (n.d.). *The impact of the Teacher Advancement Program on student achievement, teacher attitudes, and job satisfaction* Santa Monica, CA: Milken Family Foundation.

Schacter, J., Thum, Y. M., Reifsneider, D., & Schiff, T. (n.d.). *The Teacher Advancement Program report two: Year three results from Arizon and year one results from South Carolina TAP Schools.* Santa Monica, CA: Milken Family Foundation.

Shavelson, R. J., & Towne, L. (2002). *Scientific research in education.* Washington, DC: National Academies Press.

Soifer, D. (2004, October 1). AFT Attack on charter schools meets swift response from reformers. *School Reform News,* p. 1. Also available at http://www.heartland.org/Article.cfm?artId=15698

Solmon, L. C. (2003). *Findings from the 2002 survey of parents with children in Arizona charter schools: How parents grade their charter schools.* Santa Monica, CA: Human Resources Policy Corporation.

Twyman, J. S., Layng, J., Stikeleather, G., & Hobbins, K. A. (in press). A non-linear approach to curriculum design: The role of behavior analysis in building an effective reading program. In W. L. Heward et al. (Eds.), *Focus on behavior analysis in education* (Vol. 3). Upper Saddle River, NJ: Merrill/Prentice Hall.

Walberg, H. J. (1984). Quantification reconsidered. In E. Gordon (Ed.), *Review of research in education.* Washington, DC: American Educational Research Association.

Walberg, H. J. (2001). Achievement in American schools. In T. Moe, (Ed.), *A primer on American Schools: An assessment by the Koret Task Force on K-12 education* (pp. 43-67). Stanford, CA: Hoover Institution Press.

Walberg, H. J. (2002). Principles for accountability designs. In W. Evers & H. J. Walberg (Eds.), *School accountability* (pp. 155-183). Stanford, CA: Hoover Institution Press.

Walberg, H. J. (in press). Improving educational productivity: An assessment of extant research. In R. Subotnik & H. J. Walberg (Eds.), *The scientific basis of educational productivity.* Greenwich, CT: Information Age.

Walberg, H. J., Connell, D. B., Turner, R. R., & Olsen, L. K. (1986, June). Health knowledge and attitudes change before behavior: A national evaluation of health education. *Curriculum Update,* pp. 4-6.

Walberg, H. J., & Meyer, J. (2004). *The effects of core knowledge on state test achievement in North Carolina and the effects of core knowledge school factors on state test achievement in North Carolina.* Charlottesville, VA.: Core Knowledge Foundation.

Welch, W. W., & Walberg, H. J. (1972). A national experiment in curriculum evaluation. *American Educational Research Journal, 9,* 373-384.

CONFERENCE PRESENTERS

Lowell Milken

Widely known as an educational pioneer and reformer, Lowell Milken is chairman of the Milken Family Foundation (MFF), which he co-founded in 1982. Under his leadership, MFF has become one of the most innovative private foundations in the United States, creating national programs in K-12 education and medical research. Among his contributions to strengthening K-12 education, Mr. Milken conceived the Milken National Educator Awards in 1985 to recognize the importance of outstanding educators and to encourage talented young people to choose teaching as a career. Mr. Milken launched the Teacher Advancement Program (TAP) in 1999 to restructure and thus revitalize the teaching profession. Named by *Worth* magazine as one of America's most generous philanthropists, Mr. Milken is also an involved businessman who is chairman of London-based Heron International, a worldwide leader in property development, and co-founded Knowledge Universe, a company focused on meeting the life-long learning requirements of both individuals and businesses.

Kimberly Firetag Agam

As Senior Research Associate for Policy Analysis, Kimberly Firetag Agam's work focuses on a wide range of local, state, and national programs and policies aimed at improving teacher quality. Ms. Agam monitors state and federal education policy, provides her expertise to states developing teacher quality initiatives, and assists with government relations.

Joan Baratz-Snowden

Joan Baratz-Snowden is director in the Educational Issues Department of the American Federation of Teachers. In that capacity, she is responsible for developing information and materials for affiliates regarding issues related to assessment, Title I, the National Board for Professional Teaching Standards (NBPTS) and for developing a program to increase the access to and use of technology by teachers.

John A. Boehner

Elected to represent the Eighth Congressional District of Ohio for a seventh term in November 2002, John A. Boehner continues to fight for a smaller, more accountable federal government. During his tenure in the House, Boehner has been active in education reform issues and in January 2001, Boehner was selected by House Republicans to chair the House Committee on Education and the Workforce. In that post, Boehner helped to pass the No Child Left Behind Act with overwhelming bipartisan support.

Frank T. Brogan

A lifelong champion of public education, Frank T. Brogan is currently president of Florida Atlantic University. Starting his career as a fifth-grade teacher in Martin County public schools, Brogan served as dean, assistant principal, principal, and ultimately superintendent of schools in Martin County before becoming Florida's youngest-ever commissioner of education. In this post, Mr. Brogan strengthened accountability in Florida's public school system, and today continues that work in higher education.

Kevin P. Chavous

Kevin P. Chavous served three terms as the Ward Seven representative on the District of Columbia city council. As chair of the city council's committee of education, libraries, and recreation, Mr. Chavous was at the forefront of promoting change within the district public school system, and his efforts led to nearly 400 million new dollars for public education.

Cheryl L. Fagnano

Cheryl L. Fagnano is the former senior vice president of the Milken Family Foundation and associate director of the Teacher Advancement

Program (TAP). She was responsible for planning and implementation of the Teacher Advancement Program. Dr. Fagnano worked closely with the local and regional TAP executive directors to ensure that all participating schools effectively implement the TAP reform by respecting local conditions, while remaining faithful to the prescribed model.

Frederick M. Hess

Known for his work on a diverse range of educational issues, Frederick M. Hess serves as director of education policy at American Enterprise Institute (AEI), and executive editor of *Education Next*. Dr. Hess is a faculty associate of Harvard University's Program in Education Policy and Governance, and currently serves on the review board for the Broad Prize in Urban Education.

Eugene W. Hickok

Dr. Eugene W. Hickok is the former U.S. under secretary of education and principal adviser to former Secretary of Education Rod Paige. Prior to his appointment, Dr. Hickok spent 6 years as Pennsylvania's secretary of education. There, he provided oversight for the state's education system, helped implement a sweeping education reform agenda, and served on the boards of trustees of Pennsylvania's four state-related universities and on the board of governors of the state system of higher education.

Jim Horne

As former commissioner of education for the state of Florida, Jim Horne provided guidance for more than 2,000 employees of the Department of Education, and served as chief executive of Florida's new K-20 education system. Prior to his appointment as commissioner, Horne served as secretary of education.

Richard M. Ingersoll

As associate professor of education and sociology at the University of Pennsylvania, Richard M. Ingersoll researches management and organization of elementary and secondary schools, as well as issues related to the teaching profession. He has conducted extensive research on teacher shortages and under-qualified teachers.

Ken James

Ken James is the director of the Arkansas Department of Education. Starting his career as a classroom teacher, Dr. James also served as assistant principal, principal, assistant superintendent,and ultimately superintendent of schools in Fayette County Public Schools, Lexington, Kentucky, Little Rock and Van Buren, Arkansas.

Brad Jupp

Brad Jupp is a teacher in the Denver Public Schools assigned to the Design Team of the Denver Public Schools/Denver Classroom Teachers Association Pay for Performance Pilot. He has volunteered as a member of the negotiations Team for the Denver Classroom Teachers Association for more than a decade, and has been a teacher in the Denver Public Schools since 1987.

Lisa Graham Keegan

As a founding member and former chief executive officer of Education Leaders Council (ELC), Lisa Graham Keegan is one of the nation's most prominent—and outspoken—education reform advocates. Prior to working with ELC, Ms. Keegan spent a decade leading Arizona's education reform movement both in the state House and after being elected state superintendent of public instruction.

Alan Krueger

Alan Krueger is the Bendheim Professor of Economics and Public Affairs at Princeton University. He has published numerous articles in academic journals on a wide range of subjects including the economics of education, income dispersion, labor demand, unemployment, and environmental economics, and is a regular contributor to the economic science column of the *New York Times*. He is the founding director of the Princeton University Survey Research Center, director of the Princeton

University Industrial Relations Section, and a research associate of the National Bureau of Economic Research.

Mary L. Landrieu

One of the Senate's foremost leaders on education, Senator Mary L. Landrieu was the first woman from Louisiana elected to a full term in the U.S. Senate. She currently serves on the Senate Appropriations, Energy, and Natural Resources, and Small Business Committees. She worked across party lines in 2001 to craft the No Child Left Behind Act, and led a successful effort to ensure that federal Title I dollars make it to schools with the highest concentrations of poor children.

Jay Mathews

An education reporter and online columnist, Jay Mathews has been with the *Washington Post* for 33 years. He has written numerous books, including *Class Struggle: What's Wrong (and Right) with America's Best Public High Schools*, in which he created a rating system for high schools called the Challenge Index, which is used by several news organizations and school districts. Mathews' new book, *Harvard Schmarvard: Getting Beyond the Ivy League to the College that is Best for You*, challenges the notion that getting into a brand-name school will change your life, and shows how to survive the admissions process with your family and sense of humor intact.

Janice Poda

As Senior Director of the Division of Teacher Quality for the South Carolina Department of Education, Janice Poda plays a key role in helping South Carolina to implement comprehensive statewide reforms. The Division of Teacher Quality provides guidance and technical assistance to teachers in the areas of preparation, certification, and evaluation as well as No Child Left Behind.

Nina Rees

As Deputy Under Secretary for Innovation and Improvement in the newly created Office of Innovation and Improvement (OII), Nina S. Rees oversees the administration of approximately 25 competitive grant programs. Working with the Office of Elementary and Secondary Education, she also coordinates implementation of the public school choice and supplemental services provisions of the president's No Child Left Behind Act.

Ted Sanders

Ted Sanders is president of the Education Commission of the States (ECS), an interstate compact created in 1965 to improve public education by facilitating the exchange of information, ideas, and experiences among state policymakers and education leaders. As a nonprofit, nonpartisan organization involving key leaders from all levels of the education system, ECS creates unique opportunities to build partnerships, share information, and promote development of policy based on available research and strategies.

John Schacter

John Schacter is president of The Teaching Doctors, a company that conducts large-scale program evaluations and trains teachers and administrators how to recognize and coach for effective instruction. Prior to that, he served as vice president for research projects at the Milken Family Foundation. Dr. Schacter has published and created programs on such topics as performance pay, early reading, technology integration, and teacher quality.

Tamara W. Schiff

Tamara W. Schiff is vice president for the Milken Family Foundation and associate director of the Teacher Advancement Program. She has been involved in the development of TAP since its inception in 1999. In her role as associate director, she oversees the planning and implementation of the TAP in all partner states, schools, and districts. Dr. Schiff has made numerous presentations to policy, school administrative, and practitioner groups concerned about teacher quality and interested in the Teacher Advancement Program.

Ray Simon

As assistant secretary of the Office of Elementary and Secondary Education, Ray Simon plays a pivotal role in policy and management issues affecting elementary and secondary education. He directs, coordinates, and recommends policy for programs designed to assist state and local education agencies with such tasks as improving the achievement of elementary and secondary school students. Prior to his appointment by President Bush, Simon was director of the Arkansas Department of Education, and served as superintendent of the Conway School District in Arkansas.

Lewis C. Solmon

Lewis C. Solmon is executive vice president, education, at the Milken Family Foundation, a member of its Board of Trustees, and director of the Teacher Advancement Program (TAP), a major initiative of the Foundation focused on improving teacher quality. He has advised several governors and state superintendents in the areas of teacher quality, school technology funding and school finance, and served on Governor Jeb Bush's education transition team in 2002-2003.

Herbert J. Walberg

Herbert J. Walberg is professor emeritus of education and psychology at the University of Illinois at Chicago and a distinguished visiting fellow of Stanford University's Hoover Institution. Dr. Walberg has written and edited more than 55 books and written over 350 articles on such topics as educational effectiveness and exceptional human accomplishments. He currently chairs the board of Chicago's Heartland Institute, a think tank providing policy analysis for the U.S. Congress, state legislators, the media, and the public.

Susan Tave Zelman

As superintendent of public instruction for the Ohio Department of Education, Susan Tave Zelman is responsible for framing policy, advancing systemic reform, supervising implementation of laws, and providing a clear vision of progress for education in the State of Ohio. Prior to assuming duties of superintendent, Dr. Zelman served as deputy commissioner of the Missouri Department of Elementary and Secondary Education as well as chief policy and administrative consultant to the commissioner of education, where she oversaw a $3.7 billion budget.

Printed in the United States
36292LVS00001B/95